Reframing Failure in Digital

Reframing Failure in Digital Scholarship

Edited by Anna-Maria Sichani and Michael Donnay

UNIVERSITY OF LONDON PRESS

Available to purchase in print or download for
free at https://uolpress.co.uk

First published 2025 by
University of London Press
Senate House, Malet St, London WC1E 7HU

A CIP catalogue record for this book is available from The British Library.

ISBN 978-1-908590-90-9 (hardback)
ISBN 978-1-908590-91-6 (paperback)
ISBN 978-1-908590-96-1 (.epub)
ISBN 978-1-908590-94-7 (.pdf)
ISBN 978-1-908590-92-3 (.html)

DOI https://doi.org/10.14296/10.63674/yrab7358

Cover design for University of London Press by Nicky Borowiec.
Book design by Nigel French.
Text set by Westchester Publishing Services UK
in Source Sans Pro, designed by Erik Spiekermann.

Contents

List of figures

Notes on contributors

Janneke Adema (she/her) is a cultural and media theorist working in the fields of (book) publishing and digital culture and an associate professor in digital media at the Centre for Postdigital Cultures (Coventry University).

Brittany Amell (she/her) is an INKE Partnership postdoctoral fellow in Open Social Scholarship and MITACS Accelerate Industrial postdoctoral fellow in Open, Collaborative Scholarship (Arts & Humanities) at the Electronic Textual Cultures Lab (ETCL).

Arianna Ciula is director and research software senior analyst at King's Digital Lab, King's College London.

Frances Corry is an assistant professor in the Department of Information Culture and Data Stewardship at the University of Pittsburgh.

David De Roure is academic director of digital scholarship at the University of Oxford and professor of e-Research in the Oxford e-Research Centre.

Quinn Dombrowski is the academic technology specialist in the Division of Literatures, Cultures, and Languages, and the Library, at Stanford University.

Michael Donnay is a community manager with the Software Sustainability Institute.

Anisa Hawes is *Programming Historian*'s publishing manager. Beyond the project, she is a researcher and web archivist with a special interest in critical curatorial practice, and using open-source tools to preserve digital cultural memory.

Jennifer Isasi is an assistant research professor of digital scholarship at the Pennsylvania State University, where she directs the Digital Liberal Arts Research Initiative, and is also part of the editorial board of the open access journal *Programming Historian*.

Caio Mello is a postdoctoral researcher in the project Impresso – Media Monitoring of the Past at the Luxembourg Centre for Contemporary and Digital History (C^2DH).

Jenny Mitcham is chief digital preservation officer at the Digital Preservation Coalition where she works closely with members on their digital preservation challenges.

Christopher Ohge is senior lecturer in digital approaches to literature at the School of Advanced Study, University of London.

Riva Quiroga is a linguist and educator by training. Since 2019, she has been involved in *Programming Historian* as an editor of the Spanish team and as a trustee of ProgHist Ltd, the charity that runs the project.

Arran Rees is a researcher and practitioner interested in museums, digital cultural heritage collections and collaborative action research processes and currently works as the Museum Data Manager for the Museum Data Service.

Jentery Sayers is associate professor of English and director of media studies at the University of Victoria, where he also directs the Praxis Studio for Comparative Media Studies.

Anna-Maria Sichani is a media historian and a digital humanist. She is currently a BRAID fellow and a research associate in digital humanities at the Digital Humanities Research Hub, School of Advanced Study, University of London.

Nabeel Siddiqui is an assistant professor of digital media at Susquehanna University, where he also serves as the director of the Center for Teaching and Learning.

Elena Spadini is a researcher in digital humanities, with a background in romance philology. Her research interests span from medieval manuscripts to contemporary authors and born-digital literary sources.

Jennifer Stertzer is director of the Center for Digital Editing and the Washington Papers and a research associate professor at the University of Virginia.

Lauren Tuckley is director of the Center for Research and Fellowships at Georgetown University, where she leads a team administering undergraduate research programmes and mentoring students and young alumni applying for nationally competitive fellowships.

Joris J. van Zundert is senior researcher and developer in the Department of Computational Literary Studies and the Digital Humanities Lab at the Huygens Institute of the Royal Netherlands Academy of Arts and Sciences (KNAW).

Naomi Wells is senior lecturer in Italian and Spanish with digital humanities at the School of Advanced Study, University of London.

Jane Winters is professor of digital humanities and director of the Digital Humanities Research Hub at the School of Advanced Study, University of London.

Acknowledgements

This project and book would have been impossible without our wonderful contributing authors; we would like to thank them for trusting us with their inspiring reflections and for their resiliency and professionalism.

We are equally indebted to those whose writing didn't quite make it into these pages. We'd like to extend our particular thanks to the original contributors of the 2022–23 seminar who we were not – for one reason or another – able to include in this collection, but whose discussions helped shape this book nonetheless.

Special thanks to our publisher, Emma Gallon, for her attentive care and invaluable role in the production of this volume. We'd also like to thank the two anonymous peer reviewers for their thoughtful feedback early in the process.

Anna-Maria would like to thank her co-editor, Michael, for being such a terrific collaborator and for helping see this project through to the end. She would like to thank Jane Winters for being an inspiring mentor and supporting us in this seminar series and publication. Special thanks go to the entire team at DHRH, as well as colleagues from the various projects she has worked on over the years, for reinforcing her belief that digital scholarship is far from a failed discourse, practice and career choice. And to Vassilis, Loukia and David, for being a positive force in her life.

Michael is grateful to Anna-Maria for being a generous and understanding co-editor, without whom this book would not have been completed. He would also like to thank Jane Winters, Naomi Wells, and the rest of the team at the University of London for being so supportive of the project. Thanks go to his parents, Michelle and Victor, for being his first and best editors and to Chris for teaching him to think computationally. And to Lily, for all her love and support.

We hope our efforts as editors of this volume have not failed. But even if they have, this failure remains a labour of love.

Introduction: reframing failure

Anna-Maria Sichani and Michael Donnay

Failure is ordinary. Paraphrasing Raymond Williams's famous quote on culture (McGuigan 2014), this book talks about failure as an everyday, common thing both in life and in digital scholarship. The truth is that no one gets through life without failing – in both minor and often significant ways. When we fail, it may feel as if we are alone in this. However, there is nothing more human than to fail: a relationship crisis, a failed exam, a career reversal, a book proposal rejection or a bungled project. To err is human – to fail is too.

Yet, for something so central to our experience, failure often sits at the periphery of our writing, training and professional discourse. This inability to see failure as an essential part of our work does not just have the potential to leave us feeling isolated. It also leaves a sizeable hole in how we understand the process of *doing* digital scholarship. Its absence can lead to an incomplete understanding of our own research, teaching and collaborations. This book encourages us to recentre failure as a core part of our scholarship.

This book aims to do two related and interlocking things. The first is to develop a vocabulary for failure that is critical, constructive and compassionate. Much of the language associated with failure draws on negative emotions or implies a personal, moral deficiency on the part of the individual who has failed. This negative discourse discourages a critical engagement with failure, while the focus on the individual can ignore the systemic issues at play. We aim to replace that language with a vocabulary that fosters critical and constructive engagement, while at the same time speaking with an appropriate compassion for those involved.

The second is to bring a renewed critical focus to failure as an object of inquiry and contribute to the growing and increasingly diverse body of 'critical digital humanities'. In many ways, failure has been a defining element of digital scholarship in the arts and humanities over the last several decades. These failures have sparked excellent reflections from practitioners like Shawn Graham and Quinn Dombrowski, who have called for the field to explore failure more critically and seriously (Graham 2019; Dombrowski 2014). Yet despite these writings and continued technical, social and institutional failures in the field, a sustained engagement with failure has not materialised.

As other fields in the humanities begin to reassess their relationship with failure and digital scholarship begins a renewed engagement with questions of technical and environmental sustainability – or lack thereof – now seems like a particularly generative moment to return to this conversation (Coleman 2023). This collection offers an updated and richly interdisciplinary set of perspectives, drawing on recent experience and developments, while remaining rooted in the critical and reflective tradition of earlier writing in the field (Greenspan 2019).

In bringing together the reflective, personal approach with a critical perspective, we want to move away from the approach that self-improvement and motivational literature takes to failure (for example, see Lachkovic 2024). We are not offering a guide on learning to fail forward or succeed at failure. We are not going to glorify the technocratic call to 'move fast and break things'. And we aren't going to offer any secret advice about how to avoid failure.

Instead, this book offers examples of real-world failures for evaluation, discussion and critical reflection. We want to showcase the various types of failure in digital scholarship. We want to normalise a discourse of open conversation (and practice) around failure in academic and professional life. And we want to remind one another that we are not alone in making mistakes, not alone in failing.

Failure in digital scholarship

The book is structured around four major conversations within digital scholarship: innovation, technology, collaboration and institutions. These groupings represent our best (and perhaps failed) editorial effort to provide structure to the collection, but there are certainly overlaps and discussions that reach across sections. Each chapter is made up of short reflections offering the author's distinct perspective on failure relating to that issue. Every reflection stands on its own – and can be read as such – but is also in conversation with the other pieces alongside it. They are written in a variety of styles, reflecting both the practice in each author's home discipline and their personal approach to the topic.

Contributors come from a deliberately wide range of disciplinary backgrounds and work in different institutional and national contexts across the globe. Their perspectives are informed by and connected to their research, but they are also deeply grounded in their individual positionality. The reflective mode allows for a more candid approach than traditional academic writing and hopefully captures some of the generous spirit of dialogue we have found with our contributors.

While many of our contributors identify as digital humanists, not all do, and so we have chosen the more expansive term 'digital scholarship' to describe the areas of research with which this collection is concerned. Digital scholarship refers broadly to the use of digital methods and technologies, without setting a boundary around the specific disciplines they are applied to (Digital Scholarship @ Oxford n.d.). We have tried to be similarly expansive when setting the focus for this book and you will see both terms used throughout. We hope this will allow those working within digital scholarship, as well as those in other (even non-digital) communities of practice, to draw on these reflections.

When taken as a whole, the book offers a polyvocal snapshot of the 'state of failure' in digital scholarship and serves as an invitation to pull failure back from the periphery of our understanding of the field – and ourselves.

Failure and innovation

Lisa Spiro's 2012 observation – that the 'digital humanities community recognizes the value of failure in the pursuit of innovation' – also serves as a provocation for the community to examine its relationship to innovation (Spiro 2012). In many ways, the ethos of digital scholarship resembles that of the technology sector, characterised by a bias towards 'newness' (Sichani 2022). Indeed, digital humanities practitioners have often built a professional identity that celebrates risky playfulness (Nowviskie 2016) and 'screwing around' (Ramsay 2014). But when our methodological orientation leans too far in that direction, we are at risk of adopting the same techno-optimist frameworks that prioritise novelty and (disruptive) innovation which several of the reflections in this chapter critique.

Despite the crucial role failure plays in innovation, there remains a strong taboo against publicly acknowledging that side of the coin. For example, the affordances of contemporary software development – such as version control and trackable revision histories – could allow for an open-ended, extensible and constantly updated research output. While these tools offer the potential to embrace a 'culture of the perpetual prototype' (Flanders 2015) or 'perpetual beta' (Nowviskie 2012), institutional pressure from funding bodies and universities to demonstrate concrete deliverables means there is little room for the failure inherent in prototyping to be manifested as such. Some of the reflections in this section address this challenge and consider how failure might point us in the direction of a more sustainable approach to innovation and the work required to move us there.

Failure and technological obsolescence

Technical obsolescence is quickly becoming one of the main focuses for digital researchers. The field has long been aware of the challenges involved in maintaining digital projects and data, but the topic has taken on an increased urgency in recent years as major changes to foundational technologies, like the sunsetting of Adobe Flash in late 2020, and the increase in cyberattacks on cultural heritage institutions and infrastructures (Warren 2024; Keating 2024), have made the maintenance challenges even more stark. In response, there has been a growing and vivid discussion around technical sustainability and maintenance (Holmes et al. 2023).

However, these technical conversations are only just beginning to connect to the theoretical, social and institutional contexts where failure also plays a major (unacknowledged) role (Holmes et al. 2023). Specific solutions, like static websites, still tend to put the focus on technological solutions rather than addressing the people and skills required to maintain digital objects (Dombrowski 2022). Ironically, even when systemic solutions to technical obsolescence are proposed, they rarely come with the necessary funding. So even though the funding bodies in the United Kingdom now require a data management plan, they rarely if ever allow grant funding to be used to cover project maintenance beyond the end date of the project (UKRI 2018).

The reflections in this section draw on diverse experiences of technological obsolescence to consider how we can better manage the inevitable failure of our digital objects and how we might study those objects when they have failed. They pay particular attention to the role our human infrastructure plays in sustaining tools and technical systems.

Failure and collaboration

Digital research is almost always a collaborative endeavour, and so enabling and managing collaborations is a core concern for digital scholars and practitioners. Unlike many other humanities disciplines, digital projects regularly require large teams that bring together a wide range of skills, professional expertise and communities of practice. These teams often include people working in software development, cultural heritage institutions and universities – all of whom can bring different assumptions and professional languages to a project (Neubert 2020). The discipline has long been aware of the challenges in working this way, with some of the most insightful writing on the topic coming from collaborators normally relegated to the periphery of the academy (Bell and Kennan 2021).

However, for a field that prides itself on interdisciplinarity, we still spend little time discussing how to do it well (Ahnert et al. 2023). This is, in part, because humanities scholars rarely have a professional venue to discuss their research process as opposed to outputs. It's also because we are less willing to acknowledge when these collaborations go wrong (as they often can). This can often be out of an understandable desire to protect relationships. Yet this unwillingness to discuss when and how collaborations go wrong can leave future projects ill-prepared to address similar challenges. Moreover, the informal way these challenges are discussed privileges those who have access to those professional networks and excludes those who do not. Each reflection in this section takes those 'coffee break' conversations and brings a critical and constructive lens to them.

Failure and institutions

Although not unique to digital scholarship, systemic challenges within institutions are perhaps more keenly felt because of the collaborative and interdisciplinary nature of the field (Greenspan 2019). These challenges cut across the three other areas of the book, with many of the failures of innovation, technical infrastructure and collaboration directly tied to wider systemic issues. In many ways, the failure of institutional frameworks, from funding systems to postgraduate training, circumscribe all the work we do – a theme taken up by several reflections in this section.

As a field we continue to fall short of our aspirations for better utilising digital technology to create a more equitable research culture, despite any number of guidelines about citing digital outputs, assessing digital scholarship and acknowledging contributors' roles in research outputs (Editorial Process n.d.; Modern Language Association 2012; Allen et al. 2019). Reflections in this chapter take up some of these challenges and propose alternatives that leverage the affordances of digital publishing in particular to shift institutional cultures.

This section also acknowledges that failure brings different risks for different people. The privilege to fail publicly is still more likely to be afforded to white, male and permanently employed academics (Gupta in Graham 2019), while those with more precarious positions face additional barriers to publicly discussing their failures. These practitioners are also the ones most likely to be failed by existing institutional structures, compounding the issue. A number of contributors address these challenges explicitly and it's a thread we hope is evident throughout the book.

Reframing failure

In bringing together this community of authors, our hope is to make clear the important place of failure in scholarly life. We want to reflect on failure in the round, bringing critical attention to the (often unacknowledged) role it plays in shaping our response to some of the core questions in the field.

By proposing failure as a commonplace of our theoretical, critical and technological endeavours, this book aims to offer an unusual – hopefully not too failed – account of our everyday professional practice. By naturalising and normalising failure in its various iterations, we seek to promote a mode of digital scholarship that accepts, celebrates and cares for human creativity beyond success and innovation.

References

Ahnert, Ruth, Emma Griffin, Giorgia Tolfo and Mia Ridge. *Collaborative Historical Research in the Age of Big Data: Lessons from an Interdisciplinary Project*. Elements in Historical Theory and Practice. Cambridge University Press, 2023. https://doi.org/10.1017/9781009175548.

Allen, Liz, Alison O'Connell and Veronique Kiermer. 'How Can We Ensure Visibility and Diversity in Research Contributions? How the Contributor Role Taxonomy (CRediT) Is Helping the Shift from Authorship to Contributorship', *Learned Publishing* 32, no. 1 (2019): 71–4. https://doi.org/10.1002/leap.1210.

Bell, Emilia C. and Mary Anne Kennan. 'Partnering in Knowledge Production: Roles for Librarians in the Digital Humanities', *Journal of the Australian Library and Information Association* 70, no. 2 (2021): 157–76. https://www.tandfonline.com/doi/full/10.1080/24750158.2021.1907886.

Coleman, Simon. 'Preface', *Journal of the Royal Anthropological Institute* 29, S1 (2023): 6–7. https://doi.org/10.1111/1467-9655.13910.

Digital Scholarship @ Oxford. 'What Is Digital Scholarship?' (n.d.) Accessed 26 November 2024. https://digitalscholarship.web.ox.ac.uk/what-digital-scholarship.

Dombrowski, Quinn. 'Whatever Happened to Project Bamboo?' *Literary and Linguistic Computing* 29, no. 3 (2014): 326–39. https://doi.org/10.1093/llc/fqu026.

Dombrowski, Quinn. 'Minimizing Computing Maximizes Labor'. *Digital Humanities Quarterly* 16, no. 2 (2022). Accessed 24 November 2024. http://www.digitalhumanities.org/dhq/vol/16/2/000594/000594.html.

'Editorial Process: Reviews in Digital Humanities', *Reviews in Digital Humanities*. (n.d.) Accessed 26 November 2024. https://reviewsindh.pubpub.org/review-process.

Flanders, Julia. 'The Long Now of Digital Humanities'. Baker-Nord Center for the Humanities, Case Western Reserve University, 2015. Accessed 25 November 2024. https://case.edu/artsci/bakernord/events/past-events/2014-2015/long-now-digital-humanities.

Graham, Shawn. *Failing Gloriously and Other Essays*. With a Foreword by Eric Kansa and Afterword by Neha Gupta. Digital Press at the

University of North Dakota, 2019. Accessed 25 November 2024. https://thedigitalpress.org/failing-gloriously/.

Greenspan, Brian. 'The Scandal of Digital Humanities'. In *Debates in Digital Humanities 2019*, edited by Matthew K. Gold and Lauren F. Klein, 92–5. Debates in Digital Humanities. University of Minnesota Press, 2019. https://doi.org/10.5749/9781452963785.

Gupta, Neha. 'Afterword'. In *Failing Gloriously and Other Essays*, by Shawn Graham, 130–34. Digital Press at the University of North Dakota, 2019. Accessed 25 November 2024. https://thedigitalpress.org/failing-gloriously/.

Holmes, Martin, Janelle Jenstad and Matthew J. Huculak. 'Introduction to Special Issue: Project Resiliency in the Digital Humanities', *Digital Humanities Quarterly* 17, no. 1 (2023). Accessed 24 November 2024. http://www.digitalhumanities.org/dhq/vol/17/1/000671/000671.html.

Keating, Roly. 'Learning Lessons from the Cyber-Attack'. 8 March 2024. Accessed 24 November 2024. https://blogs.bl.uk/living-knowledge/2024/03/learning-lessons-from-the-cyber-attack.html.

Lachkovic, Josh. 'What I Learnt from My Failed Startup'. *Sifted*. 5 April 2024. Accessed 25 November 2024. https://sifted.eu/articles/learnings-from-my-failed-startup/.

McGuigan, Jim. *Raymond Williams on Culture & Society: Essential Writings*. SAGE Publications, 2014. https://doi.org/10.4135/9781473914766.

Modern Language Association. 'Guidelines for Evaluating Work in Digital Humanities and Digital Media Journal of Digital Humanities', *Journal of Digital Humanities* 1, no. 4 (2012). Accessed 24 November 2024. https://journalofdigitalhumanities.org/1-4/guidelines-for-evaluating-work-in-digital-humanities-and-digital-media-from-the-mla/.

Neubert, Anna Maria. 'Navigating Disciplinary Differences in (Digital) Research Projects'. In *Digital Methods in the Humanities: Challenges, Ideas, Perspectives*, edited by Silke Schwandt, 59–85. Digital Humanities Research. Bielefeld University Press, 2020. https://doi.org/10.14361/9783839454190.

Nowviskie, Bethany. 'Evaluating Collaborative Digital Scholarship (or, Where Credit Is Due)', *Journal of Digital Humanities* 1, no. 4 (2012). Accessed 24 November 2024. http://journalofdigitalhumanities.org

/1-4/evaluating-collaborative-digital-scholarship-by-bethany-nowviskie/.

Nowviskie, Bethany. 'On the Origin of "Hack" and "Yack"'. In *Debates in Digital Humanities 2016*, edited by Matthew K. Gold and Lauren F. Klein, 66–70. University of Minnesota Press, 2016. https://doi.org/10.5749/9781452963761.

Ramsay, Stephen. 'The Hermeneutics of Screwing Around; or What You Do with a Million Books'. In *Pastplay: Teaching and Learning History with Technology*, edited by Kevin Kee, 111–20. University of Michigan Press, 2014.

Sichani, Anna-Maria. 'Embracing Decline in Digital Scholarship beyond Sustainability'. In *The Bloomsbury Handbook to the Digital Humanities*, edited by James O'Sullivan, 317–24. Bloomsbury Publishing, 2022.

Spiro, Lisa. '"This Is Why We Fight": Defining the Values of the Digital Humanities'. In *Debates in the Digital Humanities*, edited by Matthew K. Gold, 16–35. University of Minnesota Press, 2012. https://doi.org/10.5749/9781452963754.

UKRI. 'Guidance on Best Practice in the Management of Research Data'. 2018. Accessed 26 November 2024. https://www.ukri.org/publications/guidance-on-best-practice-in-the-management-of-research-data/.

Warren, Tom. 'The Internet Archive Is Back as a Read-Only Service after Cyberattacks', *The Verge*. 14 October 2024. Accessed 26 November 2024. https://www.theverge.com/2024/10/14/24269741/internet-archive-online-read-only-data-breach-outage.

Part I
INNOVATION

Failure and innovation

Digital technologies have historically been embedded in narratives of experimentation, novelty and innovation that often pair with discourse around risk and failure. While discussions surrounding innovation and newness – whether in technology, culture or everyday life – often embrace failure as part of the journey towards a successful outcome, they simultaneously embed a narrative of rupture that discards previous modes and paradigms (Christensen 1997). Facebook's early motto – 'move fast and break things' – evocatively captures this duality (Blodget 2009).

These discourses have become more prominent among research funders, and programmes that prioritise experimentation, risk and novelty are increasingly common, at least in the United Kingdom and European contexts (UKRI 2019; Leptin 2024). This move might suggest that humanities disciplines have adopted a culture that is willing to easily accept the failures that will inevitably accompany that approach to research. Yet, as Quinn Dombrowski deftly argues, professional culture in the humanities – even to some extent within the digital humanities – remains highly risk averse. Jane Winters examines some of the reasons this conservative culture persists, including (somewhat ironically) the funding organisation's own approach to grant evaluation.

Definitions of innovation can shape the work we do in other ways. Christopher Ohge's reflection asks whether we are well served by an 'innovation-as-novelty' paradigm. He argues instead for an approach to innovation that recognises the importance of newness, but orients us towards a research ethic that values doing things well over doing things differently for the sake of it. This theme is picked up in David De Roure's contribution, which examines the 'software waste cycle' that many innovative digital projects fall into. The reformulation of failure as play that De Roure proposes could encourage risk-taking and innovation, while incentivising the reuse of existing tools and methods.

These reflections all acknowledge the importance of innovation in research generally, and digital scholarship particularly, while drawing attention to places where our current model of innovation fails us.

References

Blodget, Henry. 'Mark Zuckerberg On Innovation'. *Business Insider* (1 October 2009) Archived from the original on 9 February 2021. Accessed 24 November 2024. https://www.businessinsider.com/mark-zuckerberg-innovation-2009-10?r=US&IR=T.

Christensen, Clayton M. *The Innovator's Dilemma: When New Technologies Cause Great Firms to Fail.* The Management of Innovation and Change Series. Harvard Business School Press, 1997.

Leptin, Maria. 'Evaluation of Research Proposals: The Why and What of the ERC's Recent Changes'. European Research Council. 2024. Accessed 24 November 2024. https://erc.europa.eu/sites/default/files/2024-02/Evaluation_of_research_proposals.pdf.

UKRI. *UK Research and Innovation Annual Report and Accounts 2018–2019.* Dandy Booksellers Ltd, 2019.

Chapter 1

Stop lying to yourself: collective delusion and digital humanities grant funding

Quinn Dombrowski

From grant applications to curricular development, digital humanities projects and programmes are shaped by the field's perceived connection with funding.[1] Projects are often awarded small grants of money or labour with the condition – implied or explicit – that the project leader will seek external funding to continue or expand this work. And yet, the process of applying for a grant can fundamentally shift both the project and the perspective of the principal investigator (PI) applicant, exposing both to varieties of failure not previously possible.

This piece discusses the impact of applying for a grant on the development of a digital humanities project, the different scales of failure that can come into play with a 'successful' grant application, and the consequences of that success on the trajectory of an individual scholar's career. Contrasting the kind of failure that comes from self-funded projects with the multiple layers of failure often at stake in grant-funded work, it proposes steps for mitigating the damage of the current model of grant funding that could be taken at the level of the individual, the funding agency and professional organisations, all of which are implicated in different ways.

Failure in self-funded projects

A grant application is almost never the beginning of a project, except in classroom contexts where writing a grant is a pedagogical activity. A digital humanities project almost always grows out of a person's own interests, passions, frustrations or problems. It is because of this personal connection to the project content that many digital humanities projects come into existence in the absence of funding, running entirely on a person's own labour in the margins of their lives and whatever financial resources they can dedicate to the work. These projects are arguably the most fortunate, despite the constraints they face: allowed to develop in their own time and manner, without a predetermined path that has been committed to the page and shared with a broader audience. Outside of the context of research-intensive institutions, self-funded projects may be the only feasible mode of project development, with initiatives taking a distinctly different shape in the absence of institutionalised structures for project development and support (Risam 2021).

This is not to say that there is no accountability in self-supported projects: collaboration of any sort generates a network of entanglements and obligations. As soon as you involve other people – be it through working with their materials, or accepting their labour (all the more so when it is volunteer labour, as is often the case in unfunded projects) – you take on the weight of responsibility to see that something comes of those materials or work (Mann 2019; Keralis 2018). Accepting volunteer labour, or being entrusted with materials important to a person or community, or building something that other people begin to rely on (or rely on the promise of) for their own future work: these are all pathways to a form of genuine failure. The failure that is worth seriously wrestling with, and letting it shape your approach to future collaborations, is the kind that involves letting down people who were counting on you. This is not to say that one should contort one's life into knots to avoid these letdowns at all costs: some projects are simply not feasible in the end, let alone sustainable. It often feels terrible to end a project (see 'How I Lost the Crowd' in Graham 2019, 71–80) but for most projects, endings are a matter of when and how, rather than if. This is partly a consequence of the fact that long-term sustainability for digital humanities projects remains an area of concern. Not only is it not widely provided as a service even at the best-resourced institutions, it is unclear what such a thing would even look like. The diversity of tools, materials and technology underpinning digital humanities work makes it inherently resistant to any sort of automatable workflow, though a considerable amount of thought has gone into what pieces of such a thing might look like, including the work of The Endings Project.[2]

Sometimes there is truth in the meme-cliché: even if a project did not produce anything one could point to, the true digital humanities might be the friends met along the way. However, grappling with the gap between promises and results – especially when it implicates others' resources, and considering what that gap means for your collaborators – is an important kind of self-reflection for digital humanists to engage in. Particularly for projects led by faculty or senior staff, it is important to embrace honest feedback from collaborators in positions of lesser institutional power as part of this process, rather than simply speculating on the impact of the project and its demise. Done well, drawing a self-funded project to an ending can uncover lessons of value even in a project that fundamentally didn't work. When funding becomes part of the picture, however, the entire project framework shifts.

What happens when you get funding?

From the perspective of federal government grant agencies in particular, accountability is paramount when it comes to distributing funding. This is even more so in a political climate where even the existence of government-funded grants for the humanities comes under political attack with increasing frequency. It is important to be able to justify the value of the projects that are funded, and to know with reasonable certainty that the projects will, in fact, be completed.[3] Even for private funders like the Mellon Foundation where the programme officers provide more support and dialogue through the application process and after the project is funded, part of the process involves crafting a detailed set of deliverables, project plan, staffing plan and budget.

There is nothing wrong with this approach to careful and deliberate project planning, and depending on the desired scale of the project, it may be the only way forward. Problems arise when scholars feel pressured to shift their project in directions that they don't truly want in order to secure funding. This leads to grant proposals crafted out of well-meaning self-delusion: being funded, they reason, will come with a set of things they wouldn't have otherwise done, but it at least would provide institutional legitimacy and surely there will be enough funding around the margins to do the work the scholar is actually excited about.

Compromises between a scholar's ideal project and something that aligns with funder priorities are an unavoidable and even productive tension that comes out of the grant application process. It is easy to profess support for open data and sharing code; the reality is much messier when one is faced with the prospect of diverting resources (in the form of labour) from research, satisfying technical development work, or scholarly production to the distinctly tedious and stressful task of cleaning and documenting data and metadata, and wrangling them into an institutional, disciplinary or other type of repository. Funder requirements are an effective way to enforce norms like code and data sharing that have a broader value, even when it is at odds with the immediate preferences of project teams.

However, compromises like open data requirements are not the only ones in play when scholars apply for grants. In reality, the projects that make the most sense from the perspective of a scholar's own research or teaching are rarely well-aligned with major grant programmes. Even digital humanities work itself often falls between the cracks, for example, the major Canadian agency funding the humanities does not have a dedicated category for digital humanities (DH). The reward structure of academic disciplines from the perspective of career advancement is at odds with the priorities of funders, who typically look for a broader impact. At research-intensive institutions, a well-reviewed monograph that wins an award from the disciplinary society has a much greater value for a scholar's career than building a technical tool or platform that could be used by scholars in multiple fields. The latter also requires considerably more ongoing labour and infrastructure, and the scholar then faces a dilemma. Do they devote their own time to this maintenance work, at the cost of producing additional forms of legible scholarly production that will better support their career? Here, again, scholars outside research-intensive institutions may be in an advantageous position: the self-funded DH projects developed at public access and regional comprehensive institutions tend to be better received as part of the scholar's evaluation, without forcing them to contort the project to fit a set of specific expectations and outcomes.

In this way, step by step, a scholar with a grant-funded digital humanities project is sucked deeper into the cycle of having to write grants to maintain technical work that they didn't need for their original vision, but the technical work was necessary to get the grant to fund that initial vision.

This process calls to mind the children's rhyme 'There Was an Old Lady Who Swallowed a Fly', where the old lady swallows progressively larger creatures, each to catch the prior creature she'd swallowed, until she ultimately perishes. The wiser choice, at any point in this process, would be to come to peace with the set of well-intentioned but misguided choices that led to a situation of metaphorically swallowing several animals whole (that is, writing grants) and *stop swallowing ever-larger animals*, even if it means grappling with the consequences of having a 'failed' project.

The anxiety about 'failure' runs deep, with digital humanities generally following the acculturation of the humanities rather than the technical communities with which it intersects. In the humanities, failure is deeply personal, bringing with it shame and stigma, if not ostracisation. 'Failure' to secure an academic job after a PhD can still lead to scholars being written off by their former advisors and community. An article with an analysis that people feel 'failed' can be held against the writer for years. These represent fundamental, collective cultural failures within the humanities, casually discarding the years of training and mentorship and acculturation that go into graduate work in these fields. Meanwhile, failure is culturally unremarkable on the IT side because it is inevitable: IT teams do not spend years of meticulous study and work on a focused line of argumentation that draws deeply from their own insights and personal experiences. They build things – often, new things. Some of the things they build will inevitably fall apart, or fail to even come together long enough to meaningfully be described as 'falling apart'; this is the nature of the work. There is some wisdom in the humanities' efforts to interrogate the concept of 'failure', reframing efforts that one might immediately label that way in order to centre other aspects. But a tendency towards critical analysis and reframing can easily slip into pathological avoidance of the discomfort of 'failure', downplaying it and talking around it. It is worth confronting and acknowledging.

Reframing funding

Any project that involves human labour is expensive. It is expensive if you hire specialists with expertise. It is also expensive if you hire people who are learning the skills necessary to become future specialists. Learning involves failure and waste; learning is slow, and often jeopardises project timelines. In my first encounter with preparing a grant budget as part of sustaining the Digital Research Tools (DiRT) directory (Dombrowski 2021),

I was appalled when my boss took my numbers – carefully and precisely calculated to include what I felt was a realistic buffer for delays – and told me to double them. He was right.

Digital humanists tend to suffer from a surfeit of naiveté-powered optimism, and we pay dearly by closing the gaps between that optimism and reality with time and energy that would serve us better if we were to step away from this work and take a break. It precipitates burnout, and normalises this behaviour for more junior members of the team, whether or not the project leader attempts to draw clear boundaries and expectations exempting them from heroic measures to get the project done. The fact is that the scale of funds that projects are typically awarded – where $200,000 counts as a sizeable grant – is simply not commensurate with the work we commit to taking on. This is the case even if that work matches our actual needs and desires for the project, which it often does not. The discrepancy between the scale of funding available to humanists and to the sciences is not explainable in terms of the differences in material costs between the fields: labour is a primary cost driver in both cases. We do ourselves, and our collaborators, a deep disservice by pretending otherwise.

Digital humanities is long overdue for a reality check with regard to grant funding. While funding agencies have opened the door to public feedback before, the power dynamics at play inherently put constraints on honest dialogue. Scholars who are themselves potential future applicants are reluctant to raise concerns, lest it be taken as ingratitude – or worse, a reflection of their personal incompetence and inability to execute a project that others could do with ease. I write this from a position of a twisted kind of privilege: in my current role, I am not permitted to apply for grants. With grant funding off the table, I can speak more freely about what I have seen, both as a reviewer and while supporting applicants and recipients at various stages of their journeys.[4]

Funders need to be more conscientious about the assumptions that underpin their calls for proposals (CFPs). What are the benefits to the scholars who undertake this kind of work? What kinds of scholars are even in a position to undertake the work without great cost to their own careers, or spending nights and weekends on the grant in order to do the double load of traditionally legible scholarly output and a digital project? In what discipline(s) are the priorities in the CFP actually valued, beyond the mere CV bonus of receiving grant funding? For what discipline(s) do the priorities feel 'close enough' that scholars will be tempted to contort the work they want to do into the shape of the grant? How much time, realistically, is required to do a project that compellingly fulfils the CFP, and is the available funding adequate to do that work?[5]

Funding agencies have set out grant programmes as a form of indirect influence on the priorities of fields. However, the result has been an unresolved game of chicken between funders and fields, the latter of which have not broadly implemented changes to their tenure and promotion guidelines that reflect funder priorities. Professional organisations continue to fight to address this gap, issuing revision after revision to recommendations for greater recognition for digital scholarship. While this is better than simply leaving scholars to fend for themselves, both grant agencies and professional organisations need to take a more active stance in advocating for greater alignment between funding priorities, professional organisation recommendations and the actual requirements that scholars face in their own evaluation process. Otherwise, however well-meaning their actions may be, funders and professional organisations are setting up scholars for failure by incentivising them to pursue grants and start projects that will take time and energy away from work that will actually be rewarded in research-intensive institutions.

There is also a role here for scholars to do a better job of looking out for their own interests. If they see digital scholarship as an important part of their work, that should be included in the negotiations upfront around tenure and promotion requirements. Grant funding is alluring, particularly at institutions where the scholar has access to fewer resources to implement the kinds of projects they dream of, but it is crucial to be brutally honest with yourself about how far the grant expectations stray from what you actually want to do. What additional work are you taking on that you wouldn't otherwise? What will you be required to find in order to sustain the thing you create – assuming you are able to finish it? How much would you lose face if you're unable to complete the project, or unable to sustain it for long? What is the value of the project for you personally and your career, when weighed against these risks and challenges? What would you be losing out on – including factoring things like your own mental health – if (and, realistically, when) this project spills over into your nights and weekends, so you can meet the other professional expectations necessary to continue or progress in your job?

In 2023, the Association for Computers and the Humanities (ACH) sought to reimagine its seed grant programme in a direction that centred radical honesty. The outcome of the reinvisioned grant programme wouldn't be any particular *thing*, but a write-up of what the project team had learned in the process – which is to say, it would reflect what is truly the most durable outcome of most grants, and be resistant to the traps of self-delusion that so commonly accompany grants. While the implementation of this programme is still under discussion as of summer 2024, the act of discussing such a different approach to grantmaking was itself generative. On the one hand, ACH is free of the kinds of public accountability constraints that national funding agencies are. On the other hand, perhaps a radical reimagining of federal government grant programmes could also stop selling a conception of digital humanities that primarily produces platforms and tools, and shift the discourse towards digital humanities as a vehicle for developing important expertise, not unlike programmes funded under US Title VI, first introduced in 1958 under the National Defense Education Act (NDEA), which has subsequently provided support for language and area studies training (US Department of Education 2011). What if we thought of technical and analytical skills at the intersection of data and human cultures as akin to language or area studies knowledge: perhaps not relevant to all citizens at all times, but important for the country to know it has well-trained people to call upon in a crisis that would need to draw upon those skills. Alpert-Abrams (2020) movingly paints a picture of 'what the humanities do in a crisis'; as a later example, Saving Ukrainian Cultural Heritage Online (SUCHO) brought together digital humanists, librarians and everyday people to preserve Ukrainian digital cultural heritage under siege in Russia's full-scale invasion (LeBlanc et al. 2022). Ironically, the perceived risks that drove SUCHO were not realised in Ukraine, but rather, in the United States, as the Trump administration quickly undertook a ham-fisted keyword-search based effort to purge government webpages and data referencing women, ethnic minority groups, and the LGBTQ+ community. In a moment where methods commonly used – with care and thought and nuance – in digital humanities circles were being adopted to wipe out an inclusive historical narrative, digital humanities scholars in the US and beyond have found themselves in a position to apply their skills towards a social good.

This is a compelling case for the digital humanities, and there are existing grant programmes focused on training opportunities. But given the often poor alignment between grants that fund projects and what is actually to the benefit of both scholars and broader communities, it may be time to rethink the 'DH project grant' as a vehicle to prepare experts who can respond in a crisis, while simultaneously working with disciplinary organisations to develop meaningful, small-scale funding opportunities that can offset the costs of doing the kind of disciplinary digital work that can more directly lead to legible scholarly outcomes for the person doing it. If we cannot responsibly ask scholars to broaden their scope because we do not have the resources to either support or reward that kind of work, a better path forward would be to provide funding at the level where the scholar's own scope is meaningful and impactful. Even if the amount of funding were smaller, less money better targeted to the scholar's actual goals is still a better outcome than a larger grant that comes with unwanted obligations.

Conclusion

Money cuts across all disciplinary and technical boundaries, offering a form of validation legible to department chairs and deans, regardless of whether they share one's own methodological or theoretical framework. As a result, grant funding feels like the ultimate prize for many scholars, whether or not it actually makes the most sense as a way to implement the project they have in mind. The institutional value of grants – quite separate from the metrics on which scholars themselves are evaluated – further exacerbates this drive, leading scholars to partake in a collective delusion where grants are inherently good, however detrimental they may be in practice for the individual scholar.

Given the digital humanities culture of transparency and honestly reckoning with issues ranging from labour to data ethics, the role of grant funding is overdue some serious interrogation from all sides. Are funders genuinely satisfied with their existing programmes, and the incentives they lay out for scholars, even with the reasonably high probability of detrimental consequences for scholars' careers? Are scholars going into grant applications with a clear vision of metaphorically swallowing that first fly, and all the animals that are likely to follow? What are the roles of disciplinary organisations? Do they genuinely value the kinds of discipline-focused projects that scholars themselves come up with? If so, how can they support the realisation of these projects? If not, perhaps this should be made clear to scholars who can then make choices accordingly, as this has implications for their career development.

It is well past the time for looking the metaphorical gift horse of digital humanities grant funding in the mouth. Otherwise, one would be wise to recall the old lady who swallowed a horse. As the conclusion of the rhyme tells us: she died, of course.

Note from the author

This chapter was written in summer 2024. There is a painful irony in finalising a piece advocating for less reliance on grants, as a US citizen, in a moment when the Office of Digital Humanities has been eliminated from the National Endowment for the Humanities, which has experienced devastating funding cuts, along with the Institute for Museum and Library Services, another major DH funder within the US government. Regardless, I stand by these provocations, as an offering of food for thought for colleagues who find themselves in more supportive funding contexts, present and future.

Notes

1 See Allington et al. (2016) for an example of building an argument against digital humanities on the basis of that perceived connection.

2 See https://endings.uvic.ca (accessed 25 November 2024).

3 The mass cancellation of US National Endowment for the Humanities grants in spring 2025 under the Trump administration, in order to reallocate funds to a 'Garden of Heroes' featuring realistic sculptures of figures from American history from an approved list, goes to show that bad-faith political attacks are sometimes simply that. No amount of documentation and Gantt charts and carefully worked-through budgeting would have an impact on the cancellation of these grants, and the only path to reinstating these funds runs through appealing to elected representatives and lawsuits, such as ones filed by organisations including the Authors Guild, the American Council of Learned Societies, the Modern Language Association, the American Historical Association, and others.

4 Different positions come with different sets of opportunities and constraints, and in many cases, staff have a wealth of experience – across a wider range of projects than most individual faculty – and have less personally at stake in the outcome. As a result, they are more likely to be open about challenges, and can get into specifics while also maintaining an appropriate degree of anonymity.

5 The National Endowment for Humanities (NEH) has recently updated its grant application packet to require a justification of costs, which is a step in a positive direction towards surfacing how many people will be paid how much, and forcing applicants to reflect on these numbers somewhat. Programmes would benefit from even more explicit guidance about an appropriate scale for these projects.

References

Allington, Daniel, David Golumbia and Sarah Brouillette. 'Neoliberal Tools (and Archives): A Political History of Digital Humanities', *LA Review of Books* (1 May 2016). Accessed 25 November 2024. https://lareviewofbooks.org/article/neoliberal-tools-archives-political-history-digital-humanities/.

Alpert-Abrams, Hannah. 'What the Humanities Do in a Crisis'. Blog post (11 April 2020). Accessed 25 November 2024. https://halperta.medium.com/what-the-humanities-do-in-a-crisis-a7ae63263b0e.

Dombrowski, Quinn. 'The Directory Paradox'. In *People, Practice, Power: Digital Humanities Outside the Center*, edited by Anne McGrail, Angel David Nieves and Siobhan Senier, 83–98. Debates in Digital Humanities. University of Minnesota Press, 2021. https://doi.org/10.5749/9781452968346.

Graham, Shawn. 'How I Lost the Crowd'. In *Failing Gloriously and Other Essays*, 71–80. The Digital Press at the University of North Dakota, 2019. Accessed 25 November 2024. https://thedigitalpress.org/failing-gloriously/.

Keralis, Spencer. 'Disrupting Labor in Digital Humanities; or, The Classroom Is Not Your Crowd'. In *Disrupting the Digital Humanities*, edited by Dorothy Kim and Jesse Stommel, 273–94. Punctum Books, 2018.

LeBlanc, Zoe, et al. 'A Conversation with the Organizers of Saving Ukrainian Cultural Heritage Online (SUCHO)'. *Journal of Library Outreach and Engagement* 2, no. 1 (13 July 2022). https://doi.org/10.21900/j.jloe.v2i1.969.

Mann, Rachel. 'Paid to Do but Not to Think: Reevaluating the Role of Graduate Student Collaborators'. In *Debates in the Digital Humanities 2019*, edited by Matthew Gold and Lauren Klein, 268–78. Debates in Digital Humanities. University of Minnesota Press, 2019. https://doi.org/10.5749/9781452963785.

Risam, Roopika. 'Stewarding Place: Digital Humanities at the Regional Comprehensive University'. In *People, Practice, Power: Digital Humanities Outside the Center*, edited by Anne McGrail, Angel David Neives and Siobhan Senier, 304–14. Debates in Digital Humanities. University of Minnesota Press, 2021. https://doi.org/10.5749/9781452968346.

US Department of Education. 'The History of Title VI and Fulbright-Hays: An Impressive International Timeline'. 2011. Accessed 25 November 2024. https://web.archive.org/web/20240301181512/https://www2.ed.gov/about/offices/list/ope/iegps/history.html.

Chapter 2

Risk, failure and the assessment of innovative research

Jane Winters

Digital humanities research may be organised in numerous different ways within institutions – in departments, centres, hubs, institutes – but the unit of the laboratory is one that has been widely adopted. And, 'While the design lab or art studio has had a great influence on many digital humanities labs, the model of the science laboratory is most often invoked by those that imagine the digital humanities lab-space' (Earhart 2015, 392). Central to our understandings of such a laboratory is that it is a place where experiments happen, drawing on explicitly scientific methods. New knowledge is generated through experimentation, through trial and error, through what has been described as 'thinkering' – 'the action of playful experimentation with technological and digital tools for the interpretation and presentation' (C^2DH, n.d.). Such experimentation necessarily goes hand in hand not just with the potential for failure but with its inevitability. Mistakes are made. A 3D print of a complex object collapses before it is finished, the errors in a script only become apparent twenty-four hours after it was set running, a web scraper gets caught in a crawler trap, the wrong choice of stop words turns out to exclude an important set of entities during text analysis. This is the everyday experience of doing digital humanities research. It can, to say the least, be annoying, but it can also be a highly valuable learning experience or perhaps even generate new insights. The sharing of these setbacks and failures with other members of a team can prevent them from making the same mistakes, might help to explain a similar problem that has been holding them back, or might trigger a new idea or train of thought.

So far so good. This is the kind of failure that we can all get on board with. It is an acceptable, even desirable part of the research process. It is generally only talked about within a team, and often occluded by public descriptions of seamless pipelines and workflows, but there are no negative consequences were others to hear about it. But what happens when experimentation is scaled up, when it is not at the level of an individual task but at the heart of a large research project for which you are seeking funding? The stakes are suddenly much higher, both at the research proposal stage and subsequently (should you be lucky enough to get through peer review) during reporting on project delivery and outcomes. How can the possibility of failure be negotiated; how can it be acknowledged as inextricable from experimental processes, as an enabler of innovation?

To read the funding calls published by research support agencies is to be struck with enthusiasm for and interest in experimentation, innovation and interdisciplinarity. A quick glance at recent calls published by UK Research and Innovation (UKRI) open to arts and humanities researchers reveals the presence of words such as 'ambitious', 'transform', 'alternative', 'innovative', 'breakthrough', 'disruptive' and 'transcend' (UKRI, n.d.). Researchers are encouraged to think big, to push at the boundaries of current knowledge and to devise projects that will be transformative both in form and in findings. But how does this aspiration hold up in the face of traditional peer-review criteria that include value for money, feasibility and track record of success? These are, of course, important factors to consider – especially for publicly funded research – but within the strict grading systems operated by many funding bodies, they can serve almost systemically to weed out innovation and experimentation. What are the mechanisms for evaluating the feasibility of a method that cannot be fully explained at the outset of a project because it will only develop as the research unfolds? This might be the case, for example, in a project that draws on systemic action research. It is possible to outline the broad principles of the action research cycle – plan, act, observe, reflect, plan forward – but not precisely where they will lead in the context of a particular project (Heron and Reason 2006). The lack of fixity is precisely the point, but it carries with it risk, and with risk comes the potential for failure. We are encouraged to 'manage out' risk; if it is acknowledged at all it is in the reassuring form of a carefully weighted risk register. But in attempting to remove risk completely we are in danger of stifling innovative practice, discouraging interdisciplinary collaboration and holding back the development of new forms of scholarly output.

One way of addressing this challenge is to devise funding schemes that support straightforwardly exploratory and experimental research. The Curiosity Awards scheme launched by UKRI in 2023, for example, is 'intentionally flexible' and encourages proposals concerned, among other things, with 'high risk and high potential concepts' (a rare positive mention of risk!) and 'scoping and piloting . . . early-stage proof of concept for ideas or change of direction' (UKRI 2023). As might be expected, the available funding is relatively limited (up to £100,000) but that in itself removes a degree of pressure from applicants and opens the door to generative failure as a reported research finding. Such schemes will work most effectively if they are accompanied by peer-review training processes that encourage recognition of risk, uncertainty and failure as inherent in some of the most exciting and challenging research and not as an automatic indicator of unfeasibility. There has to be scope to admit that risk is present, and that a project may fail, but that it is worth supporting despite and perhaps even because of that fact.

The connection between 'high risk' and 'high potential' in some areas of research is clearly beginning to be recognised. Encouraging risk in principle, however, is not the same thing as accepting it and its companion – failure – in practice. How can institutions, funding bodies, research teams and individual researchers work together to create spaces where it becomes not just possible but essential to report on the things that have failed, and what was learnt from that failure, as well as to celebrate project successes? This is hard to do within evaluation and reporting structures that are concerned with metrics – how many journal articles were published by a project team, how many conferences did they attend, what software and datasets were created, how many people interacted with project outputs of varying kinds? There may often simply be no mechanism for telling the story of a project in official reporting, of contextualising both achievements and failure to achieve intended goals, of exploring the innovation that can arise from having to redesign an ongoing project that is not quite working.

There are, though, some positive developments in relation to the evaluation of research, including the acceptance not just that 'Research assessment shapes research culture', but that 'Funders can initiate positive culture change through careful design and implementation of research assessment' (Global Research Council 2020, 5). Initiatives such as the Declaration on Research Assessment (DORA) and the Coalition for Advancing Research Assessment (CoARA) encourage more qualitative approaches to the assessment of research and its impact, allowing complex narratives about research trajectories to be constructed, valued and evaluated. The dial is beginning to move, but it takes a long time to change a research culture, and perhaps even longer to overcome institutional aversion to risk and the public acknowledgement of failure.

Finally, it is important to recognise that the option to talk openly about risk and failure is not available to everyone, or that the potential consequences may be different depending on career stage, gender, ethnicity or a range of other factors. Established researchers are much more able to talk about their failures, about their rejected grant proposals and publications, about the projects that had to be steered back on to the rails, without damaging their careers. This brings a responsibility to do precisely that, while acknowledging that such openness reflects privilege. We can all, however, respond to consultations from funding bodies looking to design and implement responsible research assessment processes. We can all work within our institutions to raise awareness of what it means to be a DORA signatory in both principle and practice. We can all make space within our teams for the sharing of failure without judgement or consequence. It may take time, but we can change research cultures and bring failure openly into our research and practice as a positive force.

References

C²DH. ‘Thinkering’, n.d. Accessed 25 June 2024. https://www.c2dh.uni.lu/thinkering.

Earhart, Amy. ‘The Digital Humanities as a Laboratory’. In *Between Humanities and the Digital*, edited by Patrik Svensson and David Theo Goldberg. MIT Press, 2015.

Global Research Council. *Responsible Research Assessment*. 2020. Accessed 25 June 2024. https://globalresearchcouncil.org/fileadmin//documents/GRC_Publications/GRC_RRA_Conference_Summary_Report.pdf.

Heron, John and Peter Reason. ‘The Practice of Co-operative Enquiry: Research “With” Rather than “On” People’. In *Handbook of Action Research*, edited by Peter Reason and Hilary Bradbury, 179–88. Sage Publications, 2006.

UKRI. ‘AHRC Responsive Mode: Curiosity Award Round One’. 2023. Accessed 25 June 2024. https://www.ukri.org/opportunity/ahrc-responsive-mode-curiosity-award/.

UKRI. ‘Funding Finder: AHRC’, n.d. Accessed 25 June 2024. https://www.ukri.org/opportunity/?filter_council%5B%5D=814.

Chapter 3

Innovation, tools and ecology

Christopher Ohge

Innovation may seem like a new idea, but it is a sixteenth-century term that was first recorded during an era of scientific revolutions. The *Oxford English Dictionary* defines it firstly as 'The action of innovating; the introduction of novelties; the alteration of what is established by the introduction of new elements or forms' (s.v. 'Innovation, n.'). But it also includes an obsolete sense of 'political revolution; a rebellion or insurrection' exemplified by Shakespeare's King Henry IV's warning about the 'discontents' who 'gape and rub the elbow at the newes / Of hurly burly innouation' (*Henry IV, Part 1*, v. i. 78). Nowadays many people would think of its most common usage of bringing a new product into the market, but the first sense of 'novelty' and 'new forms' speaks to the ethos of many digital researchers. That lingering sense of revolution may also suggest another reason why it is so congenial to technology, whether it was the 'revolution' of print in the fifteenth century (as Elizabeth Eisenstein put it, which has since rightly been reconsidered as overly sweeping) or the digital revolution of the past few decades (Eisenstein 2012; Johns 2000; Baron et al. 2007). When resources are scarce, though, it might also seem attractive to a humble humanist to claim that they are revolutionaries now, too. (King Henry IV might suggest danger.) This relationship between innovation and revolution brings me to the core question of this polemic: is it a failure to innovate in digital humanities (DH), or a greater failure *not* to innovate? Or, better yet, under which conditions should we innovate when the idea itself seems to partake of growth-economy logic that has perpetuated the climate crisis? Should innovation be about newness as such, or about 'making it new' (namely, making something new out of tradition, or what has worked well before)?

The fact that 'Innovation' was a criterion for acceptance into the Association of Digital Humanities convention in 2023 shows its importance as a working principle in DH, even though there is still no consensus on what the term means. If innovation is about novelty, or about engaging in a logic that supports neoliberal hype, then it can become an albatross for a DH researcher or team. Innovations in DH have led to some important benefits (e.g. IIIF n.d) as well as failures (e.g. Project Bamboo), but the albatross is usually the resources required for maintaining the project (Dombrowski 2014). Yet some of the greatest achievements of DH tool-making are not 'innovative' in the sense of being sophisticated or flashy – like AntConc (Anthony n.d.) or Voyant Tools (Sinclair and Rockwell n.d.) – but simple and very useful and are nonetheless impactful and widely used.

As I worked as a coordinator for the Digital Humanities Climate Coalition Toolkit (Baillot et al. 2024), it became clear that an unthinking loyalty to innovation-as-novelty contributes to an increased carbon footprint. It also betrays the dual calamity of the climate crisis and precarity – *precarity*, in that many institutions simply cannot afford to be innovative, and that the people required to do this work are operating under the realities of insecure university staffing.

Given these considerations – the vexed implications of innovation, the environmental costs of innovation and precarious resources and labour conditions – innovation should be framed in pragmatic terms. By 'pragmatic terms' I mean making things that work and that help us cope better with the conditions of our research.[1] (This goes against a capitalist logic of innovation which valorises novelty and return on investment.) I can think of no better example of this in my own digital work than the development of a manuscript editor for the Herman Melville Electronic Library (hereafter, MEL).[2] When I started contributing to this project, in 2010, one of the project's main focuses was to develop an XML editor, called TextLab, initially to encode the complicated surviving manuscript of *Billy Budd*. Developed by Nick Laiacona, who had previously worked with Jerome McGann on the Juxta Commons platform,[3] TextLab was as innovative a manuscript editor as one could imagine: it matched TEI XML-encoded transcriptions of a manuscript to the coordinates of the manuscript's facsimile, allowing for a granular examination of inscriptions and revisions. It was also multilayered: it could view a diplomatic transcription (with mouseover pop-up

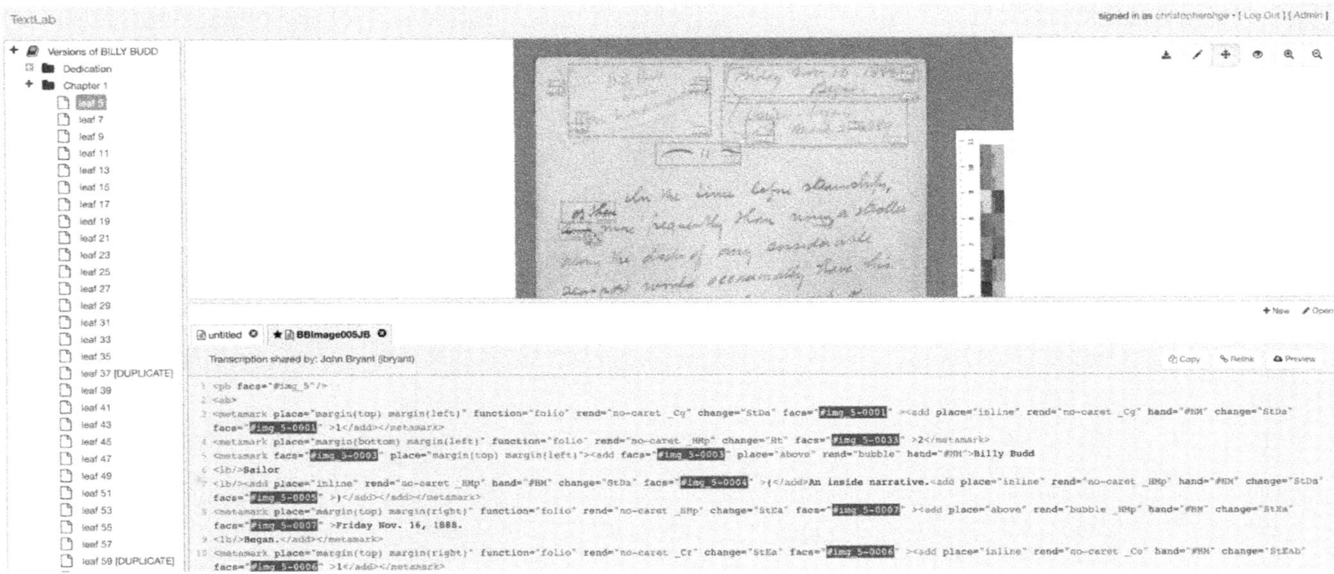

Figure 3.1: TextLab XML editing window. Public domain.

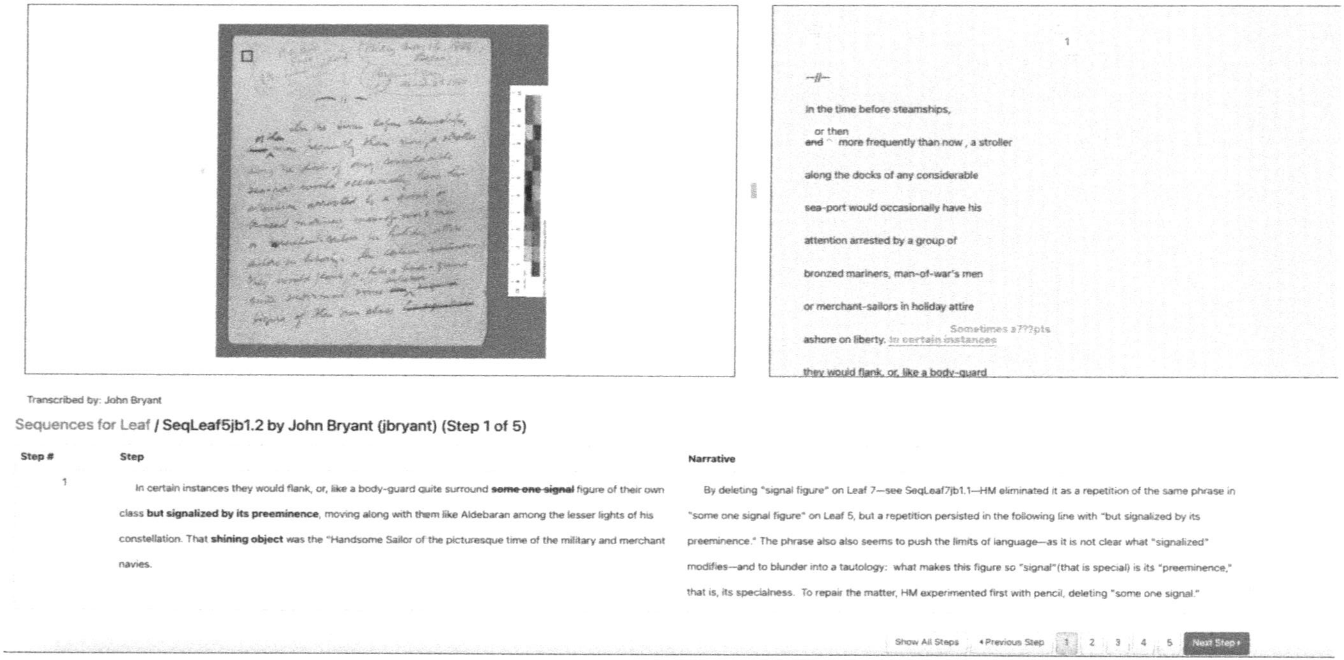

Figure 3.2: TextLab's diplomatic transcription view, with revision narrative sequences, from the Melville Electronic Library (c. 2019). Public domain.

notes that showed the TEI encoding), a base text (a cleaned-up version of the diplomatic text), as well as 'revision narrative' notes to explain how the text changed.

This all amounted to a technical implementation of John Bryant's theories in *The Fluid Text*, which argued for a new way of presenting all versions of a text in a digital interface (Bryant 2002). TextLab was brilliant: by 2019, the editors had completed a fully encoded digital edition of *Billy Budd*.

TextLab presented some serious issues, though. The first is that it was developed for one project, the Melville Electronic Library, rather than being built as a general-purpose tool. It was also a dynamic app, hosted on Heroku, that cost several hundred US dollars per month just to maintain. Then MEL lost its support from its funder. Then the director of the project, John Bryant, retired, and his former institution chose not to support the project, and its supporting research centre. MEL became the orphan that Ishmael describes at the end of *Moby-Dick*.[4] But we also faced the dilemma of innovating without being able to pay for it in the long term. By hosting a dynamic app on a third-party site, we were also not harbouring a sustainable, environmentally friendly tool. This is not the fault of anyone in particular: these were the conditions of innovation under which we were operating – conditions which were incentivised by the funding environment at the time but not supported for the long term. Like many projects that benefit from a windfall, MEL created cutting-edge tools that directly contributed to its obsolescence.

Even though we learned these lessons the hard way, we continued our conversations and collaboration with Nick Laiacona, who has since founded Performant Software to support digital humanities projects and develop tools. We agreed that what was needed was a general-purpose tool similar to TextLab but that could make use of existing innovations (such as IIIF) while also making use of minimal computing principles to ensure sustainability.[5] By combining features of MEL's TextLab with another project's lightweight manuscript interface, at the Making and Knowing Project, Laiacona released EditionCrafter in 2023.[6] Owing to the stable TEI XML source data at the Melville Electronic Library, we were able to facilitate the replacement of the TextLab software with EditionCrafter to display the *Billy Budd* manuscript.

By innovating in this pragmatic and responsible way, and with much heroic effort by Laiacona and other colleagues, we were able to build on a previous failure to ensure the stability of the project and to support a more

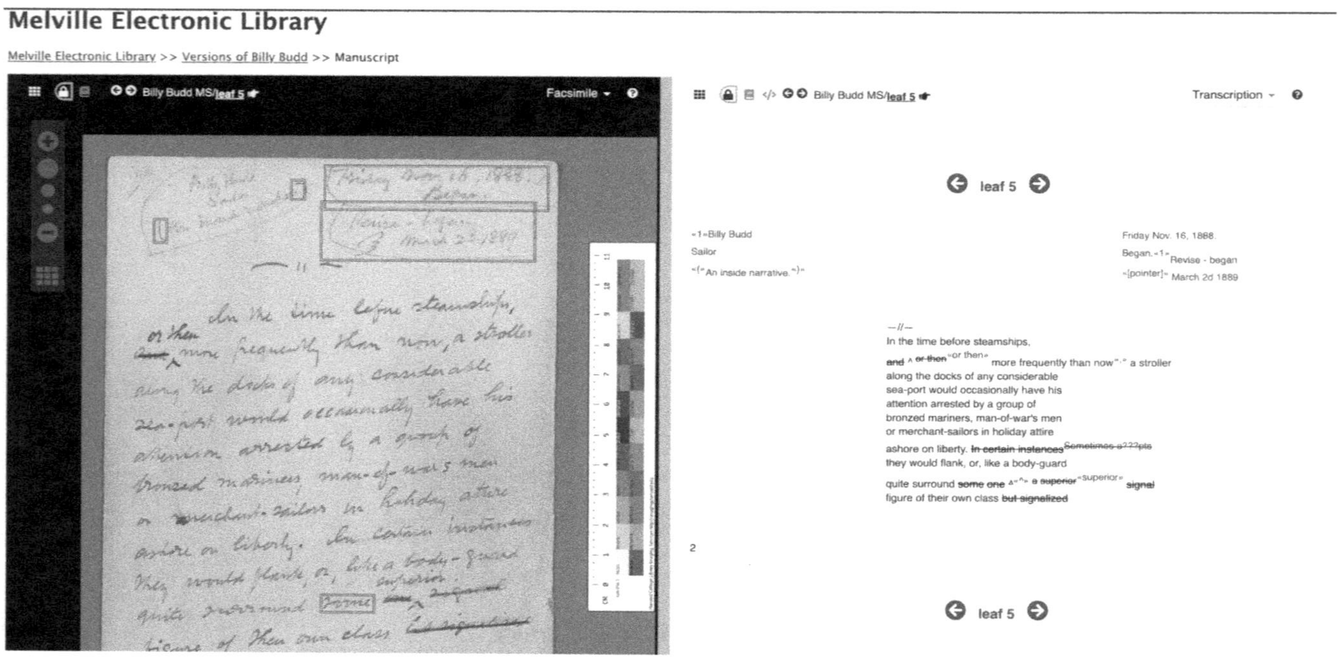

Figure 3.3: The current *Billy Budd* manuscript viewer in Edition Crafter (https://melville.electroniclibrary.org/editions/versions-of-billy-budd/billy-budd-ms.html#/ec/img_5/f/img_5/transcription). Public domain.

responsible digital tool.[7] By doing so, we were also setting an example to reduce the carbon footprint of our project.

I rather like the organic metaphor of innovation, used in botany, to describe the growth of a new shoot at the apex of a stem or branch. It reframes innovation as a process of 'making it new', or branching off from the whole – to push the metaphor further, it could entail that innovation is a new branch of the discipline which is dependent on its roots. Innovation can strengthen that which remains. What this would require, in theory, is that we innovate by branching off from what is already useful, and to think of more efficient ways of promoting healthy growth. I would hope that if we undertake the much harder work of changing our culture of innovation in digital humanities, we might see more innovative thinking instead of techno-utopian promises that contribute to the further degradation of the natural world. In practice, this would mean putting the focus on doing things well (and responsibly) rather than novelty for novelty's sake (making new things), without pressuring ourselves to introduce novelties into technology that are unnecessary to promote the core enterprise – the work, the research.

Notes

1 In Chapter 1 of my *Publishing Scholarly Editions: Archives, Computing, and Experience* (Cambridge University Press, 2021), I discuss what pragmatic approaches to editing and publishing entail.

2 See https://melville.electroniclibrary.org/ (accessed 25 November 2024).

3 See https://wiki.tei-c.org/index.php/JuxtaCommons (accessed 25 November 2024).

4 See the detailed analysis of the ongoing management, security and sustainability of roughly 100 digital humanities projects by Smithies, Westling, Sichani, Mellen and Ciula in *Digital Humanities Quarterly* (2019).

5 Minimal computing refers to computing done under some set of significant constraints of hardware, software, education, network capacity, power or other factors, as defined by the Global Outlook Digital Humanities group. See https://go-dh.github.io/mincomp/about/ (accessed 25 November 2024).

6 See https://edition640.makingandknowing.org/#/ and https://cu-mkp.github.io/editioncrafter/ (accessed 25 November 2024).

7 Before EditionCrafter was implemented, the MEL website had also been transformed into a static site, which further reduced energy usage and ensured long-term sustainability.

Indeed, supporting communities of practice in software creation, documentation and training may be a particularly effective intervention in the humanities context: it is a means of sharing practice from the 'early adopters' to build capacity. A strong example of this approach is the consortia of Huma-Num, the French Research Infrastructure for the Social Sciences and Humanities, where collective consultation defines communities and their technical resources.[2]

SSI itself has sustained for fourteen years to date, helped by its 'collaborate, not compete' ethos and wide disciplinary breadth. Its current work focuses on four of the software sustainability priorities we perceive today: capable research communities, widespread adoption of research software best practice, evidence-driven research software policy and guidance, and broadened access and contributions to the research software community.[3] In this way, SSI is building resilience against failure into the research community and addressing the software waste cycle.

The new primitives

While digital computational resources have grown over recent decades, so too has the engagement of citizens with the digital world – we were once a community of scholars with access to a small number of computers; now we operate in a world of crowd and cloud, and a new abundance of both data and computation.

This nexus is significant in the evolution of our knowledge infrastructure. It has, for example, catalysed the remarkable success and adoption of large language models (LLMs). Machine learning approaches are rapidly being adopted into our digital research methods, and into the infrastructure itself.

It is interesting to reflect on the various affordances we have identified in the context of scholarly primitives (Unsworth 2000). Some of them might suggest, or at least align with, candidates for new primitives; for example modelling, prototyping, crowdsourcing and training a machine learning model.

We suggest that another new affordance of the digital, and perhaps a scholarly primitive, is play (De Roure and Willcox 2020). Play involves observing, testing and trying; it involves imagination and, crucially, it is safe to fail. Newcomers to programming are often relieved to discover they don't break the computer if they get something wrong. Play encourages experimentation and immediate learning from failure; digital affordances mean these experiments can proceed at pace.

We can experiment easily, bringing multiple approaches to analyse a dataset and borrowing ideas from near and far: does a method of analysing a corpus of eighteenth-century French literature reveal useful insights when applied to the same genre, but in nineteenth-century Italian? Can a sequence-matching algorithm used in bioinformatics be applied to music analysis? Playing with software also underpins the hackathon as a method, and indeed is celebrated in hacker culture (Parrish 2016) – it is naturally something we can do with software, and naturally something humans do. It catalyses creativity: as Boden says, 'Creativity is the ability to come up with ideas or artefacts that are new, surprising and valuable' (Boden 2004). Play as a scholarly primitive is embedded in our scholarly practices and enables failure and innovation at the same time.

We would argue that our enduring infrastructure should also be designed for play, for example through programmatic interfaces. These new affordances empower us to create new infrastructure ourselves, and to share it. This is powerful, though we must be aware of the responsibilities that go with it. When we create infrastructure we are party to it not being agnostic, and with disaffordances in mind too, we should be transparent about the costs: both machine learning and crowdsourcing can be expensive, in energy and the time of volunteers. These are important aspects of *Responsible Innovation* (Jirotka et al. 2017), in the context of software and of research infrastructure.

Software, innovation and failure

Innovation in software tools and their application occurs right across the disciplinary landscape. This involves experiments in designing and applying digital methods, and these are possible due to the ease of creating and adapting software. Key to this process of experimentation is failure. This is not just tolerated but absolutely fundamental to the process, and the flexibility with which we can conduct these digital experiments means this can be low risk.

Does this apply equally to the sciences and humanities? To a great extent, the computational aspects are applicable, and practices can be shared. This is illustrated well by the practice of open source software development, and code sharing on GitHub. We might view GitHub as a social edition of software, which we are all able to use and to curate, with a comprehensive provenance.

Relatedly, the notion of reproducibility is promoted in the digital research world and is directly relevant to digital humanities and digital scholarship. In this context, reproducibility (which we might think of as 'computational reproducibility') means making data and code available so that the computations can be executed again with equivalent results. This is hugely valuable in sharing practice, and it enables outputs to be tested, compared and interpreted, and for new experiments to be conducted – supporting innovation.

However there is a stronger notion, and extensive history, of reproducible research in the sciences, and it is very much about failure. To test a proposed addition to the common knowledge, the scientific method requires independent replication of an experiment – by different researchers, in a different laboratory, typically implementing the same methodology. Replication is essential to give confidence in scientific results, hence repetition and failure are fundamental parts of the process.

This approach to independent replication is perhaps where the established cultures most differ. Science necessarily has a culture of documenting failure and of 'repeating', as part of an accepted and principled method. There are many comparisons to be drawn, but traditional humanities scholarship does not typically report failure in this way. We can imagine a scientific reproducibility approach to archival research: do two people get the same result from the same archive, do we build confidence in a result by going into more than one? However, we do see some practice of reproducibility, for example in archaeology where replication studies have educational benefits too (Marwick et al. 2020).

Perhaps, then, what we are proposing with the digital approaches is to support this process of interpretation and model building – augmenting our mental models with digital ones, which give us new means of observing, testing and sharing.

But for the digital part, we can innovate and play, fail and improve, and we can document this through open software practices. By sharing software, computational reproducibility demonstrates a less independent replication than science – it might be compared to sharing a lab or at least apparatus. But this is useful in an ecosystem which is growing in communities of practice and rapidly evolving – where labs are scarce and shared ones welcome.

Permission to be creative: permission to fail

At some point in the future we might lose the 'digital' prefix and digital scholarship will just be called scholarship, with the digital methods assumed where they are relevant. But the only way to get to that point is first to develop the digital methods, skills, capacity and career paths. We have shown that innovation in methods involves failing and learning from that failure. What is essential is to give people the power of play, permission to be creative and permission to fail, so that this innovation can occur.

Notes

1 See https://www.software.ac.uk/ (accessed 25 November 2024).

2 See https://documentation.huma-num.fr/humanum-en/ (accessed 25 November 2024).

3 See https://www.ukri.org/news/ukri-continues-investing-in-improving-research-software-practices/ (accessed 25 November 2024).

References

Berry, David M. and Mark C. Marino. 'Reading ELIZA: Critical Code Studies in Action', *Electronic Book Review* (3 November 2024). Accessed 25 November 2024. https://electronicbookreview.com/essay/reading-eliza-critical-code-studies-in-action/.

Boden, Margaret A. *The Creative Mind: Myths and Mechanisms*. 2nd edn. Routledge, 2004. https://doi.org/10.4324/9780203508527.

Cohen, Jeremy, Daniel S. Katz, Michelle Barker, Neil Chue Hong, Robert Haines and Caroline Jay. 'The Four Pillars of Research Software Engineering', *IEEE Software* 38, no. 1 (2021): 97–105. https://doi.org/10.1109/MS.2020.2973362.

De Roure, David and Pip Willcox. 'Scholarly Social Machines: A Web Science Perspective on Our Knowledge Infrastructure'. In *Proceedings of the 12th ACM Conference on Web Science* (WebSci '20), 49–58. New York: Association for Computing Machinery, 2020. https://doi.org/10.1145/3394231.3397915.

De Roure, David and Pip Willcox. 'Numbers into Notes: Digital Prototyping as Close Reading of Ada Lovelace's "Note A"'. Paper presented at *ADHO* 2017, McGill University, Montreal, 2017. Accessed 25 November 2024. https://dh2017.adho.org/abstracts/540/540.pdf.

Jirotka, Marina, Bastian Grimpe, Bernd Stahl, Gillian Eden and Mark Hartswood. 'Responsible Research and Innovation in the Digital Age', *Communications of the ACM* 60, no. 5 (2017): 62–8. https://doi.org/10.1145/3064940.

Ma, Bofan, Ellen Sargen, David De Roure and Emily Howard. 'Learning to Learn: A Reflexive Case Study of PRiSM SampleRNN'. Paper presented at *AIMC 2024,* Oxford, 9–11 September 2024. Accessed 25 November 2024. https://aimc2024.pubpub.org/pub/fnpykfdv.

Marwick, Ben, Li-Ying Wang, Ryan Robinson and Hope Loiselle. 'How to Use Replication Assignments for Teaching Integrity in Empirical Archaeology', *Advances in Archaeological Practice* 8, no. 1 (2020): 78–86. https://doi.org/10.1017/aap.2019.38.

Michie, Donald. 'Advances in Programming and Non-Numerical Analysis', *Nature* 200 (1963): 641–2. https://doi.org/10.1038/200641a0.

Naughton, John. 'Lecture: Getting from Here to There', *MedieKultur: Journal of Media and Communication Research* 30, no. 57 (2014). https://doi.org/10.7146/mediekultur.v30i57.18609.

Parrish, Allison. 'Programming Is Forgetting: Toward a New Hacker Ethic'. Open Transcripts, 2016. Accessed 25 November 2024. open-transcripts.org/transcript/programming-forgetting-new-hacker-ethic/.

Taylor, Rebecca, Johanna Walker, Simon Hettrick, Philippa Broadbent and David De Roure. 'Shaping Data and Software Policy in the Arts and Humanities Research Community: A Study for the AHRC'. Zenodo, 2022. https://doi.org/10.5281/ZENODO.10518740.

Unsworth, John. 'Scholarly Primitives 20 Years Later'. Video. Version 1.0.0. DARIAH-Campus, 2020. Accessed 25 November 2024. https://campus.dariah.eu/resource/posts/scholarly-primitives-20-years-later.

Unsworth, John. 'Scholarly Primitives: What Methods Do Humanities Researchers Have in Common, and How Might Our Tools Reflect This'. Paper presented at the Symposium on Humanities Computing: Formal Methods, Experimental Practice, King's College, London, May 2000. Accessed 25 November 2024. https://people.brandeis.edu/~unsworth/Kings.5-00/primitives.html.

Part II
TECHNOLOGY

Failure and technological obsolescence

Digital things constantly break. Our systems crash. An essential piece of software is no longer supported. There is an error message on the landing page of a project's website. A dataset is in an unreadable format. The computer no longer has a way to read a once-common storage device.

Media and digital technology evolve rapidly and things that were once new and innovative – devices, technical standards, programming languages – are quickly surpassed by newer ones. Technologies that once undergirded whole digital ecosystems are now semi-functional, if they are usable at all (Mladentseva 2022). Researchers working in digital scholarship encounter this challenge in two distinct areas of their work: the digital as an object of study and the digital as a tool for scholarship (Gitelman 2008). In both cases, the fragility of technical systems is keenly felt.

Those who study digital systems or digitally mediated communities are more aware than most of the constant cycle of obsolescence that seems to define digital technology in particular. This is a relatively new challenge for scholars – as Carolyn Marvin (1988, 2) reminds us, '*new technologies* is a historically relative term' – and Frances Corry reflects on the difficulties, logistical and otherwise, inherent in studying these things.

Since digital scholarship brings with it this notion of building, along-side an ethos of experimentation, we also have our own long list of technical failures to address (Dombrowski 2014; Star and Ruhleder 1996). Despite concerns dating back to the 1990s, only in the last few years have keywords like 'sustainability', 'maintenance' and 'resiliency' become *de rigueur* in project plans and funding requirements (Smithies et al. 2019; Holmes et al. 2023). Jenny Mitcham's reflection points to the role that open discussions of failure can play in encouraging these developments, while at the same time reminding us that the fetishisation of 'best practice' can sometimes detract from meaningful action.

Despite this recent focus on sustainability, the funding model for research still means that digital outputs often fall into disrepair almost the moment they are finished. Many more fail to be accessible after a few years, let alone for the decades-long timescales expected of scholarly outputs in the humanities. Arianna Ciula addresses some of these challenges in her reflection, drawing on the long history that King's Digital Lab has in maintaining legacy digital projects. Even when long-term solutions do succeed, as they did with TEI-XML, Joris van Zundert argues that we can become victims of our own (apparent) success – locked into the philosophies of these specific technologies in a way that leads to future failure.

References

Dombrowski, Quinn. 'Whatever Happened to Project Bamboo?', *Literary and Linguistic Computing* 29, no. 3 (2014): 326–39. https://doi.org/10.1093/llc/fqu026.

Gitelman, Lisa. *Always Already New: Media, History and the Data of Culture*. MIT Press, 2008.

Holmes, Martin, Janelle Jenstad and Matthew J. Huculak. 'Introduction to Special Issue: Project Resiliency in the Digital Humanities', *Digital Humanities Quarterly* 17, no. 1 (2023). http://www.digitalhumanities.org/dhq/vol/17/1/000671/000671.html.

Marvin, Carolyn. *When Old Technologies Were New: Thinking About Electric Communication in the Late Nineteenth Century*. Oxford University Press, 1988.

Mladentseva, Anna. 'Responding to Obsolescence in Flash-Based Net Art: A Case Study on Migrating Sinae Kim's *Genesis*', *Journal of the Institute of Conservation* 45, no. 1 (2022): 52–68. https://doi.org/10.1080/19455224.2021.2007412.

Smithies, James, Carina Westling, Anna-Maria Sichani, Pam Mellen and Arianna Ciula. 'Managing 100 Digital Humanities Projects: Digital Scholarship & Archiving in King's Digital Lab', *Digital Humanities Quarterly* 13, no. 1 (2019). http://www.digitalhumanities.org/dhq/vol/13/1/000411/000411.html.

Star, Susan Leigh and Karen Ruhleder. 'Steps Toward an Ecology of Infrastructure: Design and Access for Large Information Spaces', *Information Systems Research* 7, no. 1 (1996): 111–34. https://doi.org/10.1287/isre.7.1.111.

Chapter 5

Brokenness is social

Frances Corry

When I think of a piece of broken technology, it tends to be my phone, which, despite best effort and purchased protection, is always chipped, glass falling into my hands. If I don't think of my broken phone, perhaps it's my toaster – burning one side of the bread. Or there's the doorbell, which doesn't ring at all (sorry to anyone who tries to visit). If I imagine a little longer, beyond the surface of screens, broken technology could be a 404 warning on a webpage – a broken link, something at least I don't feel responsible for fixing. As numerous as these broken artefacts are, their number isn't entirely surprising: science and technology scholars, with a nod to Nigerian author Chinua Achebe (1958), have noted quite simply that, 'Things are made, and things fall apart' (Jackson 2014; Jackson et al. 2011).

The point is, that when I think of broken technology, I tend to first think of something material, or physical; something visualisable and bound to an object. A search online for images of 'broken technology' would lead you toward the same conclusion: broken technology means piles of discarded electronics with smashed screens. But this lay sense of technological brokenness has started to fall apart too, breaking, in a sense, the more research I do on sociotechnical systems as they fall into disrepair and disuse, or as they are dismantled. Instead, through this research, technological brokenness has been revealed more and more as *social*, constituted through individuals and groups, in shared discourse and ideology. Understanding technological brokenness as social, as I'll show in this chapter, allows analysts and practitioners to see brokenness as not something that is absolute and bound to an object, but rather, as a category open to contestation and interpretation.

This is not to say that brokenness has always been treated as rote or as purely technical within scholarly literature. In science and technology studies, brokenness – and its entwined practice, repair – have been animated as useful lenses for understanding technical systems and their social entanglements. Science and Technology Studies (STS) scholar Steven Jackson, for instance, has proposed 'broken-world thinking', a framework that argues 'breakdown, dissolution, and change, rather than innovation, development, or design . . . are the key themes and problems facing new media and technology scholarship today' (Jackson 2014). Brokenness serves as the background to related scholarship on repair, which likewise has proposed that looking to and through repair of sociotechnical systems can foreground the pressing issues of our time. That is, repair as a subject is framed as an analytical move that tends to usurp dominant ways of thinking (Graham and Thrift 2007), particularly ideologies of innovation and progress mapped to new technology. In doing so, repair often reveals otherwise obfuscated actors and practices, modes of political resistance and contestation (Lloveras et al. 2025), just as it foregrounds often overlooked concepts, including identity and status, the effects of capitalism, as well as infrastructure, disaster and the environment (Russell and Vinsel 2018).

Scholarship from communication and information studies has also taken up brokenness, with a critical focus on 'glitches' in data-intensive, automatic decision-making systems, whether the algorithms used by Google Search or in recidivism rulings. Rooted in Black feminist perspectives, analyses of glitches by scholars like Safiya Noble (2018), Ruha Benjamin (2019) and Meredith Broussard (2023) have shown how events often described as glitches, such as Google Images labelling Black people as gorillas, or Google Search surfacing Nazi sites when looking up the term 'Jew' (Noble 2018), are more than minor malfunctions in a technical system. Rather, these so-called glitches are indicative of structural biases in these systems, perspectives of racism, ableism and misogyny endemic to the system rather than exceptional to it. As Broussard writes, 'A glitch can be fixed. The biases embedded in technology are more than mere glitches; they're baked in from the beginning' (Broussard 2023). Other thinkers have shown how 'errors' can catalyse creative and liberatory reimagining within systems of oppression. Writers like Jack Halberstam (2011) and Legacy Russell (2020), for instance, show how bodies and ways of knowing that do not align with dominant systems necessarily fail within these matrices of power, failure in turn creating conditions for alternative forms of selfhood and community. Digital humanities projects have also played with the generative, aesthetic potential of 'mistakes' (Sample 2015).

These treatments of breaking and brokenness, whether the analytical affordances of repair from STS or the revealing nature of the glitch from communication and information studies, begin to complicate the notion of technological brokenness as something that is simply a matter of a cracked screen. Rather, they started to phrase brokenness as something that can reveal and reimagine social relations. It is a lens I took up, and then expanded from, through empirical research into the closure, or sunsetting, of social media platforms.

Over the course of 2020 and 2021, I recruited former employees of social media platforms that had closed, contacting them through publicly available emails or through their LinkedIn profiles. I ultimately interviewed fifty-three participants. I wanted to learn about how social media platforms functioned beyond moments of growth and innovation, how employees made decisions about how to handle user data as platforms declined and closed, and how these decisions would shape what was left of these sites in the long term. The platforms employees represented were typically ones that had been popular in the United States, among them Geocities, Friendster, MySpace and Vine, but I also spoke to founders of smaller platforms based in the United States and the UK (Corry 2024).

Developing a codebook that was sensitive to these themes of repair through frameworks from STS, information studies and communication, I analysed these conversations using an iterative thematic coding analysis, bringing existing themes to the texts and generating emergent themes in the analysis process. The study was approved by the University of Southern California's Institutional Review Board.

Technological brokenness pervaded this work in obvious and non-obvious ways. There was the obvious way, that related to my material imaginary of technological brokenness as cracked screens and broken toasters. Social media platforms, at end of life, had to be materially dismantled: drives had to wiped, server space vacated, hardware sold and recycled. But brokenness revealed itself in ways that were not immediately obvious when I began these interviews, too; technological brokenness instead appeared as something that was always contextual and relational. Ideas of brokenness were categories defined and mobilised by different actors in different ways depending on social context.

This came out most clearly in the case of Friendster, a social media platform founded in 2002 in San Francisco. Friendster had similar capabilities to Facebook today, with user profiles, image sharing and messaging. As I've described in other writing about this platform (Corry 2022), Friendster grew rapidly, with significant amounts of blue-chip Silicon Valley funders who were interested in the possibilities of their userbase: young, hip and well-off tech workers of Silicon Valley and other major metro centres in the United States. Concurrently, however, the platform became popular in Southeast Asia, with the userbase there exceeding that in the United States. Former employees at Friendster noted that its popularity there grew in part because a famous Filipino actress joined the site early on, just as the site supplied a useful infrastructure for close-knit groups of friends, known in Tagalog as *barkada*, to communicate with one another.

In its early years, Friendster experienced significant technical breakage. The site struggled to handle user traffic and was often down, with little time for repairs, given its around the clock global use. Yet few employees, and platform investors, thought of the platform as 'broken' or 'failed' at that point. Rather, as another interviewee who founded a mobile platform noted: 'There is this saying: growth fixes everything'. In his interpretation, no matter the technical disrepair of the system, economic fungibility of the business, or difficult interpersonal dynamics of the employees, if user numbers were growing, the platform wasn't broken. For these sociotechnical systems, from the perspective of these actors, brokenness belied my imaginary of shattered screens: it did not equate to an ability to technologically function.

It was only when user numbers started to shift – when the technical issues had stabilised – that Friendster was deemed 'broken' by its US-based users, employees and investors. In the mid 2000s, Friendster users in the United States largely switched to MySpace and Facebook. Press accounts wondered what had ever happened to Friendster. Its investors implored its newly hired leadership teams to 'fix it and flog it', as one former CEO recounted: to get the platform to a place such that it could be sold, and investment recouped. But despite these discourses around Friendster's disrepair, use in Southeast Asia had continued robustly: in 2008, Friendster was far from broken, as it was the largest social network in Asia.

In Friendster's case, a sociotechnical system could be functioning when it was technically broken, and broken when it was technically functioning, according to some US employees and investors. On the other hand, user groups may have identified the platform as broken when it was technically struggling. Later on, users – especially users in Southeast Asia – may have thought of Friendster as robust even when US investors had deemed the platform broken. In other words, the platform's brokenness was contested, open to interpretation and contextually dependent. It depended on where you stood, and what you valued. It was *social.*

At its most basic, for something to be social means that it is *in relation to others* ('Social, adj. 5e'). Despite 'technological brokenness' always conjuring thoughts of individual objects – broken phones and doorbells and toasters – my interviews showed that brokenness is always social because it is always relational. It takes on meaning in groups of people, revealing complex social linkages (and their ruptures) between humans and other humans, and between humans and artefacts.

Understanding technological brokenness as social is useful, I think: to go beyond the object itself to the relations that animate it. What can that perspective do for analyses of technology, and for the theory and practice of digital humanities? Just as analyses of repair from STS, and analyses of glitches from information studies, have revealed otherwise obfuscated social relations, understanding brokenness as social may reveal interactions with sociotechnical systems that are otherwise hard to see. Brokenness may be a means of understanding how varying social worlds can interpret the same sociotechnical system in different, and sometimes competing, ways. Importantly, it may also point to a politics of brokenness, or how labels of disrepair and failure are wielded by different actors for different ends. Taking a relational and social view of brokenness also has the potential to inflect the critical praxis at the heart of the digital humanities. In DH, it might foreground the very human work – the choices and perspectives, as well as the labour hours – that go into project, tool and knowledge maintenance. It might prompt us to ask deeper questions about the types of social worlds that are supported or failed by this scholarly work. And it might build on that longstanding DH value of experimentation (Spiro 2012), and allow projects to investigate technological brokenness as a site of exploration, broadening the category beyond meaning the ability to technically function (Donaldson 2020).

These are perspectives that have seeped into my own relations to my many broken technologies. My toaster still burns the bread on one side, which has highlighted the planned irreparability of many consumer products. Glass continues to fall from my phone screen, but I realised it still functions for my needs, despite broken appearances. As for the un-ringable doorbell: I've decided I like the solitude.

References

Achebe, Chinua. *Things Fall Apart*. African Writers Series, AWS 1. Heinemann, 1958.

Benjamin, Ruha. *Race After Technology: Abolitionist Tools for the New Jim Code*. Polity, 2019.

Broussard, Meredith. *More than a Glitch: Confronting Race, Gender, and Ability Bias in Tech*. MIT Press, 2023.

Corry, Frances. 'The Production of Destruction: How Employee Values Shape Platform Afterlives', *New Media & Society*. 2024. https://doi.org/10.1177/14614448241276382.

Corry, Frances. 'Why Does a Platform Die? Diagnosing Platform Death at Friendster's End', *Internet Histories* 6, no. 1–2 (2022): 31–47. https://doi.org/10.1080/24701475.2021.1985360.

Donaldson, Sonya. 'Singing the Nation: On Memory, Ephemerality, and the Minimal Computing Model'. *Singing the Nation* (blog). 2020. Accessed 25 November 2024. https://singingthenation.com/posts/singing-the-nation/.

Graham, Stephen and Nigel Thrift. 'Out of Order: Understanding Repair and Maintenance', *Theory, Culture & Society* 24, no. 3 (2007): 1–25. https://doi.org/10.1177/0263276407075954.

Halberstam, Jack. *The Queer Art of Failure*. Duke University Press, 2011.

Jackson, Steven J. 'Rethinking Repair'. In *Media Technologies: Essays on Communication, Materiality, and Society*, edited by Tarleton Gillespie, Pablo J. Boczkowski and Kirsten A. Foot, 221–40. MIT Press, 2014.

Jackson, Steven J., Alex Pompe and Gabriel Krieshok. 'Things Fall Apart: Maintenance, Repair, and Technology for Education Initiatives in Rural Namibia'. In *iConference '11: Proceedings of the 2011 iConference*, 83–90. ACM Press, 2011. https://doi.org/10.1145/1940761.1940773.

Lloveras, Javier, Mario Pansera and Adrian Smith. 'On "the Politics of Repair Beyond Repair": Radical Democracy and the Right to Repair Movement', *Journal of Business Ethics* 196, no. 2 (2025): 325–44. https://doi.org/10.1007/s10551-024-05705-z.

Noble, Safiya Umoja. *Algorithms of Oppression*. NYU Press, 2018.

Russell, Andrew L. and Lee Vinsel. 'After Innovation, Turn to Maintenance', *Technology and Culture* 59, no. 1 (2018): 1–25. https://doi.org/10.1353/tech.2018.0004.

Russell, Legacy. *Glitch Feminism: A Manifesto*. Verso, 2020.

Sample, Mark. 'Your Mistake Was a Vital Connection'. *Sample Reality* (blog). 5 September 2015. Accessed 25 November 2024. https://samplereality.com/2015/09/05/your-mistake-was-a-vital-strategy/.

'Social, Adj. and n'. n.d. In *OED Online*. Oxford University Press. Accessed 22 February 2019. https://www.oed.com/dictionary/social_adj?tab=factsheet#21921663.

Spiro, Lisa. '"This Is Why We Fight": Defining the Values of the Digital Humanities'. In *Debates in the Digital Humanities*, edited by Matthew K. Gold, 16–35. University of Minnesota Press, 2012. https://doi.org/10.5749/9781452963754.

Chapter 6

A career in ruins? Accepting imperfection and celebrating failures in digital preservation and digital archaeology

Jenny Mitcham

A career in (the) ruins

Digital preservation was an interesting vocational choice for me. After an early career in archaeology, it seemed I was unable to escape from what is jokingly described as a 'career in ruins'. Even as I swapped my kneeling mat and trowel for a comfy office chair and a floppy disk drive the concepts of brokenness and uncertainty have been a constant companion.

Archaeology is all about piecing together and translating partial information from the past, whilst digital preservation is all about finding a way to transmit information to the future. Both disciplines are tinged with an element of failure. As archaeologists, how do we know if we've interpreted those messages from the past correctly? As digital archivists, how do we know whether people in the future will find, read and understand the digital messages we are preserving for them today? When you work in a career full of uncertainties, unknowns and speculation, some level of failure is to be expected, and even celebrated.

These two disciplines do collide and interface when we consider the term 'digital archaeology', which can be defined as 'rescuing neglected and damaged data resources' (Ross and Gow 1999), and the process of reclaiming digital information that has been damaged or become unusable due to technological obsolescence of formats and media.[1]

Of course, 'digital archaeology' is not the only thing that digital archivists do on a day-to-day basis. It forms a very small part of the work that we undertake. When digital preservation works well, the interventions and preservation activities happen early on. We 'fix' things *before* they become broken. We take actions to collect, describe, manage and maintain the content *whilst it is still current* and usable. We carry out further activities to assess risks and plan preservation actions *before* they become an urgent necessity.

Change is inevitable and none of us can foresee the future. We make decisions about the preservation of digital content without the benefit of a crystal ball and with no way of being sure that our decisions were the best ones. As a result, uncertainty is our constant companion and the answer to nearly every question about digital preservation is 'it depends'. There is no one-size-fits-all solution to preserve our digital archives and, invariably, the details and specifics of each scenario matter (Owens 2018).

Good, better, best . . .

It surprises me when I see the term 'best practice' coming up so often in our line of work. Given the uncertainty that is typically present around what we do and how we do it, the trend to strive for 'best practice' feels neither healthy nor realistic. Do we know what 'best practice' is in the context of our work? Are we setting ourselves up for greater failure by aiming for this? It is particularly hard to claim that anything we do in this line of work could be considered 'best practice' when our workflows and strategies are ever evolving, and we have limited options to evidence our success. How can we know if preservation strategies and actions implemented today have been successful? For many, including those who are just getting started, those with limited resources and support, and those who are trying to find innovative solutions in new areas, 'good enough' is a far more achievable aim. Finding a workable solution and documenting the imperfections and opportunities for improvement doesn't necessarily align with the 'best practice' rhetoric but is often a more realistic way of working.[2]

Accepting imperfection

Consider a 'digital archaeology' scenario I faced several years ago in a previous role at the Borthwick Institute for Archives. I was given the task of preserving a series of screenplays that had been written using a legacy word processing package from the early 1990s and stored for many years on 5¼ inch floppy disks. Aside from the issue of recovering the data from an obsolete media format, and establishing which software the files had been created in, the challenge remained to preserve the information in a format that could be read and understood by users who wanted to access those screenplays both now and into the future.

This task brought with it many layers of imperfection and brokenness. Firstly, some of those original floppy disks could no longer be read. Secondly, experiments with file format conversion were not able to preserve every significant feature of the original WordStar files – a compromise ultimately had to be reached. Thirdly, the scenario became more challenging on discovering that some of the files in this collection were already damaged, having suffered from localised corruption at some point in their lifecycle. Having no route to go back and 'fix' this corruption, attention turned to how to record and document the issue. As I worked through this set of challenges I blogged about my progress, noting these observations and flagging up the many imperfections of this work (Mitcham 2018).

A contrasting digital preservation case study concerned more modern documents in native Google Document format (Micham 2017). Though exporting these 'documents' for archive tended to create an accurate copy of the words on the page, other elements were compromised. Collaborative features of the document such as comments (often a key feature of records created in this platform) were often not replicated well, and key document properties visible within Google Drive (for example, owner, creation date, last modified date) were not consistently retained. Other features of the original, such as the full revision history of the document, are also lost on export. Given there was no perfect preservation solution for these types of document, a compromise had to be reached, and the methodology and its limitations documented.

Though these early experiments could not be described as a complete success, the very process of working through and highlighting the problem areas was helpful. Indeed, subsequent work has built on these initial experiments and the conversation has moved forward in a productive way.[3]

No one likes to fail, but I see neither of these examples as a low point in my career. When working with constant change, complex problems and the lack of a single, perfect solution, we need to take a pragmatic and realistic approach, acknowledging and documenting the imperfections that come alongside this. 'Best practice' this surely isn't, but the ability to experiment and to share points of failure with the wider community can be incredibly valuable in moving our collective thinking forward.

Admitting failure

The Digital Preservation Coalition (DPC) provides a supportive network for a global community of organisations who have a need to preserve digital content for the long term. Many of our events facilitate the sharing of expert knowledge and provide opportunities for members to talk about the innovative work they are involved in – whether it was ultimately successful or not. It is so much harder to talk about failure, but many would agree that it is equally valuable.

With this in mind, we established a series of networking events with a specific goal to discuss and share failures. 'Digital Preservationists Anonymous' (also known as 'Fail Club') was set up as a support group to 'reflect on things that have not gone as well as we liked' with a goal to be 'liberating, cathartic and therapeutic'. The first meeting was held in 2017, and it has been a repeating event on our programme ever since (Middleton 2017).

I attended my first 'Fail Club' in 2018 before I joined the DPC staff team. A small group of us, led by a DPC facilitator, huddled in a top room of a pub in York, and with the door firmly shut, and in lowered tones, I was able to talk to a small group of peers about a digital preservation advocacy failure that I was experiencing. It was a cathartic experience and one that I was able to move forward from in a positive way (having realised that most of the people round the table related to the issue I was having and were able to share their own strategies to move forward).

I've since been involved in several of these events in the role of facilitator and it always turns out to be a rewarding experience. The conversation naturally flows once we provide a designated space to open up about failure. I can't say any more because (of course) 'what happens in Fail Club, stays in Fail Club', but comments received from attendees refer to it as a 'safe and enriching opportunity to share professional frustrations, mistakes and fears' and 'a great forum to chat about difficulties I've faced at work that I've not found solutions for'.[4]

Encouraging and supporting conversations around failure should happen by default at any professional forum or event. As well as 'Fail Club', the DPC facilitate member-only events where speakers and attendees are given a safe space to talk openly about the challenges. Though these are more often online and without a physical door to push shut, we build an atmosphere of safety, ensuring our inclusion and diversity policy is referenced and understood, starting with a friendly round of introductions, reassuring attendees that the meeting isn't being recorded and applying Chatham House Rules where appropriate.[5]

Success from failure

We learn a lot from failure and it is often a stepping stone to success. Even our 'Fail Club' events end up with a focus on positive steps to move forward (so much so that we recently debated rebranding them with a more positive name). Skills that are required to be successful in digital preservation include an ability to experiment, to try things out, to record and analyse results, to be resilient in the face of failure. Curiosity is a key attribute for success – the mindset that thinks 'I wonder what would happen if I tried this . . .' is encouraged. Working in this way undoubtedly leads to an element of failure, but if you don't try, you will never have a chance of succeeding.

The recent focus within the library and archives sector on a cyber-attack at the British Library has been on the negative effects of the incident and the impact on the organisation's ability to continue to run key services, but there remain glimmers of hope for the digital preservation community at least (Keating 2024). What would have happened if robust digital preservation processes were not in place at the British Library? A blog post from Andy Jackson (who was working at the British Library at the time of the attack) describes how a project to replicate the UK Web Archive 'went from being a cumbersome mitigation of a theoretical risk, to an absolutely crucial part of an active disaster recovery plan' (Jackson 2024). Is this an extreme example of what a digital preservation success might look like in the presence of catastrophe? Perhaps. But simply by talking about what went wrong and what could have been done differently, the lessons learned can be shared widely. As noted by Roly Keating (CEO of the British Library) 'some good will have come from this dreadful incident'.[6]

Last words

Since leaving archaeology my career isn't exactly in ruins, but failure has been a consistent, and not entirely unwelcome, companion. Working in an evolving field with success measures that are far into the future we need to leverage failure to our best advantage. By failing we learn how to move forward, and in talking about failure we share that learning. Curiosity and resilience in the face of failures are key qualities for practitioners in this field. With a focus on continuous improvement and by striving to meet 'good practice' rather than 'best' we can set realistic targets and goals. Understanding and documenting the elements of brokenness and imperfection in our work *is* digital preservation good practice and is something that should be celebrated.

Notes

1 The term 'digital archaeology' is also used to refer to the use of digital technologies to support the discipline of archaeology. See for example 'Digital Archaeology', Wikipedia, last modified 22 March 2025, https://en.wikipedia.org/wiki/Digital_archaeology (accessed 25 November 2024).

2 A longer discussion on the topic of good practice versus best can be found here: 'When is "Good" Better than "Best"? In Support of Digital Preservation Good Practice', Jenny Mitcham, last modified 18 April 2023, https://www.dpconline.org/blog/when-is-good-better-than-best-in-support-of-digital-preservation-good-practice (accessed 25 November 2024).

3 For example: 'What's Up, (with Google) Docs? – The Challenge of Native Cloud Formats', Paul Young, last modified 4 March 2021, https://www.dpconline.org/blog/whats-up-with-google-docs (accessed 25 November 2024).

4 'Digital Preservationists Anonymous', Digital Preservation Coalition, https://www.dpconline.org/events/eventdetail/218/-/digital-preservationists-anonymous (accessed 25 November 2024).

5 'Inclusion and Diversity Policy', Digital Preservation Coalition, August 2021, https://www.dpconline.org/docs/about-1/dpc-policies-and-forms/1807-dpc-inclusion-and-diversity-policy/file (accessed 25 November 2024).

6 Keating quoted in Connor Jones, 'British Library's candid ransomware comms driven by "emotional intelligence"', 20 May 2024. https://www.theregister.com/2024/05/20/the_british_library_owes_lauded/ (accessed 25 November 2024).

References

Jackson, Andy. 'Grasping a Petabyte: The Impact of Replicating the UK Web Archive'. 1 July 2024. Accessed 24 November 2024. https://anjackson.net/2024/07/01/grasping-a-petabyte/.

Keating, Roly. 'Learning Lessons from the Cyber-attack'. 8 March 2024. Accessed 24 November 2024. https://blogs.bl.uk/living-knowledge/2024/03/learning-lessons-from-the-cyber-attack.html.

Middleton, Sarah. 'Losing All Hope to Find Freedom: Fail Club Is Here to Help'. Last modified 3 August 2017. Accessed 24 November 2024. https://www.dpconline.org/blog/fail-club-to-help.

Mitcham, Jenny. 'How Can We Preserve Google Documents?' 28 April 2017. Accessed 24 November 2024. https://digital-archiving.blogspot.com/search?q=how%20can%20we%20preserve%20google%20documents.

Mitcham, Jenny. 'An Imperfect Migration Story'. 8 June 2018. Accessed 24 November 2024. https://digital-archiving.blogspot.com/2018/06/an-imperfect-migration-story_34.html.

Owens, Trevor. *The Theory and Craft of Digital Preservation*. Johns Hopkins University Press, 2018.

Ross, Seamus and Ann Gow. *Digital Archaeology: Rescuing Neglected and Damaged Data Resources: A JISC/NPO Study within the Electronic Libraries (eLib) Programme on the preservation of Electronic Materials*. Library Information Technology Centre, 1999. Accessed 24 November 2024. https://purehost.bath.ac.uk/ws/portalfiles/portal/11350174/p2.pdf.

Chapter 7

Living well with brokenness in an inclusive research culture: what we can learn from failures and processes in a digital humanities lab

Arianna Ciula

This chapter is informed by my role as research software analyst and director at King's Digital Lab (KDL), a Research Software Engineering (RSE) unit based in the Faculty of Arts and Humanities at King's College London in the United Kingdom. KDL core activities include the design, development and maintenance of a substantial estate of public-facing digital research outputs.

My contribution takes stock of previous reflections (Smithies et al. 2019; Smithies and Ciula 2020; Ciula 2020; Jakeman 2020; Caton and Maher 2022; Ciula and Smithies 2023) to draw a line between:

1. Failures that are *endemic* to a highly technical knowledge production context such as KDL and so need a process-oriented constructive mindset to be addressed (but not resolved since I claim this kind of brokenness is endemic and generative);
2. Failures that are *systemic* to the academic research culture such as the one KDL inhabits, a culture in need of a provocative if not activist stance to be reformed.

Failures endemic to technical production (1) are exemplified by how KDL experiences brokenness; these occurrences of failure span human and technical agencies over a *continuum* of projects' lifecycles, from long-tail digital scholarly outputs – such as web interfaces to digital scholarly editions and historical databases – to ephemeral experiments – for example a proof of concept to test a technology or a processing pipeline. For an RSE team deeply engaged with the mechanics of technical systems and processes, brokenness is recognised not only as a highly probable risk but a constant with evolving mitigations, countermeasures and playful attitudes.

The brief references to facets of research culture failures (2) which follow, on the other hand, connect to the wider digital humanities RSE context and more broadly to challenges of integrating digital Research Technical Professionals (RTPs) into inclusive research cultures.

As noted below, this analytical typology finds echo in most chapters of this book and can help us to re-imagine and drive research and policy agendas for the field.

Technical failures, living well and learning with brokenness

KDL has internal monitoring mechanisms to check on the health of servers and applications are in place with upgrades and patching occurring at regular intervals, often accelerated or intensified by incoming cybersecurity alerts or other vulnerabilities the team is made aware of. Despite these regular maintenance cycles, co-habitation with technology is prone to changes and breaks.

A recurring vehicle via which the KDL team engages with 'brokenness' is via colleagues or the public reporting that a site or a functionality is down or not working. Given the size of public-facing digital resources that we maintain (currently circa ninety) and the fact that some of those project architectures date back to the end of the 1990s, requests or problems occur quite frequently. In the last year (April 2023–April 2024), around ten issue reports were recorded per month as illustrated in Figure 7.1 (King's Digital Lab 2019; De Roure et al. 2022). Once in the pipeline, these signals of brokenness are documented, discussed and addressed within the team with predominant involvement of the lab manager or project manager and systems manager.

If the broken functionality is reported for a project that is under a Service Level Agreement (SLA) with the lab – that is, a project for which terms and costs of services such as web hosting are agreed – KDL has the responsibility to investigate and act as soon as possible.[1] It is noteworthy that the

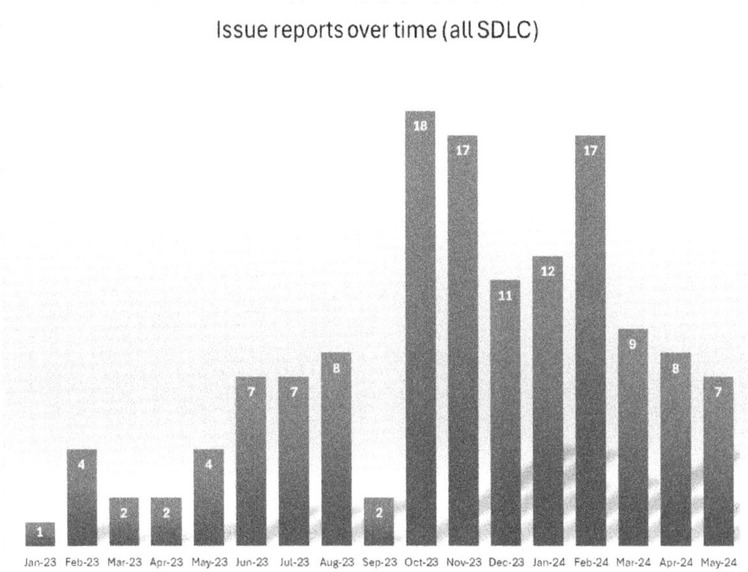

Figure 7.1: ClickUp dashboard created by Pamela Mellen on 24 June 2024 to monitor issues related to access or other broken functionalities of web environments (mainly public websites) that KDL maintains over time. © King's Digital Lab.

standard SLA language (King's Digital Lab 2019) acknowledges brokenness as a constant with usually at least a day of 'bug fix time' – human probing needed to analyse the problem and initiate a repairing action – accounted for every year of maintenance.

For an RSE team deeply engaged with the mechanics of technical systems and processes, brokenness is a risk with very high probability. Hence mitigations or countermeasures are a necessity. While solving some of these problems of brokenness can be at times hard and painful, this is also the stakes of the game, the 'beauty' of working with things that one learns to adjust and tweak. Some of the mitigations are inscribed into evolving policies and governance documentation – including SLAs but also in other phases of projects' lifecycles, such as in the formal product quote signed prior to any collaboration. For example, snippets of the standard SLA currently in use read as follows:

> The evolving nature of the online security environment can present challenges to maintaining complex software systems over the long term. KDL works to balance the interests of project partners with

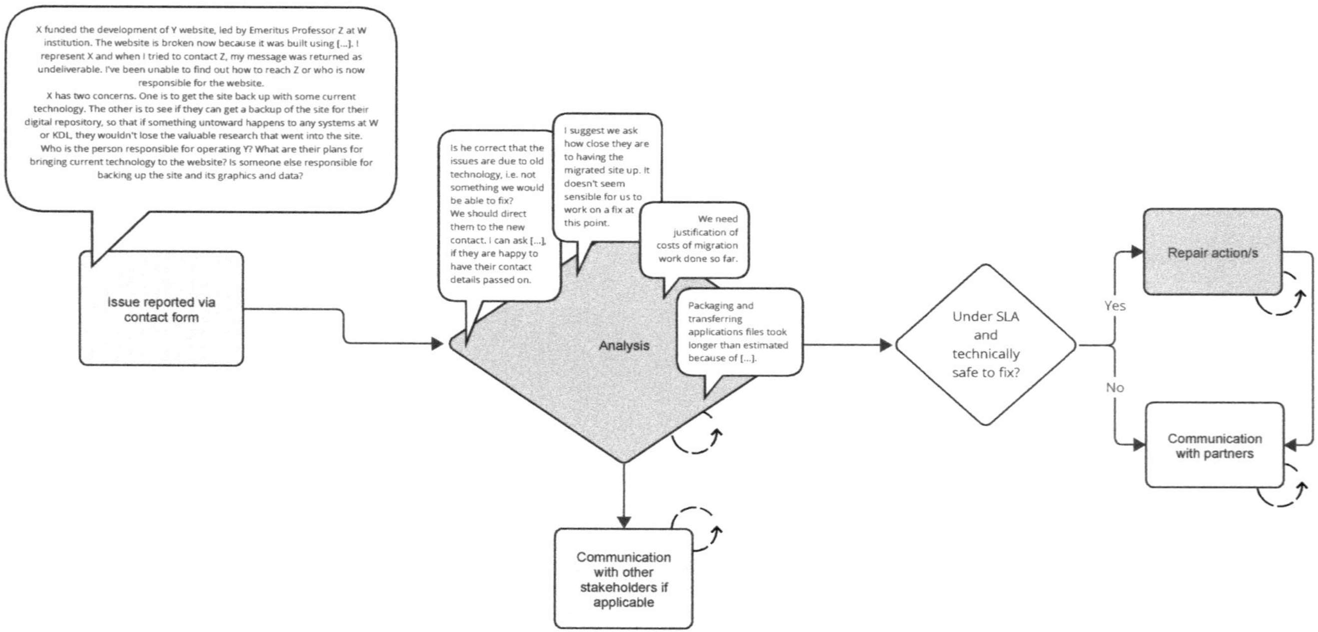

Figure 7.2: Diagram created by the author outlining the process of repair with an example of issue report and team analysis based on a real-life example. © Arianna Ciula.

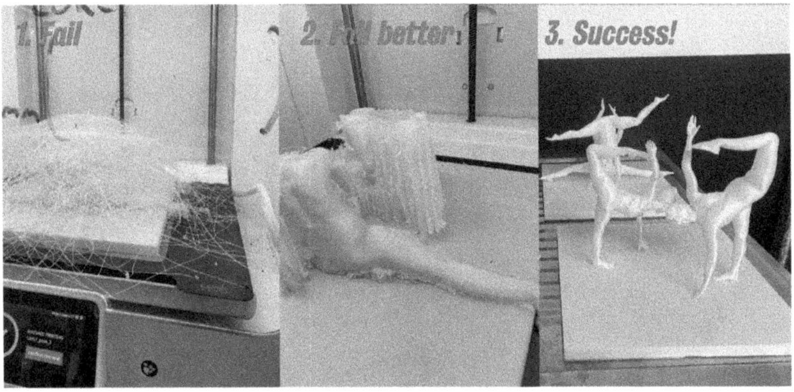

Figure 7.3: Illustration created by Neil Jakeman to exemplify a sequence of failures to adjust the 3D printing of complex forms based on sculptures designed by artist Lisa Jamhoury for her work *L'Entrée* in the Glow3 project (Jakeman and Hall 2024). © Neil Jakeman.

> the security of KCL's IT network but this is not always possible. In the unlikely event of an extended outage, KDL will notify project partners and extend this SLA by at least the length of the outage. If the project cannot be securely updated for technical reasons KDL reserves the right to end the SLA . . .
>
> . . . servers are closely monitored, but it is important that we are notified in advance if any significant increases in traffic are expected (due to the resource being profiled on national television, for example). KDL cannot be held responsible for outages caused by significant predictable increases in site traffic.

Other mitigations are enacted via monitoring processes such as the management of requests outlined above and exemplified in Figure 7.2.

However, these ad hoc repairs, maintenance cycles and governance documents do not address other elements of brokenness that are endemic to the design of software such as testing processes to assess – and on purpose break! – parts of a solution or entire systems to identify vulnerabilities and make them more robust prior to deployment. Brokenness can indeed be a very valuable feature of intermediate or ephemeral products such as proof of concept and scale models built to test a method or a technology. In the tradition of design methods (Norman 1988), this risk-averse and playful attitude to incompletion and brokenness is part of constructive and creative

SLA Evaluation Proce

Process for holistically determining recommendations for KDL digital res

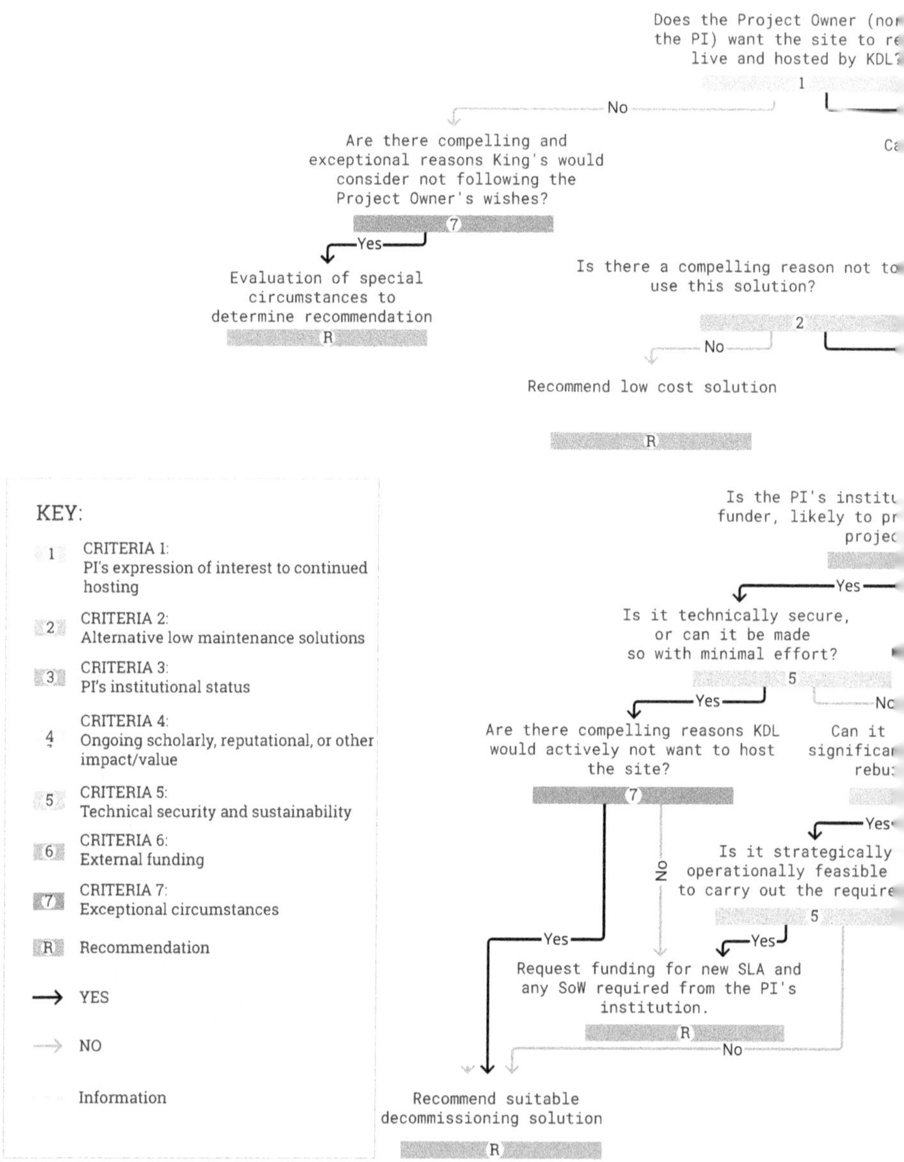

ces coming to the end of their funded hosting period.

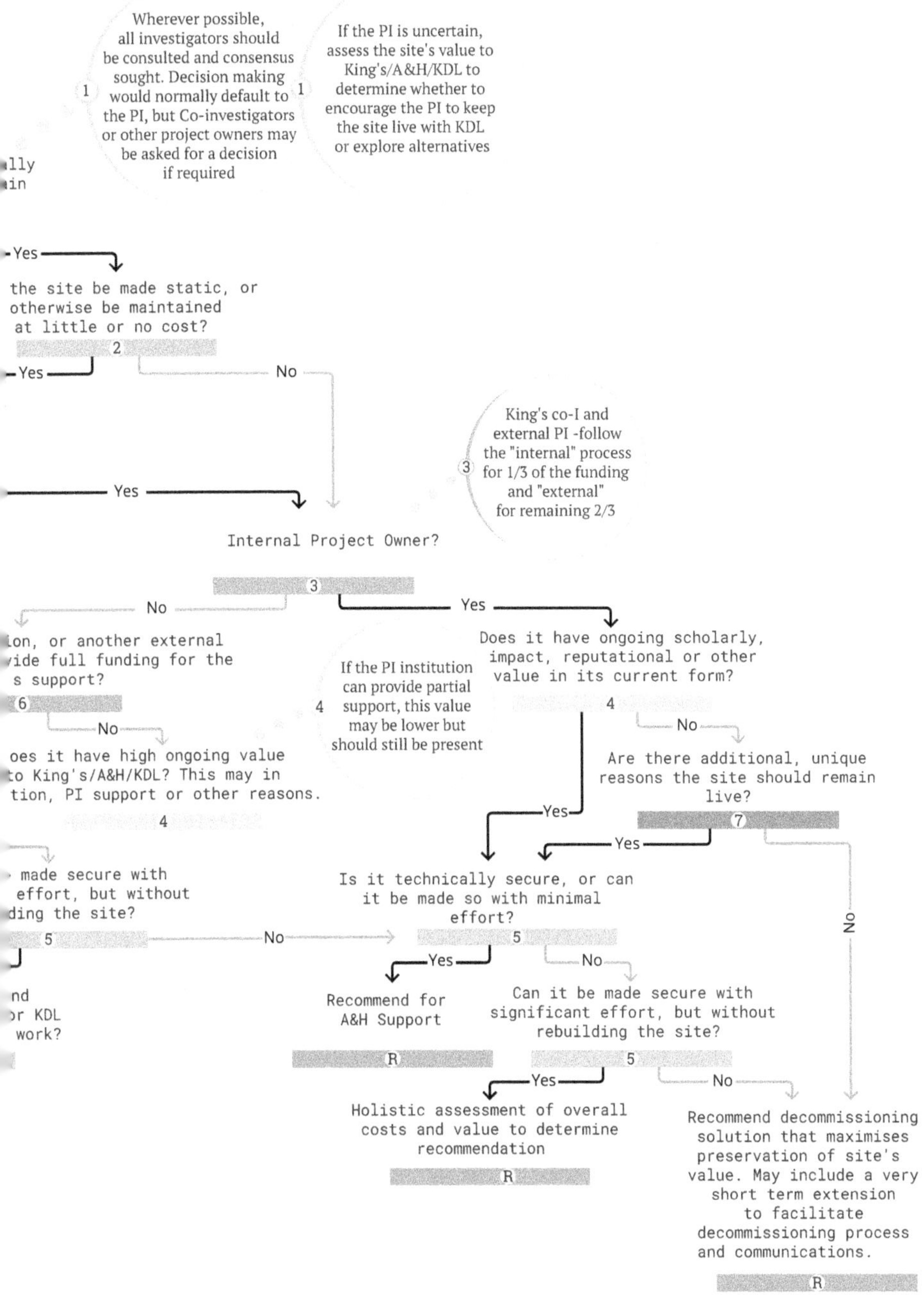

Figure 7.4: Diagram drawn by Tiffany Ong summarising KDL workflow around the decommissioning process. Recommendations are socialised with and then approved by KDL Service Level Agreement committee. © King's Digital Lab.

iterations in prototyping, where the makers of mockups and prototypes embrace the temporary, craftlike, half-broken status of these artefacts to learn, experiment, test and evolve an idea in practice as Figure 7.3 exemplifies (Ciula and Smithies 2023).

Therefore, while change and uncertainty in a research production context affect long-tail digital scholarly outputs as well as ephemeral experiments, the implications are different. There is a productive tension between embracing generative technical brokenness which is part of the evolving technical production process (such as in Figure 7.3) – very akin to the learning-by-doing spirit in maker labs but also to the production of intermediate artefacts in experimental research – and mitigating its destabilising effects when technical products have reached maturity and are expected to continue to be in use, as it is often the case for digital research outputs. The holistic Archiving and Sustainability programme KDL has developed over the years (King's Digital Lab n.d.) outlines criteria for maintenance and associated options, in particular around material obsolescence and degradation or 'sunsetting' of digital products.

These days, Software Development Lifecycles (SDLC) for new projects in KDL embed open discussions on shared responsibilities and forward planning from the outset, embracing a holistic approach to infrastructure aware of technical constraints and options, human efforts and collective costs of repairing, patching and tinkering. An archiving or static-first development approach has become a humble ambition – to reach a baseline of what should stay rather than assuming all components of a fully fledged solution deserve to last.[2] In this sobering perspective (Tucker 2022), one could say that failure to understand the financial, technical and human costs of sustaining a rich portfolio of digital projects has turned into an opportunity for the Lab, namely the opportunity to review critically and creatively its SDLC – where brokenness remains endemic, nonetheless.

KDL team members' reflections over the relatively recent history of KDL have resulted in processes to address digital (material) obsolescence, change and uncertainty in a research production context which spans long-tail digital scholarly outputs as well as ephemeral experiments. Brokenness has become an accepted constant, with mitigations and countermeasures not only enacted by local expertise in daily operations (Figure 7.2) but also inscribed in (evolving) processes (Figure 7.4), contractual obligations and institutional policies. Rather than attempt to circumnavigate failure, these efforts make brokenness emerge as endemic of the digital RTPs' creative way of working – underpinned by processes of repairing, patching and tinkering.

The role of experts in a broken research culture

I referred above to the human costs of sustaining and maintaining digital resources cognisant of the implications this has for the field as a whole. If we are serious about embedding the digital into the arts and humanities knowledge production cycle, the role of digital RTPs is essential to this endeavour (Ciula 2022; Pawlicka-Deger 2022). Failure to recognise the fundamental importance of these roles for research and training has caused several issues for the quality standards and research culture of the discipline, which we should tackle with some urgency. What follows are what I with others (Bergel et al. 2020; McGillivray et al. 2020; Romanova et al. 2021; Gambell et al. 2021) see as some examples of these failures, which are the result of substantial disinvestment in digital research infrastructures that unfortunately span the academic sector beyond DH.

- Mismatch between the increasingly digital lifecycle of projects and the career pipelines that would provide the expertise to design, develop and maintain those lifecycles. This failure bears a question and a call for action addressed mainly to those who lead teaching and training programmes: are we working towards creating the profiles of the digital RTPs we need? DH could contribute quite substantially to shaping holistic and diverse profiles by giving weight not only to data and systems but to process-oriented teaching and training and by including design and analysis skills in education strategies.
- Precarity of labour associated with technical roles. Here the overtly open critique is addressed to senior management of the higher education sector (a sector I am conscious I represent) as well as of comparable independent research organisations operating in the arts, humanities and cultural heritage research domains: can digital RTPs in these domains become more mainstream than a few laboratories and ad hoc figures with no defined roles and career progression? While we cannot compete with industry remunerations, benefits including inclusive and stimulating research environments, career paths and opportunities ought to be defined and offered systematically across institutions.

- Outdated, if not discriminatory, research cultures that are unable or unwilling to value the integral role technical objects play in knowledge production and therefore to value complementary digital research outputs including software (Hidden REF n.d.; Tasovac et al. 2023; Ciula, Esposito and Wijaya 2025) and those experts that have an intimate knowledge of how these objects work or break (Smithies et al. 2023). This borderline discriminatory research culture goes beyond DH and is reflected in our academic promotions systems and evaluation frameworks but also in funding streams and, more subtly, yet with substantial implications, in attitudes, habits and behaviours.
- Individualist research focus which discourages creative, responsible and collaborative re-use and reduces collectie impact to unidirectional dissemination activities. Linked to the point above, this relates to the difficulty of reforming research and education environments to work with (and not only for) communities. Experts cognisant of the importance of participatory and imaginative design methods are needed to achieve this reform and ultimately contribute to living well with technology collectively.[3]

It is encouraging to see – thanks in part to DH community lobbying and activism – that national funders and institutions in the UK have become sensitive to some of these failures, and that programmes and policies are emerging to address some of them.[4] However, some systemic failures inscribed in the research academic culture of fields where digital RTPs' roles are essential, such as DH, call for a more radical programme of change that integrates lessons learned by teams such as KDL and invests in fixing a destructive rather than constructive kind of brokenness, which leads to the devaluing of technical expertise and ultimately to poor research. If, in the case of KDL, the failure to understand the financial, technical and human costs of developing and sustaining a rich portfolio of digital projects has found some process-oriented mitigations, the responsibility for addressing the failure of consolidating the role of digital RTPs via adequate research and education strategies lies beyond process improvement practices in the local context. Responsible collective action – informed by DH-inspired values – is needed to foster the ethics of critical technical development, the shaping of new generations of digital RTPs and the reformation of a truly inclusive research culture.

Notes

1 For more information see https://github.com/kingsdigitallab/sdlc-for-rse/wiki/N2:-Web-Hosting-and-Infrastructure-Service-Level-Agreement-(SLA)-guidance, in King's Digital Lab, 'A Software Development Life Cycle for Research Software Engineering', sdlc-for-rse, 2019. https://github.com/kingsdigitallab/sdlc-for-rse (accessed 18 October 2024).

2 See https://kdl.kcl.ac.uk/slides/2024-london-static-first/#/ (accessed 25 November 2024).

3 KDL is now part of the College Digital Futures Institute (https://www.kcl.ac.uk/digital-futures) which has the remit of enabling research and educational programmes around the cross-disciplinary aim of living well with technology. One of the active KDL projects which exemplifies this aim is 'iREAL: Inclusive Requirements Elicitation for AI in Libraries'. This project addresses issues of participatory requirements elicitation methods in the design and use of AI models in libraries and on datasets of relevance to specific indigenous communities.

4 'STEP-UP: A Strategic TEchnical Platform for University Technical Professionals' is an example of an active project KDL is involved in, supported by the ambition of UK Research Councils to support digital research technology professionals in compliance with UKRI's 'Technician Commitment Action Plan'. The same Engineering and Physical Sciences Research Council (EPSRC) programme supported 'People in Data' at the Alan Turing Institute, while the AHRC funded 'Data/Culture: Building Sustainable Communities around Arts and Humanities Datasets and Tools' resulting in a roadmap publication (Beaven et al. 2025). Other cross-disciplinary examples include the recent UKRI *Digital RTP Skills NetworkPlus* call. Indicators of an inclusive research culture will also play a prominent role in the forthcoming UK Research Excellence Framework.

References

Alan Turing Institute. 'Data/Culture: Building Sustainable Communities around Arts and Humanities Datasets and Tools'. Accessed 18 October 2024. https://www.turing.ac.uk/research/research-projects/dataculture-building-sustainable-communities-around-arts-and-humanities.

Alan Turing Institute. 'People in Data'. Accessed 18 October 2024. https://www.turing.ac.uk/research/research-projects/people-data.

Beavan, David, Andre Piza, Stuart Gillespie, Cyara Buchuck-Wilsenach, Claire Bailey-Ross, Bickford Jake, Edward Chalstrey, et al. *Towards a National Research Software Engineering Capability in Arts and Humanities Research: A Roadmap*. Zenodo, 24 April 2025. Accessed 18 October 2024. https://zenodo.org/records/15083396.

Bergel, Giles, Pip Willcox, Guyda Armstrong, James Baker, Arianna Ciula, Nicholas Cole, Julianne Nyhan, et al. 'Sustaining Digital Humanities in the UK'. Zenodo, 25 September 2020. https://doi.org/10.5281/zenodo.4046267.

Caton, Paul and Brian Maher. 'After the Grant'. *Sixth Annual Conference for Research Software Engineering*. Newcastle Upon Tyne, 2022. Accessed 18 October 2024. https://virtual.oxfordabstracts.com/event/3101/submission/107.

Ciula, Arianna. 'Exposing Legacy Project Datasets in Digital Humanities: KDL Experience'. *King's Digital Lab – Thoughts and Reflections from the Lab* (blog), 7 July 2020. Accessed 18 October 2024. https://www.kdl.kcl.ac.uk/blog/legacy-project-datasets/.

Ciula, Arianna. 'What Does the Role of Research Technology Professional Mean to King's Digital Lab?' *King's Digital Lab—Thoughts and Reflections from the Lab* (blog), 13 October 2022. Accessed 18 October 2024. https://kdl.kcl.ac.uk/blog/rtp-rse/.

Ciula, Arianna, Øyvind Eide, Cristina Marras and Patrick Sahle. *Modelling Between Digital and Humanities: Thinking in Practice*. Open Book Publishers, 2023. https://doi.org/10.11647/obp.0369.

Ciula, Arianna, Alessandra Esposito and Fiona Wijaya. 'KDL Checklist for Digital Outputs Assessment'. 24 April 2025. Accessed 18 October 2024. https://zenodo.org/records/15147897.

Ciula, Arianna and James Smithies. 'Sustainability and Modelling at King's Digital Lab: Between Tradition and Innovation'. In *On Making in the Digital Humanities: Essays on the Scholarship of Digital Humanities Development in Honour of John Bradley*, edited by Julianne Nyhan, Geoffroy Rockwell, Stefan Sinclair and Alexandra Ortolja-Baird, 78–104. University College London Press, 2023. https://doi.org/10.14324/111.9781800084209.

De Roure, David, John Moore, Kevin Page, Toby Burrows, David Beavan, Timothy Hobson, Giles Bergel, et al. 'DigiSpec: Scoping Future Born-Digital Data Services for the Arts and Humanities: Case Reports'. 31 August 2022. https://doi.org/10.5281/zenodo.4716148.

Gambell, Sarah, Paul Gooding, Lorna Hughes, Michelle Doran, Órla Murphy, Charlotte Tupman, Jane Winters, et al. 'Communicating the Value and Impact of Digital Humanities in Teaching, Research, and Infrastructure Development'. Zenodo, 3 November 2021. https://doi.org/10.5281/zenodo.5643727.

Hidden REF. n.d. 'The Hidden REF: Celebrating All Research Outputs'. Accessed 18 October 2024. https://hidden-ref.org/.

'iREAL: Inclusive Requirements Elicitation for AI in Libraries – Inclusive Requirements Elicitation for AI in Libraries'. Accessed 18 October 2024. https://irealrai.org/.

Jakeman, Neil. 'Safeguarding an Inheritance and Ensuring a Legacy'. *King's Digital Lab—Thoughts and Reflections from the Lab* (blog), 19 August 2020. Accessed 18 October 2024. https://kdl.kcl.ac.uk/blog/sdlc-for-rse/.

Jakeman, Neil and Elliott Hall. 'Empowering Artistic Innovation'. *King's Digital Lab—Thoughts and Reflections from the Lab* (blog), 8 April 2024. Accessed 18 October 2024. https://kdl.kcl.ac.uk/blog/glow3-blog/.

King's Digital Lab. 'A Software Development Life Cycle for Research Software Engineering'. sdlc-for-rse, 2019. Accessed 18 October 2024. https://github.com/kingsdigitallab/sdlc-for-rse.

King's Digital Lab. 'Archiving and Sustainability'. n.d. Accessed 18 October 2024. https://kdl.kcl.ac.uk/about/archiving-and-sustainability/.

McGillivray, Barbara, Beatrice Alex, Sarah Ames, Guyda Armstrong, David Beavan, Arianna Ciula, Giovanni Colavizza, et al. 'The Challenges and Prospects of the Intersection of Humanities and Data Science: A White Paper from The Alan Turing Institute'. The Alan

Turing Institute, 4 August 2020. https://doi.org/10.6084/m9.figshare.12732164.v5.
Norman, Donald A. *The Psychology of Everyday Things*. Basic Books, 1988.
Pawlicka-Deger, Urszula. 'Digital Humanities Needs Equality between Humanists and Technicians'. *Times Higher Education (THE)* (blog), 9 July 2022. https://www.timeshighereducation.com/blog/digital-humanities-needs-equality-between-humanists-and-technicians.
Romanova, Natasha, Arianna Ciula, James Smithies, Neil Jakeman, Órla Murphy, Charlotte Tupman, Jane Winters, et al. 'Capacity Enhancement in Digital Humanities in the United Kingdom and Ireland: Training and Beyond'. Zenodo, 15 July 2021. https://doi.org/10.5281/zenodo.5105938.
Smithies, James and Arianna Ciula. 'Humans in the Loop: Epistemology & Method in King's Digital Lab'. In *Routledge International Handbook of Research Methods in Digital Humanities*, edited by Kristen Schuster and Stuart Dunn, 155–72. Routledge, 2020. https://doi.org/10.4324/9780429777028.
Smithies, James, Patrick ffrench and Arianna Ciula. 'Droit de Cité: The Digital Lab as Digital Milieu'. In *Digital Humanities and Laboratories: Perspectives on Knowledge, Digital Research in the Arts and Humanities Infrastructure and Culture*, edited by Urszula Pawlicka-Deger and Christopher Thompson, 52–66. Routledge, 2023. https://doi.org/10.4324/9781003185932.
Smithies, James, Anna Maria Sichani, Carina Westling, Pam Mellen and Arianna Ciula. 'Managing 100 Digital Humanities Projects: Digital Scholarship & Archiving in King's Digital Lab', *Digital Humanities Quarterly* 13, no. 1 (2019). Accessed 18 October 2024. http://www.digitalhumanities.org/dhq/vol/13/1/000411/000411.html.
'STEP-UP: A Strategic TEchnical Platform for University Technical Professionals'. Accessed 18 October 2024. http://step-up.ac.uk/.
Tasovac, Toma, Laurent Romary, Erzsébet Tóth-Czifra, Rahel C. Ackermann, Daniel Alves, Sally Chambers, Mike Cosgrave, et al. 'The Role of Research Infrastructures in the Research Assessment Reform: A DARIAH Position Paper', June 2023. Accessed 18 October 2024. https://hal.science/hal-04136772.

Tucker, Joanna. 'Facing the Challenge of Digital Sustainability as Humanities Researchers', *Journal of the British Academy* 10 (2022): 93–120. https://doi.org/10.5871/jba/010.093.

UK Research and Innovation (UKRI). 'Technician Commitment Action Plan'. 2021. Accessed 18 October 2024. https://www.ukri.org/wp-content/uploads/2022/03/UKRI-010322-TechnicianCommitmentActionPlan.pdf.

Chapter 8

Can we be failing?

Joris J. van Zundert

It cannot be failure that is bugging me. Failure is the bread and butter of research and science. Trial and error. Philology is scholarship for the brave. We mostly lack real evidence when studying historical texts. We make do with the scraps we have. We glue them together with major leaps of conjecture and imagination, and we create a story about the text that we give as an explanation of it. We build inverted pyramids of reasoning and hope they will stand. We accept that we know so little about the texts we find and their historical contexts that it would be just as well to throw them at the wall and see how the spectacular explosion of characters from the manuscript might make sense. What sticks?

In this sense philology is all about failure. We know our task is to uncover what Jerome McGann called this 'impossible truth', 'the obligation to protect human memory from neglect and erasure – as much of it as possible' (McGann 2015). An impossible truth not only because we are fighting a lack of evidence. We also cannot trust the evidence we have. Most historical texts bring us fake news, conjured up by authors in service of the politics of whomever paid them. Audaciously we assert that we can tell true intent from intentional mystification. As if we can understand the person who is a number of centuries remote from us, who lived in a society whose rationale would appal us, and whose faith, beliefs, motivations and morality would deeply confuse us.

Knowingly we set our philological selves up for failure. But there is method in the madness. *Wahrheit und methode, n'est-ce pas?* So, we ward off uncertainty and subjectivity, those devils of interpretation. Because we have method. We follow Lachmann (Ciesa 2020), Maas (1958), Greetham (1994), Tanselle (1995), Matthijsen (2003), Sahle (2013), or any other we might know and choose to be our Virgil on our journey through this hell of scholarship.

And this is what we still do in the digital era. Our texts may have been transmedialised (Sahle 2016, 32) as bundles of ones and zeroes, but we treat them as the books we see in these. Online we rebuild the world we know. We produce books. Page through the digital scholarly editions that we have produced (for instance via Steinkrüger et al. 2013), and one finds that we still produce books. The convention is: a scan of a page side by side with a transcription, annotations pop up or show up in an additional column. Do not be fooled by added media, pictures and sounds as illustrations. They are books. They are page based. They have indices, in a time of full text search.

For sure these are marvellous scholarly achievements! I will be the last to condemn them. We should celebrate these wonderful fruits of hard and precarious digital scholarly labour. More praise unto them. They brought us wonderful things. Access anywhere, anytime, to texts long hidden in dusty archives and dark corners of library depositories. We can argue with the transcription now that the facsimiles are before our eyes, we can freely search the texts, we may be supported by an excellent register or faceted search to quickly take us to mentions of persons, places, events, and what have you. It is all a glorious marvel.

Still, I wonder. Is this new world of digital data and computational power merely a new way of presenting us the same document? Or should it push our envelope harder? When we entered this realm of digital scholarly editing in the early 1990s, what did we expect? Did we really assume it would just be a new way of finding the text and reading it? The Poughkeepsie Principles (Fortier 1987) on which the Text Encoding Initiative (TEI) was built, read: 'The guidelines are intended to provide a standard format for data interchange in humanities research.' What fascinates me here is that word 'interchange'. It suggests some dynamic, right? We see scholars 'interchanging' the texts they created in TEI. It suggests something like 'I'll let you use my XML source if you'll let me use yours'. And fair enough, the TEI-XML download button is more or less a must-have for state-of-the-art web-based digital scholarly editions.

But that's it? We went through some three decades and more of digital technology development for a download button? That seems underwhelming.

Let's back up a little: we have wonderful worldwide access, anytime, we can search, and we can link to other resources. Great! Just saying, with PDF or ePub we would have had that too. Which means we have built infrastructure and text models at very high costs to add a download button for XML sources. Mind you, the cost and effort are staggering (cf. Beavan et al. 2025; Drucker 2021; Hinsen 2019; Otis 2023; Smithies et al. 2019). PDFs or ePubs merely require some server and maybe some tailored, tinkered off-the-shelf database if you want to have some smart library lookalike catalogue access. Really mundane requirements that can be supported by any decently skilled IT support staff. But to power our XML-y workflows we demand dedicated web-based XML production and publication environments. It is not just Oxygen and TEI Publisher we want. We convinced our institutes that there should be onsite integrated workflows for real serious digital scholarly editing: XML databases, document servers, XSLT transformers, document templates, encoding schemas, web servers, web development frameworks, and so forth. The stack is deep and wide. To keep things up and running, to keep pace (at least a little bit) with GUI and UX design fads and fashions, we need skilled data stewards, web engineers, frontend developers, GUI designers. And we all suffer from 'not invented here' syndrome: the list of reinvented scholarly editing platforms and supporting large-scale digital research infrastructures is long, because every institution wants its own. If you take out your pocket calculator and start adding, your screen might not be wide enough to report the staggering costs of the duplicated effort in the name of sustainability. Per annum. For a download button.

In my own cluster of institutes I know of at least three parallel attempts at providing some scholarly editing platform, workflow, tool set, or whatever you want to call them. Please do not let my director read this. In defence of the three: they all have different and well-motivated angles of attack. One is standoff markup based, embraces 'IIIF' model philosophy, and believes in distributed services for text, data and annotations. I hope they bear in mind that the devil is in the detail, such as the base encoding of a text file switching from UTF-8 to CP-1252. Another puts the money on standardised TEI models and templates for different categories of text, trusting that 80 per cent of digital editions can be covered by 20 per cent of the TEI guidelines. They might be in for a surprise when they discover how the Pareto principle actually works, which in the scholarly digital editing arena pans out to the fact that 80 per cent of the scholarly value (but likely even more) is always in the 20 per cent of any edited document that does not fit into the template. The third effort promises a next generation markup language supporting overlap and the kitchen sink, backed by a new computational grammar built from the ground up. The last one is a daring and fundamental move, no doubt revolutionary if successful. But so was Livingstone's mission, I presume. These attempts follow at least three earlier attempts made since 2004, all failing, one of my very own making (Beaulieu et al. 2012).

I am not arguing that these attempts are misinformed, misguided or failures waiting to happen. To be perfectly honest I do think most of them will fail for the most part, but beautiful knowledge and lessons will be learned in the process. The salient point for me is that these continuous attempts all over the globe do signal that in the domain of digital scholarly editing we are not in it just for a mere download button. Apparently, we feel that there is more to digital editions than the flat surface of the page and the screen. Given the enormous and repeated efforts, I suspect there is some subliminal motivation other than just the obligatory 'access' and 'preservation'. Are we subconsciously convinced that our digital editions ought to be more than just flat representations of a text stream, living isolated on web pages?

If I can take a stab at what is in store, I would argue that we dream of digital scholarly editions that are dynamic knowledge sites. Editions that are much closer to the ideals that Vanevar Bush (1945), Douglas Engelbart and William English (1968) and Theodor Nelson (1993) had in mind, and of which Tim Berners-Lee's variant, known as the Web, is a mere shadow. Digital editions that allow themselves to be connected to other digitally represented knowledge anywhere available. I do not mean mere hyperlinks pointing out from a digital edition's text towards other sites, but semantically and scholarly meaningful relations connecting very specific localities in one edition to very specific loci in other digital editions or resources. The scholarly meaningfulness of those relations should be expressed explicitly by the scholar or the computational tools the researcher is applying to create such links. So, imagine links that express things like 'This paragraph in this text source here in Tokyo University's Komaba Library says that this verse in this digital transcript of this Old-Frisian law text on the site of the Frisian Academy of Arts and Sciences in Leeuwarden in the Netherlands expresses that Frisian kings recognized private ownership of pastures'. And, for another example: 'This digitized seal in the collection of Sankt Gallen

Abbey's library evidences that Frisian kings did not acknowledge private ownership of pastures'. One can see that there is a logical contradiction between those two. Now, imagine that it would be possible for anyone to express such interpretations by creating links between loci deeply and specifically in arbitrary online scholarly resources. Scholars would be able to express competing conjectures, and we would be able to actually calculate the relative support for one or another automatically. We would, for a fact, be building a giant scholarly reasoning engine. We would be expressing and connecting the knowledge that we create everyday explicitly and in a collective way to make our knowledge more insightful for a common understanding.

Now, before you run away screaming from this 'commune-like enforced dictatorship of majority interpretation': no, this idea does not assert that there must be one common authoritative interpretation. Anyone can express any interpretation. The idea would merely be to express interpretations in a formal and explicit language that links interpretations to supporting evidence. Or one could even not link to supporting materials because one wanted to express a pure conjecture. All that would be perfectly fine. But the major pay-off of such a system would be that it enables us to really compute how strong our individual and aggregate reasoning is. Automatically being notified of new corroborating or opposing evidence would be a bonus thrown in for free.

Obviously, these possibilities are far beyond our current digital editing scholarship ecosystem. But they are very much not beyond our current digital and computational technologies. Although I am not a big fan of RDF and semantic web technology for boring but fundamental technical reasons (hint: it is not read and write, but read-only), the technology shows that interpretative language can be formalised. Knowledge graphs, which have all the dynamics we speak about, are a technology now so well understood that they make serious computer science people yawn. Moreover, even people within our community are theorising about and experimenting with these more advanced knowledge representations (Vogeler 2019; Andrews at al. 2024; Cugliana et al. 2024).

But can we be failing? So far, I think no digital scholarly edition has resulted in any significant epistemological gain. Again, improved access and discoverability are great, but they scale what we did, they do not change our praxis. For all the angle brackets that we have produced in the last four decades, we have not changed how we think about how we come to know things in philology and textual scholarship. Apart from having an add-on course in TEI-XML, any newly arrived student can still get ahead in the field by taking Greetham to hand. Is this a problem? In some ways, no. We might choose to be perfectly fine with being a conservative field, and in the end we are also about conservation of intellectual history, so why not? On the other hand: should we not also explore the potential of the textual tools that the twenty-first century throws at us? Do we have an intellectual obligation to investigate if they provide us better means of creating and representing our editions and the knowledge we create in the process?

I often worry that the field has been technologically locked in by one technology (XML) and one model (TEI), and that we are victims of our own huge success. Neither XML or TEI is very concomitant to networking and combining information dynamically across digital sources. It is not in the bones of these technologies, it is not their philosophy. But that 'interchange' thing keeps bugging me. I think the motivation behind it must have been genuine and deeply felt: a possibility to have different scholarly sources and resources interact. To have them 'talk', 'inform', and 'enlighten' each other, so that the sum would return more knowledge than the individual nodes represented. But somehow we turned our model and markup into a rather omphalocentric technology focused at representing one document in isolation, more like a static book, less like active knowledge.

If the aim is new ways to gain knowledge from philology by applying different techniques to model, connect, infer and evaluate information, then I think we are indeed failing. If this is truly the aim, we need to think vastly differently about our digital and computational scholarly editing infrastructure. Otherwise we are just building glorified digital shelves for our digitised books.

References

Andrews, Tara, Márton Rózsa, Katalin Prajda, Lewis Read and Aleksandar Anđelović. 'Re-Evaluating the Eleventh Century through Linked Events and Entities', *Historical Studies on Central Europe* 4, no. 1 (2024): 217–45. https://doi.org/10.47074/HSCE.2024-1.12.

Beaulieu, Anne, Karina Van Dalen-Oskam and Joris Van Zundert. 'Between Tradition and Web 2.0: eLaborate as a Social Experiment in Humanities Scholarship'. In *Social Software and the Evolution of User Expertise: Future Trends in Knowledge Creation and Dissemination*, edited by Tatjana Takševa, 112–29. IGI Global, 2012. Accessed 24 November 2024. https://pure.knaw.nl/portal/en/publications/between-tradition-and-web-20-elaborate-as-a-social-experiment-in-.

Beavan, David, Andre Piza, Stuart Gillespie, Cyara Buchuck-Wilsenach, Claire Bailey-Ross, Bickford Jake, Edward Chalstrey, et al. 'Towards a National Research Software Engineering Capability in Arts and Humanities Research: A Roadmap'. The Alan Turing Institute. Zenodo. 2025. https://doi.org/10.5281/zenodo.15083396.

Bush, Vannevar. 'As We May Think', *The Atlantic*, 1 July 1945. Accessed 24 November 2024. http://www.theatlantic.com/magazine/archive/1945/07/as-we-may-think/303881/.

Ciesa, Paolo. 'Principles and Practice'. In *Handbook of Stemmatology*, edited by Philipp Roelli, 292–356. De Gruyter, 2020. Accessed 24 November 2024. https://www.degruyter.com/view/title/569065.

Cugliana, Elisa, Aengus Ward, Joris J. van Zundert, Andreas Kuczera and Max Grüntgens. 'Computational Approaches and the Epistemology of Scholarly Editing', *International Journal of Digital Humanities* 6 (2024): 169–88. https://doi.org/10.1007/s42803-024-00088-z.

Drucker, Johanna. 'Sustainability and Complexity: Knowledge and Authority in the Digital Humanities', *Digital Scholarship in the Humanities* 36, Supplement_2 (2021): ii86–94. https://doi.org/10.1093/llc/fqab025.

Engelbart, Douglas C. and William K. English. 'A Research Center for Augmenting Human Intellect'. In AFIPS Conference Proceedings of the 1968 Fall Joint Computer Conference, 395–410. AFIPS, 1968. Accessed 24 November 2024. https://dougengelbart.org/content/view/140/#.

Fortier, P.A. 'The Preparation of Text Encoding Guidelines – Closing Statement of the Vassar Planning Conference'. Paper presented at Text Encoding Initiative, Poughkeepsie, 13 November 1987. view-source:https://tei-c.org/Vault/PC/pcp1.tei.

Greetham, David. *Textual Scholarship: An Introduction*. Garland Reference Library of the Humanities 1417. Garland Publishing Inc., 1994.

Hinsen, K. 'Dealing With Software Collapse', *Computing in Science & Engineering* 21, no. 3 (2019): 104–8. https://doi.org/10.1109/MCSE.2019.2900945.

Maas, Paul. *Textual Criticism*. Translated by Barbara Flower. Clarendon Press, 1958.

Mathijsen, Marita. 'Een knieval voor de luie lezer? Hertaling als enig redmiddel voor historische literatuur'. *Nederlandse Letterkunde* no. 2 (2003): 116–29. Accessed 24 November 2024. https://www.dbnl.org/tekst/_ned021200301_01/_ned021200301_01_0010.php.

McGann, Jerome. 'Truth and Method: Humanities Scholarship as a Science of Exceptions.' *Interdisciplinary Science Review* 40, no. 2 (2015): 204–18. https://doi.org/10.1179/0308018815Z.000000000113.

Nelson, Theodor Holm. *Literary Machines. The Report on, and of, Project Xanadu Concerning Word Processing, Electronic Publishing, Hypertext, Thinkertoys, Tomorrow's Intellectual Revolution, and Certain Other Topics Including Knowledge, Education and Freedom*. First published 1981. Mindfull Press, 1993.

Otis, Jessica. '"Follow the Money?": Funding and Digital Sustainability', *Digital Humanities Quarterly* 17, no. 1 (2023): 000666. Accessed 24 November 2024. https://www.digitalhumanities.org/dhq/vol/17/1/000666/000666.html.

Sahle, Patrick. *Digitale Editionsformen, Zum Umgang mit der Überlieferung unter den Bedingungen des Medienwandels. 3 Teilen.* [Finale Print-Fassung]. Schriften des Instituts für Dokumentologie und Editorik. Norderstedt Books on Demand, 2013. Accessed 24 November 2024. https://kups.ub.uni-koeln.de/5352/.

Sahle, Patrick. 'What Is a Scholarly Digital Edition?'. In *Digital Scholarly Editing: Theories and Practices*, edited by Matthew James Driscoll and Elena Pierazzo, 19–40. Open Book Publishers, 2016. Accessed 24 November 2024. http://www.openbookpublishers.com/reader/483.

Smithies, James, Carina Westling, Anna-Maria Sichani, Pam Mellen and Arianna Ciula. 'Managing 100 Digital Humanities Projects: Digital Scholarship & Archiving in King's Digital Lab', *Digital Humanities Quarterly* 13, no. 1 (2019): 000411. Accessed 24 November 2024. https://www.digitalhumanities.org/dhq/vol/13/1/000411/000411.html.

Steinkrüger, Philipp, Ulrike Henny-Krahmer and Frederike Neuber. 'Editorial – State of Play', *RIDE – A Review Journal for Digital Editions and Resources* (2013). Accessed 24 November 2024. https://ride.i-d-e.de/about/editorial/.

Tanselle, Thomas G. 'The Varieties of Scholarly Editing'. In *Scholarly Editing: A Guide to Research*, edited by D.C. Greetham, 9–32. The Modern Language Association of America, 1995. Accessed 24 November 2024. https://cmohge1.github.io/lrbs-digital-scholarly-editing/readings/tanselle_varieties_of_editing.pdf.

Vogeler, Georg. 'The "Assertive Edition"', *International Journal of Digital Humanities* 1, (2019): 309–22. https://doi.org/10.1007/s42803-019-00025-5.

Part III
COLLABORATION

Failure and collaboration

While we often celebrate ground-breaking partnerships involving multiple stakeholders from various sectors, these collaborations are incredibly complex. More often than not, they are fraught with challenges that are not always visible or discussed. Tensions in collaborations and failed partnerships can often arise from the personalities of those involved; just as in life, not everyone will be an ideal match. However, it's not always a clash of personalities that causes collaborations to struggle or fail. Often, failure results from poorly designed or inadequately considered frameworks, protocols and working models. Despite the relative ubiquity of these issues, failed or challenging collaborations – and the reasons behind them – are seldom shared (Nowviskie 2012). On the contrary, the lessons learned from these struggles are often kept hidden and failures are repeated as new teams grapple with the same challenges.

Arran J. Rees, in his reflection, emphasises the importance of communicating the challenges faced in professional practice within a more structured framework of iterative and self-reflective practical experimentation, and not just in informal settings like 'candid conversations over coffee'. He introduces the action research methodology as one way to deal with project complexities and collaboration struggles. In a similar vein, Jennifer Stertzer argues that a flexible, iterative mindset can enable a team to transform setbacks, challenges and failures – arising from both institutional and disciplinary contexts – into valuable learning experiences.

Recent reflections from the UK-based Living with Machines project, however, point to many of the challenges of collaboration that still remain for complex, large-scale collaborations, from communication channels and meeting culture protocols to authorship attribution (Ahnert et al. 2023). Some have tried to ameliorate these challenges by drawing on project management approaches from other disciplines, but differences between communities of practice have meant these borrowings have seen mixed success (Neubert 2020).

Caio Mello argues that the pipeline model, for example – a concept and project approach borrowed from data science – is particularly vulnerable to failure in data-intensive, interdisciplinary and collaborative projects. Jentery Sayers points to the failings of two other techniques – waterfall and agile – and advocates instead for a cooperative model that puts relationships at the heart of the process. This cooperative approach is also central to Lauren Tuckley's reflection, in which she proposes a community- and values-based approach to funding applications as an antidote to the hyper individualistic, trophy-hunting mentality that can pervade those spaces. Each of these reflections recognises a core tenet of failure – it always happens in relationship with other people.

References

Ahnert, Ruth, Emma Griffin, Mia Ridge and Giorgia Tolfo. *Collaborative Historical Research in the Age of Big Data: Lessons from an Interdisciplinary Project*. Cambridge University Press, 2023.

Neubert, Anna Maria. 'Navigating Disciplinary Differences in (Digital) Research Projects'. In *Digital Methods in the Humanities: Challenges, Ideas, Perspectives*, edited by Silke Schwandt, 59–86. 1st edition, vol. 1, Digital Humanities Research. Bielefeld University Press, 2020. Accessed 25 November 2024. https://www.jstor.org/stable/j.ctv2f9xskk.5.

Nowviskie, Bethany. 'Too Small to Fail'. (blog) 13 October 2012. Accessed 25 November 2024. https://nowviskie.org/2012/too-small-to-fail/.

Chapter 9

Doing, failing, learning: understanding what didn't work as a key research finding in action research

Arran J. Rees

As a researcher and a practitioner in cultural heritage, and even as a person full stop, I've always had a natural inclination to just get stuck in, whether it be ignoring the instructions and learning by doing (and often re-doing when it goes wrong), joining professional committees and steering groups, or wanting to actively experiment with scenarios I am thinking about with regards to my research. Some of what I learn is based on what worked, but much more is based on what didn't. Knowing what didn't work, what was hard, what failed, has always been a part of how knowledge is generated and exchanged, but too often this is confined to 'candid conversations' that are performed around coffees and side discussions, facilitated through social and professional networks. It is rare to find an honest reflection on what didn't work, focusing on what we can learn from that, in any of the formal presentations of findings that research and professional practice expect us to produce.

I get the sense that much of what we find written about in academic and professional contexts is sanitised. Is there perhaps a presumption that funders don't want to know what you found difficult? That admitting that you failed or didn't manage to do all that you'd planned will somehow affect your chances of getting funding again or a promotion at work? More often than not, our written accounts tend to tell stories of how our findings align neatly with our theories, how newly minted research insights will revolutionise

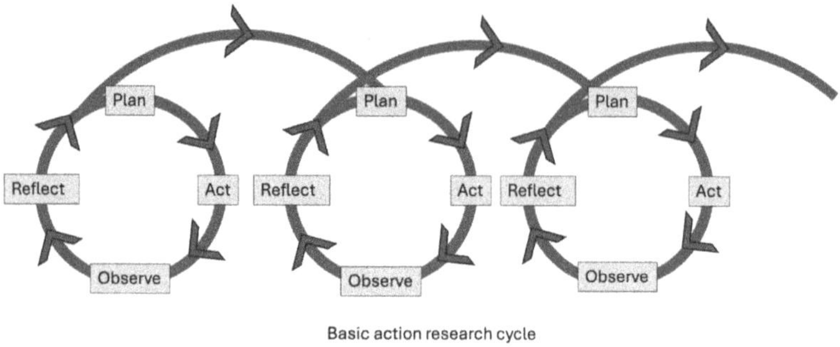

Figure 9.1: A plan, act, observe, reflect action research cycle diagram. © Arran J. Rees.

practices in museum education or exhibition design. For me, I always found this type of writing difficult to resonate with as it did not match my experiences of working in the sector beforehand. I still remember the internal battles I had with myself during my PhD, wanting to push back against overly theoretical texts, branding them as out of touch with the complex, nuanced and contextual realities of working in cultural heritage; or as Duncan Grewcock notes about heavily theoretical studies of museums, 'one could be forgiven for thinking that visiting a museum has not actually formed any part of the study' (2014, 190).

However, over time, I came to better appreciate that throughout my professional career, every activity, process or procedure I had undertaken had come to be through a theory or set of assumptions that had been derived to give them meaning (McCarthy 2016). All of these have been informed by what did and what did not work, based on an experiment that was attached to a theory. Therefore, if we are trying to make change, to influence practice through sharing what we learn in our research, it is about time we started sharing more openly what didn't work, and what didn't support our initial theories, paying attention to the particular contexts we were in, and learning from those experiences.

It was through seeking a way to do practical research that acknowledged my insights working in cultural heritage, as well as enabling my research experiences, both positive and negative, to inform my eventual findings, that I came to action research. Action research is best understood as a broad orientation towards inquiry, rather than a specific methodology. The action research cycle sets up the research as having a series of stages that repeat iteratively as you learn more. These are traditionally talked about as planning, acting, observing, reflecting and re-planning based on what you learnt during the first cycle (see Figure 9.1). Action research is an orientation towards research that seeks different ways of knowing as deeply related to practice, grounding itself in pragmatism and the practical forms of knowing (Reason 2003; Brydon-Miller and Coghlan 2019). It is in this orientation towards practical knowing and taking care to understand contextual relevance that my reflections on the idea of 'failure' come into play.

Failure as research development in action

Within the phases of an action research cycle, there are multiple points at which failure happens, and where we have opportunities to treat these points as generative learning experiences. To illustrate this, I will discuss an example from the recent 'Congruence Engine' project, which sought to use systemic action research to explore approaches to develop a united digital collection as part of the larger 'Towards a National Collection' funding programme.[1] From the beginning, Helen Graham, my action research co-facilitator, and I sought to build structures for the project that would allow for a degree of self-organising – recognising that everyone will have a different starting place on the project, have different forms of knowledge and have different motivations for being involved. In doing this we embraced a complexity worldview in the project: one that 'reminds us of the limits to certainty, [that] emphasises that things are in a continual process of "becoming" and that there is potential for startlingly new futures where what emerges can be unexpected and astonishing' (Boulton et al. 2015). In understanding that things are in a 'continual process of becoming' we immediately open ourselves to seeing everything we do, whether it works or not, as part of that process.

It is difficult to begin from a place of collective understanding in an interdisciplinary project the size of Congruence Engine. The project itself is large and complex, with over fifteen organisations and around sixty people involved to various degrees. We started out by developing a working group model, taking insights from literature on the positives and critiques of Holacracy's forms of organising (Bernstein et al. 2016; Schell and Bischof 2021), on the role of distributed leadership and open boundaries between inquiry streams in systemic action research (Burns 2007) and on collaborating in cultural heritage (Knudsen and Olesen 2018). We specified that each of these needed a facilitator who was responsible for feeding the group's work back into central team meetings which, in theory, would work to cohere a sense of direction for the whole project. We dedicated time at the beginning of the project to making space for divergence, as well as congruence, and veered away from articulating collective agreement or understanding as the only way forward for the project. In doing this we were seeking to enable parallel and distributed action that would really help unleash people's potential to innovate – both practically and conceptually.

From the onset we were upfront that this approach was not static and would probably need to change as the project evolved. This is an admission and an allowance to fail; we knew that things wouldn't work, but that we had to start somewhere. This approach to iterative development, knowing something won't work properly at first, is central to an action research approach. It builds failure in as part of the learning process.

Nine months in, after observing and reflecting on how the working groups were developing, we noticed that they were not as dynamic as we had hoped they might be. It is difficult to pinpoint exact reasons for this; there were no doubt multiple factors that inhibited their adoption, from the unfamiliarity of working in less directed and hierarchically structured ways, to the strength of disciplinary silos, but I want to focus on the hybrid nature of our project. Congruence Engine was hybrid from the onset – starting in November 2021, the opening project conference in February 2022 was, for some, the first in-person event of that ilk since the COVID-19 pandemic began. Pre-pandemic, both the project's action research facilitators had been facilitating in-person inquiry groups, being physically present, noticing the atmosphere of a room, paying attention to body language and to slight intonations in a person's voice. These were important factors for us in facilitating, improvising and cultivating relationships in action research. Attempting to do this type of work, to manifest energy and dynamism through working groups, is much harder to do digitally, and this is potentially one of the stumbling blocks we encountered. For Congruence Engine, whilst there are many pre-existing connections between some colleagues, the majority of us had never worked together, and come from different disciplines and working cultures. So, whilst we knew parallel work was happening, we realised we needed more active facilitation methods that acknowledged the differing environmental and communicative dynamics that are possible through digital and hybrid working. This was, in a more traditionalist sense, a failure of our first attempt.

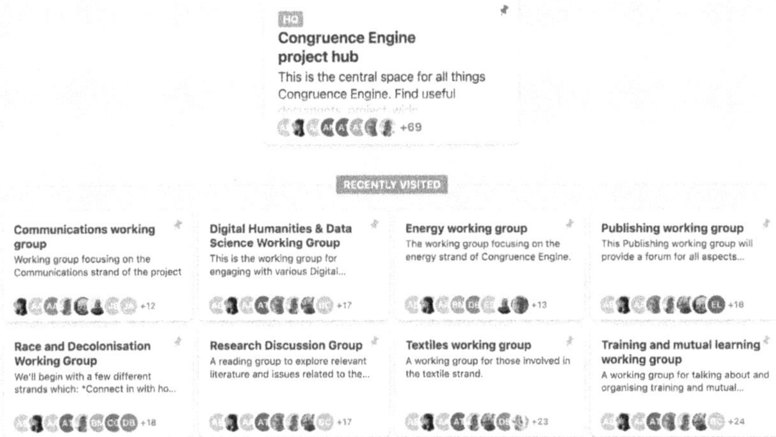

Figure 9.2: The Congruence Engine Basecamp, showing the different project working groups. © Arran J. Rees.

Keen to adapt our approach, maintaining the core principles of parallel, distributed action, led by those who the work resonates with, we devised a new structure for the project that built in a directed digitally led engagement with each other, and more facilitated cross-project meetings. Within the context of the action research's cycle structure, this was a planning forward, based on what we'd learnt during our first phase of the project. Utilising the language of iterative, incremental and adaptive change, the action research facilitators actively sought to communicate that nothing was fixed and that structures could be changed throughout the course of the project without it needing to be framed as a failure of one approach.

The project had been using Basecamp to try and facilitate the working groups in their original instantiation (Figure 9.2), but the platform had not enabled the open and generative form of collaboration we had hoped for.[2] Research on undertaking action research in online environments points to benefits of rapid and open communication services whilst acknowledging the incompleteness of communicating online, but also to the potential to work both synchronously and asynchronously across digital platforms (Embury 2015). Knowing we had groups of researchers who worked on different days, on different fractional contracts, and with Congruence Engine being a larger and smaller proportion of their focus, encouraged us to focus on developing synchronous and asynchronous modes, opting to introduce Notion to support our work.[3] For some, this added yet another digital system into the mix; something new to learn, something else to keep an eye on, but for others, it opened up the project and enabled far more openly and collectively developed ideas to be shared. Alongside the introduction of Notion, we formed a new Action Research and Project Management group and designed a new central meeting to cohere all the investigations, embedding collaborative and live documentation as part of those meetings. One of the the intentions here was to provide a new digital space for synchronous and asynchronous documentation and research development, alongside a more actively facilitated set of meetings to more explicitly encourage sharing across strands of investigation.

This second cycle of the project's structure and management was no doubt disorientating for those who had adopted and got used to the working groups model, but there was a lot to be learnt about the dynamics of a new interdisciplinary project and the types of structure that were needed to support a wide variety of researchers and practitioners. Whilst the structure of using Notion, supported by two ongoing meetings to actively facilitate the movement of the research inquiries continued throughout the project, the approach continued to be tweaked, acknowledging when a meeting, a form of organising or an approach wasn't working as intended. Instead of seeing these as a series of failures, we saw them as a step closer to understanding what is necessary for the context of our research.

Writing about action research as a mode for talking about failure

Action research is an inherently pragmatic approach to managing a research process, grounded in learning through practical experimentation. It sees any form of action as deeply contingent on the individual contexts you are operating within, and this means that the strategies put in place for Congruence Engine were a product of the people, institutions and wider political, social and economic realities we found ourselves in. This will be different each time, and therefore the approach will need to be different each time. This orientation towards learning by doing, seeing and observing what works and what doesn't is an alternative to the negative connotations of failure. It is a generative reframing of failure enabled by the iterative and complexity-embracing nature of action research.

Difficulties arise when we are asked to write about the project methodology and give overviews or accounts of how the project developed. Judi Marshall and Peter Reason argue that it is easy for accounts of action research to become bland and prosaic and urge quality action research to respect the aliveness of the method – its wildness at times (Marshall and Reason 2008). With that in mind, how can we use the opportunity of an action research framing of failure to write productively about what didn't go to plan?

As a mode of doing research, it does not necessarily align with the same models of success and significance found in traditional forms of academic inquiry. Rather than looking for 'truth' and replicability, action research is concerned with engagement, dialogue, pragmatic and locally useful outcomes, and an 'emergent, reflexive sense of what is important' (Bradbury and Reason 2001). Here we begin to step away from reportage of what was successful to what the learning was from moments of tension, from changes of process, from what was difficult and impossible to get done. Marshall and Reason sum up the potential of not knowing, or of failing to know, when they note that 'if you think you know what you are doing as an action researcher, have it comfortably in hand, you are really not doing it, are not on a learning edge' (Marshall and Reason 2008). Capturing the liveliness of the research that pushes you and your collaborators to the edge of your learning and comfort zone is the sign that significant research and learning experiences are taking place.

In talking about, and writing about Congruence Engine, I have always attempted to be (painfully, at times) self-reflexive and critical about the urge to tell a good story – of glossing over the complexity, the tensions and the failures. There is always an underlying fear that surfacing the challenges and the improvisations you made along the way will eclipse the traditional success stories we wish to tell our funders. However, in using action research as method, in demonstrating the challenges through defining what didn't work, we have the opportunity to release ourselves from that urge.

Action research is an orientation towards research that undermines the traditionalist sense of failure. Instead of defining what didn't work as a failure, action researchers see it as a development in their research, a finding that will help us move towards a better understanding of how to create a more effective research intervention during the next cycle of work. Knowing what doesn't work is as useful as knowing what does work in a complex and changeable environment.

Acknowledgements

My thanks to Helen Graham, my co-facilitator in the action research of the Congruence Engine project, whose insights on the action research methodology and the forms of investigation this chapter is based on, are forever helping me learn.

Notes

1 Towards a National Collections (TaNC) was a five-year, £18.9 million investment by the UK Arts and Humanities Research Council, looking to understand the requirements of developing a united digital collection made up of the cultural heritage materials held in the UK's museums, libraries, archives and heritage organisations. https://www.nationalcollection.org.uk/Discovery_Projects (accessed 24 November 2024).

2 Basecamp is a project management tool by 37signals. It was used by the Congruence Engine team from March 2022 until the end of the project in January 2025.

3 Notion is a documentation tool and wiki developed by Notion Labs Inc. It was used by the Congruence Engine project from January 2023 until the end of the project in January 2025.

References

Bernstein, E., J. Bunch, N. Canner and M. Lee. 'Beyond the Holocracy Hype', *Harvard Business Review* (July–August 2016): 38–49.

Boulton, J.G., P.M. Allen and C. Bowman. *Embracing Complexity: Strategic Perspectives for an Age of Turbulence*. Oxford University Press, 2015.

Bradbury, H. and P. Reason. 'Conclusion: Broadening the Bandwidth of Validity: Issues and Choice-Points for Improving the Quality of Action Research'. In *The Handbook of Action Research: Participative Inquiry and Practice*, edited by P. Reason and H. Bradbury, 695–707. SAGE Publications, 2001.

Brydon-Miller, M.. and D. Coghlan. 'First-, Second- and Third-Person Values-Based Ethics in Educational Action Research: Personal Resonance, Mutual Regard and Social Responsibility', *Educational Action Research* 27 (2019): 303–17.

Burns, D. *Systemic Action Research: A Strategy for Whole System Change*. Policy, 2007.

Embury, D. 'Action Research in an Online World'. In *The SAGE Handbook of Action Research*, edited by H. Bradbury, 529–35. SAGE Publications Ltd 2015. Accessed 24 November 2024. https://methods.sagepub.com/book/the-sage-handbook-of-action-research-3e.

Grewcock, D. *Doing Museology Differently*. Routledge, 2014.

Knudsen, L.V. and A.R. Olesen. 'Complexities of Collaborating: Understanding and Managing Difference in Collaborative Design of Museum Communications'. In *The Routledge Handbook of Museums, Media and Communication*, edited by Kirsten Drotner, Vince Dziekan, Ross Parry and Kim Christian Schrøder, 205–18. Routledge, 2018.

Marshall, J. and P. Reason. 'Taking an Attitude of Inquiry'. In *Towards Quality Improvement of Action Research: Developing Ethics and Standards*, edited by B. Boog et al. Sense Publishers, 2008.

McCarthy, C. 'Theorising Museum Practice Through Practice Theory: Museum Studies as Intercultural Practice'. In *The Routledge International Handbook of Intercultural Arts Research*, edited by P. Burnard, E. Mackinlay and K. Powell, 24–34. Routledge, 2016.

Reason, P. 'Pragmatist Philosophy and Action Research: Readings and Conversation with Richard Rorty', *Action Research* 1 (2003): 103–23.

Schell, S. and N. Bischof. 'Change the Way of Working. Ways into Self-Organization with the Use of Holacracy: An Empirical Investigation', *European Management Review* 19 (2021): 123–37.

Chapter 10

Navigating the challenges and opportunities of collaboration

Jennifer Stertzer

The Center for Digital Editing (CDE) was established at the University of Virginia in 2016 after several years of experimenting with and developing digital tools and publishing solutions at the Papers of George Washington project. Conceptualising and building the CDE involved several components: deliberating on the outcomes of the trials, explorations and advancements of digital tools and projects made over the years at the Washington Papers; assessing the state of the field of documentary editing; exploring the potential of collaboration and shared resources/expertise; thinking about how editorial projects engage with their users; experimenting with tools and platforms; and exploring the intersection between documentary editing and digital humanities.

From the outset, collaboration has been at the heart of our mission. The landscape of documentary editing is changing, with smaller, shorter-term projects increasingly replacing large, long-term endeavours. Primarily due to funding availability and evolving requirements, such as open-access digital publication and extensive public outreach, this shift has inspired us to embrace a new collaboration model that leverages various partners' strengths to maximise funding and enhance efficiency. I've witnessed first-hand how these partnerships not only create immediate benefits but also build a reservoir of technical and editorial expertise that we can draw upon for future initiatives.

However, the path of collaboration is not always smooth. Each project brings its own unique set of challenges, which we can categorise as institutional and disciplinary. Navigating these differences has not always been easy; we've faced setbacks and 'failures' that, while frustrating, have often transformed into profound learning experiences. Each hurdle has provided insights that enrich our understanding and refine our processes.

At the organisational level, I've come to appreciate the importance of coordination and cooperation among institutions. Since most of our work is grant-funded, administering projects – preparing proposals, developing and managing budgets, implementing work and reporting on progress – consumes quite a bit of time. Over time, we've sought to streamline these administrative processes, developing standardised procedures and fostering robust communication channels. This intentionality has made our collaborations more productive and less cumbersome. Yet, institutional support for digital projects can vary widely. Some partners have access to robust internal support, while others rely heavily on the CDE for essential services. Developing standardised procedures for proposal and budget development and clear timelines and workflows have helped. Additionally, fostering strong communication channels between institutions can help manage expectations and responsibilities.

Institutional support of editing and publishing technologies also varies. Some of our partner projects receive internal support, such as site hosting, platform installation and maintenance. Others need the CDE to provide some or all of those services. This reality is one of the reasons we have pursued the development of a Drupal-based editorial and publication platform. Working in a platform that provides out-of-the-box functionality (technical infrastructure, editing tools, content displays, pre-built search/browse/query options) and supports project-specific features helps ensure a predictable and efficient implementation. In turn, technical maintenance and updating have become more manageable and less time-consuming. It's been rewarding to see how this platform has enabled projects to thrive without the burden of excessive technical challenges.

Hosting, or 'publishing', content raises sustainability and institutional responsibility issues. In the realm of digital projects, planning for long-term preservation and access is paramount. Unlike print editions that find a permanent home on library shelves, digital materials require ongoing commitment and strategic planning. We have worked with projects and their host institutions to develop preservation strategies; for example, the Pinckney Papers Projects at the University of South Carolina, in collaboration with the South Caroliniana Library, devised a plan to preserve the project's research and source materials (USC, 'Pinckney Papers Projects' and 'South Caroliniana Library'). I had the opportunity to sit in on these meetings and experience how these relationships are cultivated.

At the opposite end of the spectrum, we've participated in other project meetings where the editors are incredibly wary of external support and solutions. These concerns revolve mainly around who ultimately 'owns' the project and its content. Our experiences have led us to create options, including pathways for preserving and archiving content and linking our projects to established repositories like LibraData and Rotunda (University of Virginia, 'LibraData' and 'About Rotunda').[1] Crafting a clear preservation and sustainability plan, utilising established pipelines and digital repositories, and adopting protocols for regular updates and backups are essential in ensuring that the work we do remains accessible for generations to come.

Working collaboratively also involves bridging various disciplinary, linguistic or operational gaps. Like the challenges and outcomes of navigating institutional support, interdisciplinary collaborations are both complicated and immensely rewarding. We have been fortunate to work with various practitioners, including editors, archivists, community activists, documentary filmmakers, digital humanists, public historians and curators. However, with this diversity come different methods, vocabularies and project management strategies. These collaborations require intentional communication, active listening and a willingness to adapt. I've learned that fostering a cooperative environment requires patience and a genuine openness to different perspectives. It's in these spaces that innovation flourishes. However, I've also witnessed how different terminologies can create barriers to understanding and alignment. Despite our shared mission of making content accessible, variations in language across disciplines can lead to confusion. We've encountered practitioners who struggle to find their work reflected in grant guidelines that seem rigid and exclusionary. Two projects in particular come to mind: the Chinese American WWII Veterans Digital Resource and Archive and the Yokohama Specie Bank Collaborative Digital Edition project.

The Chinese American WWII Veterans Digital Resource and Archive project grew out of a book – *Honor and Duty: The Chinese American WWII Veterans* – and a documentary film project – *Honor and Duty: The Mississippi Delta Chinese* – developed, written and directed by E. Samantha Cheng of Heritage Series, LLC.[2] The project aims to create the first digital resource and archive of public and private records acknowledging Chinese and Chinese American veterans of World War II. The CDE partnered with Cheng and her team in 2020 to help conceptualise and plan the digital project and develop a grant proposal to support that work. Since this project was built on previous endeavours, workflow and research processes were already in place.

The project team also had a solid understanding of how the data they collected could be used and displayed in the digital resource. These ideas pushed the boundaries of our ideas about data and presentation, which were primarily driven by traditional workflows and processes. The challenge was figuring out how to map the project's workflow, data structuring and publication goals to grant guidelines that required detailed descriptions of editorial methodologies (defined by traditional editing activities like cataloguing, transcribing and annotating). We initially experimented with mapping a project's practices, methods and desired outcomes to the terminology used in grant guidelines. The process was tedious and, to be honest, sometimes detrimental; instead of spending time and energy advancing work, we were talking past each other in an attempt to contort the work to better align with the guidelines. Stepping back and regrouping, we refocused on the underlying goals and processes rather than specific terminology. We drafted a proposal explaining these in detail, using language that fully represents the project.

We also had to figure out how to match the project's data, research work and interface ideas to components of our technical infrastructure. Further complicating the matter was the platform itself; the primary building blocks of a Drupal site – content types, views, blocks, themes, and so on – are not easy to understand. While every project element is reflected in the platform, articulating those connections and relationships is not always easy. We failed more times than I'd like to admit at explaining and demonstrating how the project team worked and envisioned the resource could – and did – map to the data model and content views. And while I think we were ultimately successful, the experience was fraught with frustration and exasperation.

The Yokohama Specie Bank Collaborative Digital Edition at the Japanese Cultural Community Center of Northern California (JCCCNC) in San Francisco is working to develop and make accessible documents and financial records drawn primarily from the Bank's collection. During the project's planning phase, I was invited to participate and help the team think about digital editing and platforms. We confronted two challenges from the start: how to create processes and tools that could involve community members in every phase of the work and what technical solutions were feasible for the JCCCNC to engage with, manage and sustain. Some team members felt that the CDE's (and, more generally, the field's) methods and tools were too scholarly, complex and inaccessible. We made several attempts at mitigating these concerns, from demonstrating the technology's ease of use to, again, trying to map and connect different terminologies. However, these efforts ultimately failed; the project team and the JCCCNC decided they needed to organically create methods and solutions that reflected their values and skills.

Despite this failure, we respected their decision and learned from the process. In working with other community-driven projects, we now avoid unsolicited problem-solving and instead help identify specific, appropriate areas for support. We also feel that more space needs to be made for these projects; while their methods, tools and source materials might differ, the work is no less critical. Experiences like this continue to inform another one of our projects – eLaboratories. ELabs is a 'diverse community of practitioners engaged in making source materials accessible, discoverable, or (re)imaginable' (CDE, 'eLaboratories'). Conceptualising and growing eLabs has allowed us to work with various projects and practitioners, who, in turn, have shared their work with the community (Matsuda 2019). We developed eLabs to be an open ecosystem where 'practices of editing and recovery span numerous communities and disciplines . . . a space for cross-fertilization, co-creation, and collaboration—a place where all practitioners are encouraged to grow by listening to and learning from each other' (CDE, 'About eLabs'). This ethos also aligns with the CDE's mission and is very much influenced by our collaborative successes and failures.

Not every collaborative effort reaches its intended outcome, but each experience is a chance for growth. Reflecting on what worked and what didn't is vital for shaping future endeavours. By documenting lessons learned and engaging in post-project evaluations, we've honed our ability to be better partners. Sharing the knowledge and tools we develop along the way has the potential to amplify our collective impact. As I look ahead, I'm reminded that the landscape of documentary editing and digital humanities is ever evolving. Embracing flexibility, open communication and an iterative mindset can transform challenges into opportunities. By centring our work on shared goals and adapting to the unique needs of each project, we can cultivate partnerships that advance our field and enhance access to primary source materials. It's an exciting time to be part of this dynamic community, and I'm eager to see where our collaborative spirit will take us next.

Notes

1 LibraData is UVA's local instance of the Dataverse software, originally developed and used by Harvard University. Any projects associated with the University of Virginia – Digital Publishing Cooperative (UVA-DPC; https://uvadigitalpublishingcoop.org/) can make use of this repository. The UVA-DPC ecosystem also includes Rotunda, offering another digital publication and preservation option for our partner projects.

2 See https://www.heritageseries.us/honor-and-duty-book and https://ww2cavets.com/ (accessed 25 November 2024).

References

Center for Digital Editing. 'About eLabs'. n.d. Accessed 4 November 2024. https://elaboratories.org/about/about-elabs/.

Center for Digital Editing. 'eLaboratories'. n.d. Accessed 4 November 2024. https://elaboratories.org/.

Heritage Series. 'Chinese American WWII Veterans Online Resource'. n.d. Accessed 4 November 2024. https://ww2cavets.com/.

Heritage Series. 'Honor and Duty: The Chinese American WWII Veterans Book'. 2020. Accessed 4 November 2024. https://www.heritageseries.us/honor-and-duty-book.

Matsuda, Diane. 'Caring for Community Collections: Insights from Working with the Seizo Oka Collection at the Japanese Cultural and Community Center of Northern California'. 2019. Accessed 4 November 2024. https://elaboratories.org/event/caring-for-community-collections-insights-from-working-with-the-seizo-oka-collection-at-the-japanese-cultural-and-community-center-of-northern-california/.

University of South Carolina. 'Pinckney Papers Projects'. n.d. Accessed 4 November 2024. https://sc.edu/study/colleges_schools/artsandsciences/history/research/pinkney_papers_projects/.

University of South Carolina. 'South Caroliniana Library'. n.d. Accessed 4 November 2024. https://sc.edu/about/offices_and_divisions/university_libraries/browse/south_caroliniana/index.php.

University of Virginia. 'LibraData'. n.d. Accessed 4 November 2024. https://library.virginia.edu/libra/datasets.

University of Virginia Press. 'About Rotunda'. n.d. Accessed 4 November 2024. https://www.upress.virginia.edu/rotunda/.

Chapter 11

Challenging the pipeline structure: a reflection on the organisational flow of interdisciplinary projects

Caio Mello

The use of new terminologies in research projects, especially when it comes to interdisciplinary ones, is expected and, sometimes, desirable. It helps scholars to develop better terms to refer to new phenomena, processes and methods, as well as to improve communication across disciplines. This is the case of an expression that has become increasingly common in the field of digital humanities: 'pipelines'.

Pipelines refer to 'a very long large tube, often underground, through which liquid or gas can flow for long distances' ('Pipeline', n.d.). When used in the context of digital humanities (DH), however, it is a metaphor, borrowed from data science. In computing, the term 'pipeline' is used to describe the processes of data transformation from acquisition to output – the expected outcome. In this sense, data is thought of as a fluid that flows through 'pipes', which are different stages of the processes, such as data acquisition, filtering, cleaning and visualisation, among others.

When designing research projects in DH, which very often involve a 'data pipeline', it becomes useful for scholars to think of the project's structure as pipelines themselves. It seems to be a natural and easy way of dividing the work of multiple collaborators, where someone is expected to focus on data acquisition and data management, for example, while others focus on data analysis. When we think of a truly interdisciplinary project, however, things become even more complex. This chapter questions whether

Figure 11.1: Example of a data pipeline. © Caio Mello.

'pipelines' are the most suitable form of organising an interdisciplinary project in DH and why a pipeline model of project organisation can fail.

Being truly collaborative, and truly interdisciplinary

The emergence of projects that bring together computer scientists and humanists has become increasingly frequent and encouraged by funding agencies. In this scenario, a common challenge is to define how each of the project's members can contribute to the project's aims by being part of a specific stage of the pipeline. An easy, and problematic solution for this challenge, is simply relying on computer scientists to focus on the data collection and processing steps, while humanists would contribute to the data analysis by interpreting the outputs. This form of organisation, however, brings some issues.

Van Atteveldt, Trilling and Calderón (2022) present the concept of pipeline by using an example where a researcher is interested in testing a hypothesis about 'personalisation in the news'. For this task, the authors design a pipeline that involves collecting – or scrapping – news articles published online, processing the data using Named Entity Recognition (NER), and verifying to what extent people mentioned in the texts influence the news stories. The authors then divide the pipeline into two parts, one that they believe is of interest, the final stage of verifying the hypothesis, and another that is classified as 'necessary but not inherently interesting' to them, the use of NER. In this case, although it is important to consider potential biases involved in the use of Natural Language Processing techniques, they understand that, as their work is not interested in studying NER per se, it should be taken just as a tool to be used to respond to their questions.

This approach to the use of digital methods can be easily transferred to the design of a research project resulting in a series of problems. Interpreting the result of a tool that researchers are not able to deeply understand, becomes, in a project pipeline, the same as receiving data processed by another person or group, and expecting to be able to retrieve meaningful insights out of the interpretative work. As pointed out by Viola (2023, 59), from data collection to data processing, the curatorial work is paramount, as each decision 'triggers different chain reactions and will therefore output different versions of the material'. Dividing researchers between a more 'technical' and a more 'interpretative' workgroup not only causes inefficiency in the project but can also create errors.

Fry (2007, 6) refers to the division of work on data in different segments as a 'telephone game', where something is always lost at each stage. Fry's work is particularly focused on the work of designers to represent data: if they are not involved in the early stages, they become unable to display a visualisation that accurately seeks to respond to the initial question stated by the project.

Being truly collaborative and truly interdisciplinary is challenging. It requires devoted time for scholars to reflect on how they can work together, translate specific terminology to colleagues with different backgrounds and find common terms to be used in the group work. Scarce time, resources and appropriate knowledge to conduct this reflection is, unfortunately, commonplace.

Ahnert and others (2023, 17) discuss how researchers have created space for these reflections on the project 'Living With Machines'. They considered the importance of providing researchers with the possibility to give their input in every stage of the project, aiming at responding to a common historical research question, while they should also have space to produce outputs that would benefit their particular careers in different fields of research. The authors highlight the importance of 'knowing what your data looks like, and understanding how it will be manipulated – what will be lost or added, where ambiguity may harden into certainty – before it is analysed in a specific research context' (Ahnert et al. 2023, 44).

Some of the issues related to the separation of work across a pipeline might not be directly caused by the pipeline structure itself, but I argue that the linearity of that structure reinforces the difficulties found when seeking to produce a more collaborative environment.

A critique of 'pipelines' as a representation of research planning

One way of looking at the use of pipelines as a figurative representation of processes is their use to illustrate the steps of data processing, as discussed above. In this case, for example, developers present a pipeline to inform how a certain tool works, through which the audience is capable of identifying each of the steps undertaken that lead to the results. When using this logic, in advance, to design a research project, pipelines are not part of the final stages – a representation of results – but rather a representation of the project's structural planning.

The challenge is then to avoid interpreting the project's pipeline by the logic of Taylorism, principles of labour developed by Frederick Taylor in 1911, based on the segmentation of the workforce ('Taylorism' n.d.). Among the consequences of having researchers working on a linear pipeline is the risk of having the interpretative work projecting their own beliefs and expectations onto the data outputs generated by another person or workgroup, especially when the data processing is a black box.

Moreover, it can also create obstacles to dealing with failure more efficiently. Dealing with failure requires, very often, the knowledge of the data, the context in which it was produced, the lenses through which it has been observed, and by which research questions it is motivated. Besides identifying failure, it is necessary to have the means to address it. That's when a rigid linear pipeline may cause difficulties, as it does not necessarily allow the time, resources and possibility of returning to previous steps multiple times to refine and correct them.

When thinking of a more collaborative project design, we can think beyond linearity, emphasising the necessity of integration. This way, taking as an example a data pipeline such as the one proposed by Van Atteveldt, Trilling and Calderón (2022), the participation of social scientists and humanists should be expected in the design of the data collection and data processing steps, including the work of interrogating the tool, in this case, NER. I also see as desirable the participation of data scientists in the interpretative work, which can help validate whether the output corroborates (or doesn't) the formulated conclusions.

Beyond that, thinking of non-linearity also means expecting to re-collect and re-process data more than once, or even, several times. Understanding that processes do not need to occur necessarily one after the other – and that they need to be integrated – implies a different way of understanding the role that each scholar plays in the project. The participation of the entire team in the early stages of decision-making is crucial as it raises awareness of how results are affected by each stage of the process.

Conclusion: distorting the pipes

If fluids in a linear pipeline flow in just one direction, it would be a case of distorting the pipes. The idea is to create space, within the project planning, for a collective construction that seeks less linearity and more of an integrated system. In the pipe metaphor, this space is a call for more time to be dedicated to collective planning, which can hopefully mean the construction of better tools for dealing with failure.

The pipeline model of project organisation increases opportunities for failure because individuals do not have the necessary knowledge of the other processes, the data and the choices made by collaborators. Moreover, this model has the potential to make addressing failure more difficult because it discourages iterative working between sections of the pipeline.

Truly collaborative and interdisciplinary projects are challenging and require effort from the scholars involved to devote time and resources to reflect on how to make it work. A critical look at how pipelines have been used and their potential to confine researchers into rigid processes is, therefore, a useful exercise to produce more efficient project planning that will lead to better results.

References

Ahnert, Ruth, Emma Griffin, Mia Ridge and Giorgia Tolfo. *Collaborative Historical Research in the Age of Big Data: Lessons from an Interdisciplinary Project*. Cambridge University Press, 2023. https://doi.org/10.1017/9781009175548.

Fry, Ben. *Visualizing Data: Exploring and Explaining Data with the Processing Environment*. O'Reilly Media, 2007.

'Pipeline'. n.d. In *Cambridge Dictionary*. Accessed 20 June 2024. https://dictionary.cambridge.org/dictionary/english-portuguese/pipeline.

'Taylorism'. n.d. In *Munich Business School Dictionary*. Accessed 20 June 2024. https://www.munich-business-school.de/en/l/business-studies-dictionary/taylorism.

Van Atteveldt, Wouter, Damian Trilling and Carlos Arcila Calderón. *Computational Analysis of Communication*. John Wiley & Sons, 2022.

Viola, Lorella. *The Humanities in the Digital: Beyond Critical Digital Humanities*. Springer Nature, 2023.

Chapter 12

When optimisation fails us

Jentery Sayers

I've proposed that project. Okay, I've proposed quite a few of them: the ones that promise to deliver all the digital things. An app. An interactive map. An online exhibit. Data visualisations. A blog and social media presence. Open-access data repositories and peer-reviewed articles. Such promises reflect institutional demands on the humanities to remain relevant online while doing a lot with very little. Practitioners spread themselves and their projects thin whenever funding is scarce, and the norm in today's content industry is to diversify the channels of communication to maximise circulation and reach everyone (Eichhorn 2022, 4–8). An app engages one audience, a journal article addresses another, a short video offers the tl;dr, and so it goes. Digital projects never rely on a single publication format, and their relevance is assessed by academic citation counts as well as internet performance metrics such as site visits, page views, clicks, downloads, subscriptions and search engine rankings. Publishing across these attention economies is a challenge, partly because citation and performance metrics cannot measure the quality of engagement. They are also plagued by assumptions that digital publishing is – or should be – fast and easy (Fitzpatrick 2011, 48, 191). An emphasis on the immediacy of digital content has, for instance, neglected matters of project maintenance and long-term care. Several projects I published in the early 2010s are inaccessible today. The map doesn't load. The exhibit returns a 404 error. Data disappeared. Software was deprecated. I forgot to renew the domain.

The intent of this reflection is not to lament the rise of the content industry and its fetish for metrics. It is to briefly outline why management paradigms from that industry may not transfer well to the academy or, stronger, why academics may want to reject or resist those paradigms. I am not implying that colleges and universities exist outside capitalism in a life-of-the-mind utopia. I am asserting that cooperative projects are among the most meaningful contributions practitioners can make to their scholarly fields. Although sceptics may claim that cooperative projects are bespoke and thus fail to scale, a collective awareness of predominant management paradigms helps practitioners avoid neoliberal principles of optimisation that ultimately fail us. We can approach failure by focusing on substance – when an article or exhibit is not as compelling or thorough as we hoped it would be. We can also understand it in terms of promise and timing – when we miss due dates or opportunities to flip prototypes into products. Yet, a more generative framework underscores design: an attention to process, its structures and formats and how failure is defined in the first place.

Some projects don't have much of a plan; or, more precisely, the plan circulates mostly in the head of the principal investigator (PI). This paradigm echoes the auteur theory of film, and it's feasible when someone works alone. For example, I maintain my own online portfolio, which I can update or fix whenever the mood strikes me. Opacity emerges when a single person – the 'ideas person' – oversees a project and hires research assistants, staff and other team members. Trajectories can change rapidly, collaborators may be unsure what to do and when, and tensions likely arise between concept and practice. A team is expected to read the mind of the PI, who is also the primary stakeholder. Project management software doesn't solve the problem, either. It's conducive to busywork and PI detachment from the team. Worse, it becomes 'bossware' that lowers team morale and gives members the (perhaps accurate) impression that their activities are being monitored to optimise productivity (Corbyn 2022; Munn 2024). It's not a stretch, then, to associate this PI model of leadership with toxicity.

Waterfall management paradigms are meant to correct the leadership problems linked to the lone ideas person. A waterfall plan is prescriptive. It's shared among the team, as are milestones for achieving it (Mokhtar and Khayyat 2002, 53). In the parlance of game design, the project runs on 'rails', like a train from origin to destination. Instructions are clear, and the vision and its trajectories should be, too; however, most everything is fixed to optimise time. Team members cannot be enticed by detours and must quickly resolve hiccups to maintain course. They must also refrain from iteratively releasing components of the project, meaning most public feedback is suspended until the entire project is complete (Thesig et al. 2021). Even though waterfall management motivates teams to avoid scope creep and stick to their budgets, it often pushes researcher curiosity and experimentation to the margins. Such tunnel vision fails a team if it results in monotony, high turnover rates, burnout or alienation from the project itself.

While the waterfall model privileges the project, the agile model foregrounds the process. It is flexible, thrives on iterative development and adapts to feedback throughout a project's lifecycle. The nonlinearity of agile methods appeals to practitioners who need to test multiple prototypes before settling on one, and prototyping can unfold across several publication formats. Indeed, the agile model may take its time, venturing off rails to pursue sidequests that weren't mentioned in the initial plan. For these reasons and many more, it is adopted partly or fully by many digital humanities teams (Tabak 2017). The problem, though, is that the agile model appeals to users of products and thus to customers (Beck et al. 2001). This orientation means the quality and content of agile projects are easily determined by internet traffic and online performance metrics, with management optimising attention and service provision rather than time or productivity. The agile model gives as many users as possible what they want, tracks their engagement and quantifies it for stakeholders or investors, who tend to be risk-averse.

A cooperative model learns from these three approaches to identify when and why neoliberal management paradigms that prevail in industry fail us as academic researchers and practitioners. Against the grain of optimisation, the cooperative model highlights the culture of a project, the relations within it, how it brings people together, and whether it alienates them from each other and the work they're doing. One example is what Tiffany Chan and I call 'minimal computing from the labour perspective', which does not reinvest a team's surplus labour in increased productivity (Chan and Sayers 2022). It invests instead in shared structures and knowledge. Examples include *Archipelagos: A Journal of Caribbean Digital Praxis* (supported by Columbia University Libraries and Yale University) and Vault (developed by University of Victoria Libraries). Both projects commit to sustainability by design, and they persist not as effects of their technical particulars – such as elegant code or static site generation – but as matters of habit driven by cultivation and collective expertise.

Yet another example appears in research by Liz Lane and Kristen R. Moore. They demonstrate how aspects of the agile model can be repurposed to foster a 'multivocal critical imagination' that encourages 'collaboration and coalition building across disciplines to promote equity and justice' in the academy and attends to issues that matter deeply to people's communities and daily lives (Lane and Moore 2023, 43–4). Here, the context of a project matters as a lived experience. It has agency, even, and thus there is no one-size-fits-all approach to care or design.

Against the maximisation of productivity and attention, the cooperative model reveals that neoliberal paradigms of optimisation strategically absorb the time, space, thought and mechanisms we require to interrogate the values of project management in today's content industry (Nissenbaum 2005, lxvi–lxx). That is, optimisation becomes a distraction. Slowing down the research process counters that neoliberal tendency and so, too, does organising to support cultures that routinely remind people they can't do all the things – and they don't have to.

References

Archipelagos: A Journal of Caribbean Digital Praxis. Accessed 24 November 2024. https://archipelagosjournal.org/.

Beck, Kent, et al. 'Manifesto for Agile Software Development'. 2001. Accessed 24 November 2024. https://agilemanifesto.org/.

Chan, Tiffany and Jentery Sayers. 'Minimal Computing from the Labor Perspective', *Digital Humanities Quarterly* 16, no. 2 (2022). Accessed 24 November 2024. http://www.digitalhumanities.org/dhq/vol/16/2/000600/000600.html.

Corbyn, Zoë. '"Bossware Is Coming for Almost Every Worker": The Software You Might Not Realize Is Watching You', *The Guardian*, 27 April 2022. Accessed 24 November 2024. https://www.theguardian.com/technology/2022/apr/27/remote-work-software-home-surveillance-computer-monitoring-pandemic.

Eichhorn, Kate. *Content*. MIT Press, 2022.

Fitzpatrick, Kathleen. *Planned Obsolescence: Publishing, Technology, and the Future of the Academy*. New York University Press, 2011.

Lane, Liz and Kristen R. Moore. 'The Invisible Work of Iterative Design in Addressing Design Injustices', *Technical Communication and Social Justice* 1, no. 2 (2023): 28–48. Accessed 24 November 2024. https://techcommsocialjustice.org/index.php/tcsj/article/view/11.

Mokhtar, Renad and Mashael Khayyat. 'A Comparative Case Study of Waterfall and Agile Management', *SAR Journal* 5, no. 1 (2022): 52–62. https://doi.org/10.18421/SAR51-07.

Munn, Luke. 'More than Monitoring: Grappling with Bossware', *International Journal of Communication* 18 (2024): 3128–39. Accessed 24 November 2024. https://ijoc.org/index.php/ijoc/article/viewFile/21399/4663.

Nissenbaum, Helen. 'Values in Technical Design'. In *Encyclopedia of Science, Technology, and Ethics*, edited by Carl Mitcham, lxvi–lxx. Macmillan, 2005.

Tabak, Edin. 'A Hybrid Model for Managing DH Projects', *Digital Humanities Quarterly* 11, no. 1 (2017). Accessed 24 November 2024. http://digitalhumanities.org:8081/dhq/vol/11/1/000284/000284.html.

Thesig, Theo, Carsten Feldmann and Martin Burchardt. 'Agile Versus Waterfall Project Management: Decision Model for Selecting the Appropriate Approach to a Project', *Procedia Computer Science* 181 (2021): 746–56. https://doi.org/10.1016/j.procs.2021.01.227.

Vault. n.d. Accessed 24 November 2024. https://vault.library.uvic.ca/.

Chapter 13

Reframing 'reframing': a holistic approach to understanding failure

Lauren Tuckley

Introduction

Sometimes I feel like my job is to convince people to apply for opportunities that they don't have a shot at winning. Probability bears that out. The odds of winning a highly competitive academic fellowship, like those I recruit and train undergraduate students to apply for, is around 2–4 per cent. While the competitiveness of undergraduate admissions at elite universities is widely known and hotly debated, relatively few, even within academia, might know what these fellowships are – and fewer still would be familiar with the low probability of winning one. That was the case for me, even after I'd accepted a position responsible for identifying and training students to compete for them. In other words, I hadn't heard of the Rhodes or Marshall Scholarships before it was my job to help my university's students win them.

In the United States, nationally competitive fellowships work with universities to identify top-performing American undergraduates and young alumni, offering recipients fully funded graduate study, often in the United Kingdom. Beyond funding, these fellowships provide access to elite networks, a social capital that often defines their value, offering incalculable long-term professional benefits. They're also valuable for the recipients' undergraduate institutions, which promote their students' success as a marker for institutional excellence and prestige.

The growth and value of academic fellowships over the past two decades led to the establishment of dedicated offices at universities focused solely on identifying and developing applicants. This is how I found myself working as a fellowships advisor without fully understanding the 'game'. Along the way, I've learned a few lessons about success – and failure – that have shaped my approach as an advisor: first, that to win, applicants must understand that winning isn't the ultimate goal; and second, that the competitive, individualistic nature of these processes should be reframed as a team effort. In the model I've developed, paradoxically, applicants have the best shot at winning when they're willing to help their peers – those they're in direct competition with – even at a risk to their own success. In other words, I've had to teach applicants how to embrace failure, care about the success of others as much as their own and walk away with a positive experience, win or lose.

Failure frameworks

As a fellowship advisor, I found myself constantly grappling with questions about failure. I saw students pour everything into their applications, only to face overwhelming odds – odds that meant most of them would not win. How could I prepare them to handle rejection in a way that would not discourage them from pursuing their goals?

I turned to my colleagues in the field for guidance, reaching out to our national listserv with a simple request: 'I need any and all resources you use to teach failure'. The response was remarkable. Colleagues from across the country sent me reading lists, TED Talks and academic articles, each framing failure in a unique way. As I reviewed their suggestions, three distinct approaches to understanding failure emerged, which loosely fell into three categories: psychological, ideological and political lenses.

The psychological framework was rooted in mindset, emphasising the power of belief in shaping our responses to failure. This approach, influenced heavily by Carol Dweck's 'growth mindset' theory (Dweck 2016), encourages individuals to view setbacks as learning opportunities rather than final judgements on their abilities. The psychological lens offered useful tools for self-reflection, suggesting that reframing our beliefs about failure could reduce anxiety and build confidence. But I found it incomplete; it placed responsibility on individuals without fully accounting for the broader context in which competition occurs.

The ideological framework focused on grit and perseverance, suggesting that determination is the key to overcoming failure. This approach resonated with American meritocratic values – the idea that hard work and resilience can lead to success, regardless of circumstances. Books like Angela Duckworth's *Grit* and popular stories of relentless pursuit reinforce this belief (Duckworth 2016). While this framework celebrates tenacity, I worried that it could burden students with unrealistic expectations, ignoring the structural barriers that some face and leading them to blame themselves if hard work wasn't enough to secure a win.

The political framework offered a more critical perspective, examining how societal structures define success and failure. One of the most thought-provoking recommendations came from Judith Halberstam's *The Queer Art of Failure* (2011), which views failure as a form of resistance against rigid societal norms. Halberstam's approach critiques the systems that privilege certain definitions of success, highlighting how marginalised groups often find power in embracing failure as a rejection of dominant narratives. This political lens allowed me to see failure as something that could be redefined and even celebrated in defiance of societal expectations. However, while compelling, this framework seemed difficult to apply in the context of fellowship advising, where students must still navigate traditional competitive structures to achieve their goals.

While so many of the works suggested offered valuable insights, I found none of them fully addressed my students' needs. Ultimately, I wanted an approach that balanced individual resilience with a sense of purpose that extended beyond winning. This search led me to develop my own framework, one that helps students reframe failure as part of a values-oriented, community-driven process.

Beyond winning: a values-oriented approach to competition

There's a saying that goes, 'second place is the first loser'. Our culture's competitive nature is individualistic and outcome-oriented, leading to adverse effects across all sectors – from universities misrepresenting data to boost their rankings to the Houston Astros' use of 'sign-stealing' technology to gain an unfair advantage.[1] These examples highlight how the desire to be 'the best' can compromise ethics, often with far-reaching societal harm. While these examples are extreme, the mindset behind them is deeply rooted in late capitalist society, showing up in subtle ways even in academia.

In my office, this winning mentality often manifests as 'trophy hunting'. Many students at elite universities have been competing relentlessly since middle school. Nearly every academic encounter they've had – whether excelling in standardised tests or gaining admission to a top university – involves a cutthroat pursuit of success over others. This means I often see students who want to know about the Rhodes Scholarship but lack clarity on what they hope to gain from graduate study. When I ask what graduate degree programme they want the Rhodes to fund, they frequently ask what I think would make them more likely to win. This approach is driven by the desire for an achievement signal rather than a genuine educational purpose.

In many ways, the intense competitiveness and 'trophy hunting' mentality among students aligns with broader ideological pressures embedded in our society. As I work with students pursuing fellowships, I frequently encounter the idea that winning is the only path to validation and achievement. Many of my students – bright and driven as they are – have internalised these ideals, viewing success as a narrow path that requires outperforming peers rather than exploring how their goals align with their own values and aspirations.

The dominance of this outcome-oriented perspective creates significant challenges for students, often exacerbating anxieties about failure and diminishing the joy of pursuing their genuine interests. When students view fellowships solely as milestones of personal success, their motivations can become overly transactional, focused on building résumés or collecting accolades rather than deepening their understanding or fostering their long-term goals.

This ideology also reinforces systemic inequities, favouring those who can best navigate these competitive spaces rather than those most committed to the field or cause. For students from marginalised backgrounds, the relentless pursuit of external markers of success can feel particularly burdensome, as they may face additional obstacles in a system that privileges certain forms of capital – be it social, financial or academic. In a society that already amplifies disparities, equating personal worth with outcomes like fellowship wins risks sidelining students who bring different, but equally valuable, perspectives and experiences.

To counteract these pressures, I began shifting from outcome-driven conversations to values-oriented advising, encouraging students to focus on the purpose behind their aspirations rather than the prestige of specific awards. By centring their 'why', students can approach their applications with an intrinsic commitment to their goals, making the process itself more rewarding. Instead of viewing fellowships as validation, they start to see them as potential means for advancing their core values – turning applications into opportunities for growth rather than simply high-stakes competitions.

Of course, not all students are purely 'trophy hunters'. Most apply to fellowships because they care about advancing their education and are passionate about their field, but ambition plays a role, too. My job is to help them balance these motivations. To address this, I've moved away from questions about which programme would make them more competitive and instead ask, 'Who do you want to become, and why does it matter?' Conversations focused on values and purpose often lead students to reconsider their reasons for applying, resulting in goals that are more grounded in personal motivation.

This values-oriented approach isn't limited to fellowship applications; it applies equally well to other application-based opportunities. For example, consider Leah, a senior psychology major preparing to apply for graduate school. Like many fellowship applicants, Leah initially focused on securing admission to a top-ranked programme, seeing it as validation of her hard work. Through conversations with her mentor, Leah shifted her focus from prestige to purpose, concentrating on programmes that aligned with her mission to improve mental health access in underserved communities. Ultimately, this reframing helped her find a graduate programme that resonated with her values, reducing the pressure of achieving a 'win' and allowing her to find satisfaction in the process.

All for one: reorienting traditional notions of competition

In response to these competitive complications, I developed the 'failure-as-process' method for advising prospective applicants. This approach has become one of the most successful interventions I've implemented. Ironically, I've observed that the less applicants focus on winning, the more they engage with their broader goals, and, ultimately, the more likely they are to win. This is a win–win for me as an advisor – helping students clarify their purpose and build a meaningful vision is rewarding, regardless of the outcome.

This insight led me to experiment with a community-based approach to application development – one that encouraged direct competitors to support each other's candidacies. Typically, when a university nominates multiple students for a fellowship like the Rhodes, each applicant works individually, often fostering a competitive mindset. However, I believed that a collaborative approach could strengthen each applicant's work and create a more positive experience overall. But the thing is, this approach was born out of necessity.

In March 2020, the isolation of remote learning and the burnout from endless Zoom meetings tested everyone's limits. That year, I introduced 'write-ins', where students gathered virtually to work on their applications together. During these write-ins students often dropped questions about their writing process in the chat or shared light-hearted remarks unrelated to essay writing. They were building community. These sessions created a support network, with students sharing insights that were as valuable as my own.

Initially, I worried that bringing applicants together might amplify competitive tension. But the benefits of community quickly outweighed my concerns. The 2020 UK fellowship cycle turned out to be historic for my university, with nearly every nominee advancing to a final interview and five receiving prestigious fellowship offers. But beyond the wins, it was the connections formed among the nominees that validated the approach. Working together fostered a sense of mutual support. For unsuccessful candidates, the sting of failure was softened. For those who won, the joy was amplified.

I'm now in my fourth year of using the community-based model, and the results continue to prove its effectiveness. While we achieve more wins as a group, what happens when students don't win reinforces the benefits of this approach. When applicants invest in one another's success, they walk away with more than just a single outcome – they gain friendships and future colleagues. Many have told me they felt genuinely happy to lose to a friend they'd bonded with. When everyone loses, which statistically happens most often, they still have each other to lean on. In this way, reframing failure as a shared experience helps students build a network that extends far beyond the fellowship competition.

Reframing failure: a few takeaways

Writing studies scholar Alison Carr finds failure an 'ongoing process filled with potential for tactical insight' (2023). This resonates deeply with my approach. In her work, Carr emphasises that failure should not be seen as an endpoint but rather as a complex, evolving experience that invites continual learning. Carr's reflections reinforce the idea that failure is most productive when we see it not as a conclusion but as a source of actionable feedback – fuel for future attempts rather than evidence of inadequacy. By reframing failure as a dynamic process, applicants can maintain resilience and stay aligned with their larger goals, finding purpose even in moments of setback.

Competition is an inescapable part of life, and so is failure. If failure is inevitable, reframing it becomes essential. From my work with students pursuing scholarships with long odds, I offer three ways to reframe failure that apply to innumerable competitive settings.

1) Reframe the 'why'
   Early on, I learned that one of the biggest barriers to success is allowing an achievement – or the lack of it – to define self-worth. Some students feel so anxious about failure that they choose not to apply at all. This is especially true for students who seek external validation, as the stakes of failure feel particularly high. To counter this, I encourage students to shift from focusing on themselves to focusing on something larger.

2) Reframe the goal
   A values-based approach to achievement moves the emphasis from immediate goals to long-term objectives, reducing the impact of any single failure. When students see a fellowship as a step toward a broader mission – such as fighting climate change – failure becomes less discouraging. By focusing on long-term objectives, students can maintain their commitment even when individual efforts don't succeed.

3) Reframe the 'how'
   Building a support system among peers fundamentally transforms the competitive process. While individual achievements remain important, working within a community fosters

> collective growth and resilience. The camaraderie of fellowship cohorts creates an environment where failure is shared, not isolating. When students include others in their journey, they gain both practical advice and emotional support, making the process of failing less isolating and more constructive.

By reframing competition and fostering community, we can shift from an individualistic view of success and failure to one that values resilience, learning and collective growth. The question we should be asking isn't 'How do I overcome failure?' but 'How do I stay committed to my goals and values, and what did I learn from failing *this* time?'

Note

1 In 2019 the Houston Astros, a Major League Baseball team in the United States, were revealed to have been using cameras and audio signals to communicate the details of upcoming pitches to their batters – in direct violation of league rules.

References

Carr, Alison. 'In Support of Failure', *Composition Forum* 27 (2023). Accessed 24 November 2024. https://compositionforum.com/issue/27/failure.php.

Dweck, Carol S. *Mindset: The New Psychology of Success*. Random House, 2016.

Duckworth, Angela. *Grit: The Power of Passion and Perseverance*. Scribner, 2016.

Halberstam, Jack. *The Queer Art of Failure*. Duke University Press, 2011.

Part IV
INSTITUTIONS

Failure and institutions

Institutional frameworks are failing (us). The pillars of our research and professional culture – from university operational frameworks, evaluative frameworks and peer review, research funding mechanisms, career progression structures, to publishing models and professional associations – are falling apart while they fail to address evolving concerns and needs of a community and a field that are in constant motion. These failures are deeply historical and rooted in, among many other things, the neoliberal marketisation of the public sphere (Slaughter and Rhoades 2000; Fitzpatrick 2019). In this context, failure can be a useful heuristic for identifying the places where things are not working, particularly when we want to examine systems that might otherwise resist analysis, let alone change.

Using failure this way is one of the distinctive contributions of digital humanities – 'the digital humanities . . . scandalously reveal the system's components, while focusing critical attention on the mechanisms needed to maintain them' (Greenspan 2019). The reflections in this section take up that tradition, examining failures in our institutions and systems – including within digital humanities organisations themselves.

These failures begin early in the career of many practitioners, as postgraduate training programmes fail to adequately support the digital researcher. Jennifer Isasi describes how exploring (the possibility of) failure as a pathway to success was an eye-opening experience for her, beginning in her PhD years. This perspective encouraged her to experiment with an alternative career path that offered the flexibility to pursue her chosen, often risky, scholarly questions. Many students don't receive that kind of support and, as Britt Amell argues, even traditional narratives of failure can leave specific students without sufficient scaffolding for their experimental or alternative approaches to scholarship. Elena Spadini extends these reflections further along the career pathway, drawing on examples from the *critique génétique* to remind us that what truly defines a career are the failures and rejections.

A major undercurrent facing digital scholars is that higher education institutions, as well as research funders, fail to truly understand interdisciplinary research. In practice, interdisciplinary research carries significant risk and a higher chance of failure, as Naomi Wells highlights in her reflection. According to Wells, although research funders are starting to address this issue, these efforts remain misaligned with evaluation and assessment mechanisms that still focus primarily on outcome-based metrics.

The dominance of a metrics-based culture has also played a major role in the crisis facing academic publishing. Academic professional culture – as well as formal promotion criteria – has been built on a publishing model that emphasises quantitative proxies for quality such as impact factors and citations metrics (Declaration on Research Assessment 2024). Experimental publishing has been proposed by Janneke Adema as a creative and counterhegemonic response to the systemic failure of the academic publishing system. This commitment to experiment, while holding on to key academic values, is similarly emphasised by Anisa Hawes and Riva Quiroga in their piece on changes to the publishing workflow at the *Programming Historian* aimed at addressing failures which emerged as the journal expanded.

Digital scholarship organisations are not immune from these systemic failures, as Hawes and Quiroga make clear. One area where the original optimism surrounding digital humanities has fallen far short is the field's professional organisations. Using conference attendance as a proxy for inclusion in the Alliance of Digital Humanities Organizations, the umbrella organisation for national digital humanities associations, Nabeel Siddiqui reminds us of the unfulfilled promise of inclusivity in the field. He uncovers a 'geographical failure of DH' that highlights a geography of power that the community has frequently failed to adequately acknowledge.

References

Declaration on Research Assessment. 'Guidance on the Responsible Use of Quantitative Indicators in Research Assessment'. DORA. 2024. https://doi.org/10.5281/ZENODO.10979643.

Fitzpatrick, Kathleen. *Generous Thinking: A Radical Approach to Saving the University*. Johns Hopkins University Press, 2021.

Greenspan, Brian. 'The Scandal of Digital Humanities'. In *Debates in Digital Humanities 2019*, edited by Matthew K. Gold and Lauren F. Klein, 92–5. Debates in Digital Humanities. University of Minnesota Press, 2019. https://doi.org/10.5749/9781452963785.

Slaughter, Sheila and Gary Rhoades. 'The Neo-Liberal University', *New Labor Forum* 6, (2020): 73–9.

Chapter 14

Permission to experiment with literature as data and fail in the process

Jennifer Isasi

Set for failure: plot twist

In the discipline of Hispanic studies, and most specifically, the field of Spanish literature, success is traditionally measured by achieving three key milestones: publishing an academic book, securing tenure and contributing to the field through a series of single-author scholarly articles. More often than not, said milestones are achieved by close reading and becoming an expert in a few authors or works. However, lacking a rigid plan – as a first-generation international student who didn't really know what she was getting into – I opted for an unconventional path: I would mix literature written in Spanish, in general, with computers to engage in more experimental readings. This divergence, which hasn't led me to a tenure-track position nor a book, is often perceived as a failure. Yet to me, this rather different path has been a place for personal and professional growth – with its privileges and risks – offering space to experiment in my scholarship and to support inquiry-based learning and teaching.

This was not solely my decision. I was explicitly given permission to venture into more experimental academic territories in my scholarship and 'fail' if it came to it. This key learning moment that I'll never forget took place when I defended my dissertation proposal in early 2016. While articulating my idea to employ social network analysis methods to analyse nineteenth-century Spanish historical novels, Matthew Jockers, the digital humanist on my committee who was helping me with the computational analysis, posed a crucial question. More or less, he asked, 'Jenn, you keep saying "if I am able to . . ." or "if I get to . . ." So, what if you fail to extract character mentions in a manner conducive to a meaningful application of SNA and, thus, are left without results?'

Caught off guard, I found myself for a few seconds at a loss for words. Luckily, and to my complete surprise, my advisor, Óscar Pereira Zazo, quickly interjected with a reassuring response: 'She can write about the research process and the reasons for failing at the experiment and she can still successfully graduate'. The learning process was more important than the results.

Automatic Natural Language Processing models did fail me: they were not accurate enough for my purposes back then. However, through persistent trial and error (and running against the student funding clock), I was able to find a workaround to the challenge of employing existing NLP models for character name identification, normalisation and counting. My solution involved turning a printed index of characters from a 1940s edition into a comprehensive data dictionary of characters enriched with metadata for many variables (Isasi 2017). This approach allowed an algorithm to locate the names in the novels, count their (co)occurrence, and later run social network analysis and visualisations on the data. Contrary to initial expectations, the experiment proved fruitful, as I not only avoided failing in my idea but also managed to establish meaningful connections to canonical readings of the works by established *galdosistas*. I think it was a pleasant surprise for everyone.

Comfortable with experimenting

Since then, I've been actively engaged in or advised on various data curation and research experiments that tried to replicate my dissertation model or explore new methods to analyse text-as-data. In most instances, I have had to create new datasets either independently or through collaboration due to factors such as: no previous investment in creating data about the question that crossed our mind; the absence of digitised records in an organised or clean data-collection format; the information being housed in different spaces and formats; data restrictions within academic systems for purposes of review and promotion; and more. And so, when it is time to apply a method to probe a (research or for fun) question, the only thing I have time and energy to do is something that is smaller than I envisioned. I mostly create visualisations or write some provocation, if I produce anything at all. Although I often don't produce a traditional paper, I persist in running experiments, gaining valuable insight into both the subject matter and, most importantly, the methodology employed.

This persistence is inspired by the words of my advisor, who challenged the notion of failure in a department of Modern Languages. These words have remained central to my approach to research, mentoring, workshop instruction and service. It is the perspective through which I guide students (and faculty when they are adventurous enough), urging them to enter the world of digital scholarship in any shape or form. The phrase 'she can write about the research process and the reasons for failing' has evolved over the years in my various roles into a commitment to engage, document the process, acknowledge and celebrate successes, and to take note to learn from things that didn't unfold as anticipated. As Graham puts it, this process is not just 'messing around the Internet' or with digital methods, because 'there's a cycle of exploration, documentation, experimentation, documentation, experimentation . . . [we] write it down. Blog it. Turn it into an article. Share' (2019, 85). This process is a form of scholarship as well.

Teaching from lessons learned

I see the opportunity of being able to share this knowledge with others as a professional accomplishment. Whether in my official position first as a CLIR postdoc at University of Texas-Austin (USA) and now as a director of the Digital Liberal Arts Research Initiatives at Penn State University (USA), my role as editor of *Programming Historian en español*, a journal that shares digital methods with a global audience, or as a consultant for collaborators and colleagues – primarily friends of the global majority – I strive to guide the selection of the most appropriate and ethical project workflows and tools, taking into account context and resources for courses or projects.[1] And the way said plans are developed usually has a learning goal, rather than being a simple prescription. Often, although at the beginning most students and faculty seem reluctant to 'play' in class or project meetings, we together discover that embedding digital tools to explore the cultural record invariably leads us to pose thought-provoking questions, beginning with the datasets (How was this collected?) and ending, usually, with visualisations (Are they meaningful? Are they respectful?), running through questions about the subject matter.

I must admit that, sometimes, experimenting or suggesting to experiment is also accompanied by moments of frustration. How can it be otherwise? Sometimes, the dataset is not available or is dirty; or the tool you thought could be useful cannot process text-as-data in different languages; or it is no longer updated and supported because it runs out of funding, and it doesn't work anymore (see Dombrowski's reflection in this volume). Or you have to let the idea go, because it won't count towards academic promotion. But this experimenting is critical in the context of a digital humanities pedagogy 'that centers concepts and inquiry-based learning' where mostly everyone comes into the field with different skills and knowledges (Walsh 2023, 198). And, I would add, everyone leaves the learning environments also with different skills and knowledges, forcing us to collaborate with each other and succeed or fail and learn together.

In closing: embrace the possibility of failure

Since it doesn't always lead to a traditionally readable work, the idea that experimenting with digital scholarship methods within the discipline of literature is often deemed a failure persists among many. For example, a colleague that I had not seen in a decade asked me recently: 'I don't know what you do but a director [position] sounds good. *Are you happy?*' The concern about my happiness was prompted, I know, because in their minds, I've failed. I am not a tenure-track assistant professor of Spanish; rather, I am an assistant research professor of digital scholarship.[2]

I am happy, indeed. As I fight for changes where we find there should be changes, personally, I am grateful every day for the opportunities I have to participate in them. In my teaching and sharing knowledge, I am happy. I learn something new every day, and in collaborating with other scholars in many fields I also learn from their wins and failures – because we now often share both cases (Dombrowski 2019, with special notice to its Addendum). The flexibility to pursue scholarly questions within my work responsibilities is also a privilege I cherish. Moreover, the landscape has changed and if one chooses or needs to publish, there are now numerous avenues to present projects at various stages – be it in the inception phase in journals like *Startwords*, method-focused contributions on *Programming Historian*, or reviewing projects on *Reviews in DH*. At the same time, in teaching, and as shown in *What We Teach When We Teach DH*, we are making strides towards fostering a more inclusive environment where success is not, and cannot be, uniformly measured. We are seeing a collective effort that is underway – such as the one seen in this volume – to challenge conventional norms of success in (our parts of) academia.

And, as much as I can, I am dedicated to advocating for the inclusion of this type of scholarship in our academic and disciplines' system and guiding future generations. Inspired by my mentor's advice, I embrace the idea that permission to fail is, in itself, a pathway to success. ¡Gracias, Óscar!

Notes

1 'The CLIR Postdoctoral Fellowship Program offers recent Ph.D. graduates the chance to develop research tools, resources, and services while exploring new career opportunities', usually in libraries (Council on Library and Information Resources).

2 Needless to say, this perception is based on a widespread elitism about academic ranks that is reflected both at the individual level and in the system of benefits and opportunities.

References

Dombrowski, Quinn. 'Towards a Taxonomy of Failure' (blog). 2019. Accessed 24 November 2024. https://quinndombrowski.com/blog/2019/01/30/towards-taxonomy-failure/.

Graham, Shawn. *Failing Gloriously and Other Essays*. Digital Press at the University of North Dakota, 2019. Accessed 24 November 2024. https://thedigitalpress.org/failing-gloriously/.

Isasi, Jennifer. 'Acercamiento al Análisis del Sistema de los Personajes en la Narrativa Escrita en Español: El Caso de Zumalacárregui y Mendizábal de Pérez Galdós', *Caracteres: Estudios Culturales y Críticos de La Esfera Digital* 6, no. 2 (2017): 107–37.

Walsh, Brandon. 'The Three-Speed Problem in Digital Humanities Pedagogy'. In *What We Teach When We Teach DH: Digital Humanities in the Classroom*, edited by Brian Croxall and Diane K. Jakacki, 197–206. Debated in Digital Humanities. University of Minnesota Press, 2023. https://doi.org/10.5749/9781452969558.

Chapter 15

What to do with failure? (What does failure do?)

Brittany Amell

Frequently celebrated for its potential to inspire growth, resilience and eventual success, failure continues to play a role in academic and cultural narratives. Yet, such imperatives to transmute failure into something positive – referred to in this chapter as 'failure-as-usual' – frequently overlook the broader structural inequities that are both embedded in academic systems and influential in determining who is or is not able to rebrand a failure as something else. This reflection interrogates these dominant narratives, challenging notions that failure can be universally normalised or redeemed without attending to its social, political and cultural contexts.

Each of the sections in this reflection responds to a key question. The first section asks 'What, exactly, are we asking each other and ourselves to normalise?' The second reflects on 'What, exactly, are we asking each other and ourselves to be okay with?' The final section concludes with a reflection on 'What, if anything, can we do with failure?' By drawing attention to these questions, along with the limitations of failure-as-usual narratives, the reflection aims to join others in retrieving the potential of failure as a galvaniser for meaningful social change.

What, exactly, are we asking each other and ourselves to normalise?

In a paper about ecological memoirs, grief and restorying, Willis (2009) recounts a memory of a commercial that depicted a woman in a 'romanticized version of an office space' with wood panelling and glass partitions. The woman's forearms began to burn (signified by a red glow that spread up her forearms) as a result of too much typing but then, miraculously, a solution in the form of an analgesic appears on the screen. With the help of this analgesic, the red glow is totally erased and 'the woman returns happily to her keyboard' (Willis 2009, 86). Using this example, Willis argues that there is a prevailing societal tendency to portray anything that prevents us from returning 'happily to keyboards', thus disrupting business-as-usual, as something that ought to be removed or rubbed out. This issue with defaulting to this stance is that rather than confronting the underlying conditions that led to the painful burning red glow in the first place, it palliates. Further, disruptive, unruly feelings and physical symptoms can be important catalysts for transformation and healing – but only if they're attended to. While not about failure per se, Willis's argument offers valuable insights and entryways for those interested in contemplating further the emancipatory potentials of failure.

Many efforts to retrieve failure often end up framing it as a temporary setback in storylines that otherwise inevitably seem to culminate in triumphant endings (Leary 2018). We also see efforts to retrieve failure storying it as the dues we must pay in order to succeed in academia – often characterised by stories meant to 'inspire' others that they too can overcome failure if they keep trying or, if not, to see failure as a teacher that builds character and hands out badges for effort (Brien et al. 2013; Cao and Ngetich 2023; Eckstein et al. 2023; Holdsworth 2020; Stefan 2020). It would seem that, at least in part, a persistent belief in the need to 'normalise' failure motivates these framings. In this telling, everyone fails and 'feels like an imposter, so really no-one is', and the solution is 'to individually just believe in yourself' (Breeze and Taylor 2020, 100).

On the face of it, efforts to make failure 'okay', whether by opening up conversations about it, lowering its stakes or reframing failure as desirable and pedagogical, would seem to resonate with feminist strategies to politicise individual or personal problems (Breeze and Taylor 2020). However, these framings typically have the opposite effect – that is, failure becomes *depoliticised* and the broader structural inequities that are embedded in academic systems become further invisibilised (Ahmed 2012; Dolmage 2017; Henry et al. 2017).

What, exactly, are we asking each other and ourselves to be okay with?

Attending to the stories that bodies and emotions tell us about being unruly or disruptive is necessary, even amidst pressure to 'return happily to keyboards', but only if these stories are also understood as connected to each other and to their social and political contexts. To demonstrate this, and provide some further background for this argument, this section will focus on (recontextualising) some examples of failure.

The first example comes to us from Tyler Hallmark (2018) who, in an article for the *Chronicle of Higher Education*, shares his experience as a sophomore student in the US, captivated by the world of entrepreneurship and entrepreneurs. Attending 'countless' talks, Hallmark would listen to CEOs and 'start-up wizards' painting pictures of a business world he initially thought included him – someone from a low-income background (para 2). However, Hallmark began to reconsider this thought after attending a particular talk given by an entrepreneur who shared with the audience how 'he had borrowed $50,000 from his parents to launch his first start-up and then proceeded to go bankrupt in his first year' (para 2). The takeaway, according to Hallmark? That risks are necessary and failure is okay. But, for Hallmark, this advice was irreconcilable:

> The recurring theme of 'It's OK to fail' didn't (and still doesn't) resonate with me, because I couldn't afford to fail. I didn't have parents who could lend me $50,000. In fact, $50,000 was more than my single mother could make in three years at her near-minimum-wage job. The lesson I learned was that if I didn't have money to risk losing, I shouldn't be in business. (para 3)

Hallmark's response reminds us that the framing failure as 'okay' often relies upon the illusion that there is a separation between failure, the social and political context, and the differential distribution of the consequences associated with failure (see also Feigenbaum 2021a, 2021b). In other words, failure becomes individualised and depoliticised, thus obscuring the structural inequities within academic systems that determine who can reframe failure as something else. Further, for students who face poverty, housing concerns and financial insecurity, success can feel like a matter of life or death (Feigenbaum 2021a). And, for members of historically and systemically marginalised communities, failure and its associated complement of negative feelings are neither fleeting nor simply unfortunate, but 'unavoidable' reminders of 'exclusionary social realities' (Comstock 2023, 704).

While 'failure is okay' stories may counter tendencies to leave failure unspoken, the relations between failure and normative notions of success are left unquestioned. Consequently, failure's disruptive potential is left unfulfilled. At the same time, adopting failure as a stance (situated in its social and political circumstances) does not have to require the rejection of success. For instance, for some, conforming or 'blending in' can signify both 'assimilation and a lack of recognition' and thus in many ways feel like a failure (Denny 2010, 110). However, for others, conformity is another way to subvert normative ideals and thus 'blending in' can feel like a success.

For another example, I return to my MA thesis – a multiple case study that explored the experiences Indigenous students had with learning to write in contexts of higher education in Canada, where settler-colonial legacies of dispossession and marginalisation continue to shape institutional structures and practices. Throughout our interviews, students recalled numerous encounters with direct and indirect messaging that seemed to be saying they needed to separate their identities and cultures from their writing and learning process if they wanted to be 'successful'. They recounted experiences with feedback that, in their view, criticised their writing as overly driven by storytelling and, in turn, felt like a swipe at their identity and cultural practices. Consequently, conforming to suggestions that they remove or limit the amount of storytelling in their papers felt like a failure to accept who they are (for example, 'It's me. It's in my identity. If others don't understand, it's their loss'). Thus, they felt compelled to resist notions of success (Amell 2016, 85).

One last example, this time from Stewart (2015), whose aim to prioritise Indigenous knowledge(s) and experiences in his dissertation necessitated flouting certain academic writing conventions. In the preface of his dissertation, Stewart shares how he received an initial rejection from his institution's ethics board because his application was written in a way that conformed with (and affirmed) Stewart's experience and positionality as a member of the Nisga'a nation. 'The BREB [Behavioural Research Ethics Board]', he writes, 'found the writing style of the original application to be deficient and questioned my writing ability and knowledge of English, suggesting that I hire an editor' (Stewart 2015, x). Stewart describes having to decide between resubmitting the application in standard edited academic English or to proceed without clearance, and face a 'high possibility' of rejection. Weighing the potential for a rejected dissertation, Stewart decided to resubmit the ethics application 'using standard academic conventions' (2019, 9).

These examples suggest that the meanings for both failure and success are neither fixed nor singular, nor are they universally shared. In contexts like Canada, where there is a history of eroding social safety nets, settler colonialism and many other systemic inequities, there is a real risk of doing further damage when we attempt to normalise failures without addressing the reality that 'failure affects people differently, and that privilege plays an important role in who is allowed to fail – and who isn't' (Hallmark 2018, para 1).

Equally important are questions that open up notions of success to examine their normative underpinnings. Talking about failure in ways that focus only on failure's transmutation (for example, we all fail sometimes, what matters is that we've transformed failure into something triumphant or otherwise 'good') does nothing to *open failure up* if we leave other problematic premises intact. Thus, we would do well to question the premise that transforming failure into something synonymous with success is or ought to be the goal. Similarly, we would also do well to question assumptions that pin success and its consequences down as desirable, positive and good for us – much like the 'cruel optimism' Lauren Berlant (2011) uses as a term to gesture at the ways in which definitions of success are entwined with the status quo, and both success and the status quo are portrayed as a state that is attainable, desirable and obligatory.

Beyond failure-as-usual, or what to do with failure

Failure's potential for disruption, critique and transformation is frequently undermined by narratives that depoliticise failure, treating it as an individualised experience rather than a product of structural inequalities. Without situating failure within its broader social and political contexts, efforts to normalise failure risk reinforcing the very systems they attempt to challenge.

Many scholars have emphasised the importance of 'failing failure' as a way to open up alternatives to oppressive templates of success (Burford 2017; Cvetkovich 2012; Halberstam 2011; O'Gorman and Werry 2012). This framing urges us to see failure as an opportunity for critique, a point of entry into examining the power structures and normative discourses that shape our lives (Gross and Alexander 2016). By moving away from ideologies rooted in individualism, competition and privatisation, failure can become a generative space where we challenge inequitable systems and confront the role we may play in perpetuating them.

Future directions for engaging with failure might involve focusing on failure beyond-the-usual – an understanding of failure that goes beyond personal responsibility narratives and delves into systemic critique (see Chapters 13 and 17, this volume). In educational contexts, for example, this might entail a care-full approach to failure that acknowledges how students' lived experiences shape their relationship with and understanding of failure and success. It might also involve tailoring course policies to explicitly communicate why *failure is okay* in specific, situated terms (Feigenbaum 2021a). Key to these approaches is their resistance to universalising failure, or framing it as a stepping stone to individual success. This includes examining how failure can be used to dismantle the ideologies of meritocracy and cruel optimism (Berlant 2011) that tie success to the status quo, and as an entry point for collective action, solidarity and the development of equitable alternatives.

Ultimately, by contextualising failure and interrogating its relation to success, we can better engage with its emancipatory potential – its capacity to inspire not only reflection but transformation. Failure, then, becomes less about individual shortcomings and more about a collective opportunity to confront and renovate the systems that structure our lives in order to redistribute resources and possibilities.

References

Ahmed, Sara. *On Being Included: Racism and Diversity in Institutional Life*. Duke University Press, 2012. https://doi.org/10.1515/9780822395324.

Amell, Brittany. '"The First [Draft] Was a Lot of Me . . . but the Second One Is What They Want": A Multiple-Case Study of Four Indigenous Students' Experiences with Academic Writing'. MA dissertation, Carleton University, 2016. https://doi.org/10.22215/etd/2016-11503.

Berlant, Lauren. *Cruel Optimism*. Duke University Press, 2011. https://doi.org/10.1215/9780822394716.

Breeze, Maddie and Yvette Taylor. 'Knowing Feminists: The (Mis)Use of (Our)Selves'. In *Feminist Repetitions in Higher Education*, edited by Maddie Breeze and Yvette Taylor. Springer International Publishing, 2020. https://doi.org/10.1007/978-3-030-53661-9_5.

Brien, Donna Lee, Sandra Burr and Jen Webb. '"Fail Better": Doctoral Examination and the Creative Field', *TEXT* 17, Issue Special 22 (2013): 1–12. https://doi.org/10.52086/001c.28306.

Burford, J. 'Not Writing, and Giving "Zero-F**ks" about It: Queer(y)ing Doctoral "Failure"', *Discourse: Studies in the Cultural Politics of Education*, 38, no. 4 (2017): 473–84. https://doi.org/10.1080/01596306.2015.1105788.

Cao, Xiangkun Elvis and Gladys Chepkirui Ngetich. 'The Need to Normalize Failure', *Nature Reviews Chemistry* 7, no. 2 (2023): 69–70. https://doi.org/10.1038/s41570-022-00454-x.

Comstock, Edward. 'Toward a New Neurobiology of Writing: Plasticity and the Feeling of Failure', *College Composition & Communication* 74, no. 4 (2023): 695–730. https://doi.org/10.58680/ccc202332523.

Cvetkovich, Ann. *Depression a Public Feeling*. E-Duke Books Scholarly Collection. Duke University Press, 2012. https://doi.org/10.1515/9780822391852.

Denny, Harry. 'Queering the Writing Center', *Writing Center Journal* 30, no. 1 (2010): 94–124. Accessed 24 November 2024. http://go.gale.com/ps/i.do?p=AONE&sw=w&issn=08896143&v=2.1&it=r&id=GALE%7CA360608867&sid=googleScholar&linkaccess=abs.

Dolmage, Jay. *Academic Ableism: Disability and Higher Education*. University of Michigan Press, 2017. https://doi.org/10.3998/mpub.9708722.

Eckstein, Lydia E., Amelia B. Finaret and Lisa B. Whitenack. 'Teaching the Inevitable: Embracing a Pedagogy of Failure', *Teaching and Learning Inquiry* 11 (2023). https://doi.org/10.20343/teachlearninqu.11.16.

Feigenbaum, Paul. 'Telling Students It's O.K. To Fail, but Showing Them It Isn't: Dissonant Paradigms of Failure in Higher Education', *All Faculty* 9, no. 1 (2021a): 13–26. https://doi.org/10.20343/TEACHLEARNINQU.9.1.3.

Feigenbaum, Paul. 'Welcome to "Failure Club": Supporting Intrinsic Motivation, Sort of, in College Writing', *Pedagogy* 21, no. 3 (2021b): 403–26. https://doi.org/10.1215/15314200-9132039.

Gross, D.M. and J. Alexander. 'Frameworks for Failure', *Pedagogy* 16, no. 2 (2016): 273–95. https://doi.org/10.1215/15314200-3435884.

Halberstam, Jack. *The Queer Art of Failure*. Duke University Press, 2011. https://doi.org/10.1215/9780822394358.

Hallmark, Tyler. 'When "Failure Is OK" Is Not OK', *Chronicle of Higher Education* (11 February 2018). Accessed 24 November 2024. https://www.chronicle.com/article/when-failure-is-ok-is-not-ok/.

Henry, Frances, Carl E. James, Peter S. Li, Audrey Kobayashi, Malinda Sharon Smith, Howard Ramos and Dua Enakshi. *The Equity Myth: Racialization and Indigeneity at Canadian Universities*. UBC Press, 2017.

Holdsworth, Clare. 'A Manifesto for Failure: Depersonalising, Collectivising and Embracing Failure in Research Funding', *Emotion, Space and Society* 37 (November 2020): 1–4. https://doi.org/10.1016/j.emospa.2020.100744.

Leary, J.P. *Keywords: The New Language of Capitalism*. Fernwood Publishing, 2018.

O'Gorman, R. and M. Werry. 'On Failure (On Pedagogy): Editorial Introduction', *Performance Research* 17, no. 1 (2012): 1–8. https://doi.org/10.1080/13528165.2012.651857.

Stefan, Melanie. 'If You Sing Wrong, Sing Louder: How We Learn from Failure'. TEDx Talk presented at the TEDxKuchl, Kuchl, Salzburg Austria, 19 February 2020. Accessed 24 November 2024. https://www.youtube.com/watch?v=XBZ7It51WlY.

Stewart, Patrick. 'Decolonizing Syntax: An Indigenous Dissertation', *The Journal of Unschooling and Alternative Learning* 13, no. 25 (2019): 1–14.

Stewart, Patrick Robert Reid. 'Indigenous Architecture through Indigenous Knowledge: Dim Sagalts'apkw Nisiḿ [Together We Will Build a Village]'. PhD dissertation, University of British Columbia, 2015. https://doi.library.ubc.ca/10.14288/1.0167274.

Willis, Alette. 'Restorying the Self, Restoring Place: Healing through Grief in Everyday Places', *Emotion, Space and Society* 2, no. 2 (2009): 86–91. https://doi.org/10.1016/j.emospa.2009.09.001.

Chapter 16

The remaining alternatives

Elena Spadini

I am where I am, I think, because I have failed (it happens that I am happy where I am, but that is not the point, nor does it reflect the amount of luck involved). Failure has shaped my professional profile: I could have ended up in very different places, I have not done this or that. I failed at things I really wanted: PhD positions, grants and so on. This was undeniably bad, at least at the time. When I was preparing a grant application, a colleague from the grants office told us all: if you fail, allow yourself time to grieve and to process. That was a good piece of advice.

In "L'art d'accommoder les restes" (a chapter of *Logiques du brouillon*, a classic of French *critique génétique*), Daniel Ferrer reminds us that a value judgement is made by the writer, when something is deleted and replaced by a better alternative, where 'better' is measured in artistic, ethical, political, commercial or other terms: 'C'est parce qu'on juge que B est d'un certain point de vue "mieux" que A qu'on rature A et ajoute B' (2011, 51).[1] In digital scholarly editing, a field of research I am active in, this notion is often neglected, or even unintentionally hidden. The emphasis in the last decades of digital editions, for good reasons of renovation, has been more on restoring the value of all variants and moving beyond the inaccessible 'critical apparatus' as a graveyard of deserted readings, as it has been called, than on representing what Ferrer calls 'la véritable dimension axiologique de la genèse' (2011, 51),[2] that is the dynamics of value between A and B.

This reminds me of a misconception about failure that can be exemplified by the misunderstanding of the 'Fail better' quote from Beckett's *Worstward Ho*: no, failure is not always – and certainly not in Beckett's work

– a useful event on the path to success, as self-help books proclaim.[3] It is just bad, something bad for which there would have been a better alternative, however better is defined (and this is obviously not Beckett, who focuses on the inevitable human condition of failure and does not venture into better alternatives).

But then what? What after asserting that failure is bad? We can look again at the creative process of writers to find some consolation and perhaps inspiration. I have recently been working on the Swiss author Gustave Roud (1897–1976), a writer, photographer, translator and literary critic. Roud's diary is full of pages in which he doubts himself and hints at failure. He writes: 'Mes phrases sont mortes. Ce n'est pas fatigue d'esprit, car dès le début j'ai senti cette sournoise résistance. Abandonner? Quel échec, quel aveu d'impuissance!'; [4] or: 'Je viens de relire quelques poèmes de Penna, l'envie me prend de les traduire . . . Mais n'est-ce pas, par avance, l'échec certain? . . . il me reste une infime espérance de vaincre'.[5] Apologies for helplessness are very common among writers, if not creators in general.

In his book *On Writing and Failure*, Stephen Marche recalls the many failures of famous writers. The opening sentence of an article in *The Atlantic* adapted from the book may sound familiar to more than one scholar:

> English has provided a precise term of art to describe the writerly condition: submission. Writers live in a state of submission. Submission means rejection. Rejection is the condition of the practice of submission, which is the practice of writing. Rejection, not acceptance, is what defines the life of a writer. (2023c)

He even has a direct suggestion for academics: 'The next time you're rejected from some grant or some job, remember James Joyce in 1912' (Marche 2023a). That year, Joyce failed to get a job as an English teacher at a technical college in Italy, a job he needed to pay his long overdue rent, while he also failed to get *Dubliners* published. How to fail better?, one is tempted to ask.

The new wave of talking and writing about failure (the 'fail-lit' of Lindsay Baker 2019), including this welcome anthology, hopefully contributes to a better understanding of failure as something very common, something that happens all the time – at least, it seems, in the professional lives of scholars and writers. As an early career researcher, I was surprised when a distinguished professor once told me: 'You're just seeing the tip of the iceberg: you don't see the thousands of projects that are rejected all the time, but only the few that are successful'. This was enlightening for my younger self. The necessity and frequency of debugging in programming also points in the same direction, because a bug is definitely something bad, but it happens all the time, so that we say 'programming is debugging'.

If failure is so common, we would do better to accept it as something bad but almost inevitable, and, as my colleague suggested, be prepared to grieve. What we do next is up to each of us, in that particular circumstance, in that particular moment: to return to the first person, when I fail, I want to find my better alternative, which might be to try again, or to give up, or something in between.

A note on the first person: overcoming failure, whether of a word, of a sentence or of an application, need not be a solitary activity. But again, it is up to us to decide who is right: in rejection letters I have found some remarks valuable and others less so. Of course, it is not always easy to tell, and my reaction and understanding change over time. In an interview for *The Paris Review*, writer Mary Robison talks about working with the famous and controversial editor Gordon Lish: 'In "Yours," a woman dies', Robison says, 'She wasn't even sick in his version. I had to be fierce about that one. But there were times when I just squeezed my eyes shut and signed my name'.[6] The interviewer goes on asking about the relationships between Gordon and Raymond Carver (Carver 2009, 990): 'Ray knew he was right, but he was scared that if Lish vehemently thought his versions were better, then maybe they were better'. After failure, after submission and rejection, after careful consideration of feedback and reviews, we are free to choose the next step from the remaining alternatives.

Notes

1 'It's because B is judged to be "better" than A from a certain point of view that A is crossed out and B added'. All translations are mine.

2 'the true axiological dimension of the genesis'.

3 In its original context, the phrase 'Ever tried. Ever failed. No matter. Try again. Fail again. Fail better' is part of a bleak and minimalist work concerned with the inevitability of failure in human endeavours, but it has been widely adopted as an inspirational mantra and as encouragement to persist in the face of setbacks. See Beauman 2012.

4 'My sentences are dead. It's not fatigue of spirit, because I felt this sly resistance right from the start. Give up? What a failure, what an admission of powerlessness!' Gustave Roud, *Œuvres complètes*, vol. 3, 867.

5 'I've just reread some of Penna's poems, and I'm tempted to translate them . . . But isn't that, in advance, certain failure? . . . I still have a tiny hope of winning'. Roud, *Œuvres complètes*, vol. 3, 997.

6 Interview in Bengal 2024. Gordon Lish (b. 1934) has been an influential editor working with prominent writers in the United States, mainly during his periods at *Esquire*, Knopf and *The Quarterly*. An overview of Gordon Lish's 'literary legacy' is in Groenland 2015. See also Lorentzen 2015a and 2015b and Winters and Lucarelli 2018.

References

Baker, Lindsay. 'Is Failure the New Literary Success?' *BBC Culture*, 8 July 2019. Accessed 24 November 2024. https://www.bbc.com/culture/article/20190620-is-failure-the-new-literary-success.

Beauman, Ned. 'Fail Worse', *The New Inquiry*, 9 February 2012. Accessed 24 November 2024. https://thenewinquiry.com/fail-worse/.

Bengal, Rebecca. 'Mary Robison, The Art of Fiction No. 263', *The Paris Review*, 2024. Accessed 24 November 2024. https://www.theparisreview.org/interviews/8311/the-art-of-fiction-no-263-mary-robison.

Carver, Raymond. *Collected Stories*, edited by William Stull and Maureen Carroll. Library of America, 2009.

Ferrer, Daniel. *Logiques du brouillon: modèles pour une critique génétique*. Seuil, 2011.

Groenland, Tim. 'The Poetics of the Sentence: Examining Gordon Lish's Literary Legacy', *Irish Journal of American Studies* 4 (2015): 36–49.

Lorentzen, Christian. 'Gordon Lish, The Art of Editing No. 2', *The Paris Review*, 2015a. Accessed 24 November 2024. https://www.theparisreview.org/interviews/6423/the-art-of-editing-no-2-gordon-lish.

Lorentzen, Christian. 'Gordon Lish: "Had I Not Revised Carver, Would He Be Paid the Attention Given Him? Baloney!"', *The Guardian*, 5 December 2015b.

Marche, Stephen. 'A Writer's Lament: The Better You Write, the More You Will Fail', *The New York Times*, 11 February 2023a, Books section.

Marche, Stephen. *On Writing and Failure: Or, on the Peculiar Perseverance Required to Endure the Life of a Writer*. Biblioasis, 2023b.

Marche, Stephen. 'The Fine Art of Failure', *The Atlantic*, 21 February 2023c.

Roud, Gustave. *Œuvres complètes*, vol 3, edited by Claire Jaquier and Daniel Maggetti. Zoé, 2022.

Winters, David and Jason Lucarelli, eds. *Conversations with Gordon Lish*. Literary Conversations Series. University Press of Mississippi, 2018.

Chapter 17

Who fails and why? Understanding the systemic causes of failure within and beyond the digital humanities

Naomi Wells

The increasing openness towards failure and how we can productively learn from and build on our own experiences of failure is undoubtedly a positive development. Nevertheless, it is vital that alongside individual or project-specific experiences of failure we also account for the wider structures and systems in which such failures take place. We must acknowledge failure does not always fall evenly – and most importantly equitably – on different people, and that repeated experiences of failure can stall or even block individuals from advancing their careers. This chapter seeks to look beyond the individual to highlight some of the wider issues in the research landscape that contribute to failure and to address how those working in the field of digital humanities (DH) might contribute to tackling such challenges. These reflections are predominantly grounded in the UK research landscape with which I am most familiar, but it is hoped that at least some of these experiences might also translate to other contexts.

It is particularly important that we turn our critical attention to the assessment and evaluation systems within which funding grants, publications or job applications fail. Given the inherent interdisciplinarity of DH research and researchers, the widely acknowledged limitations of these systems in fairly assessing inter- or transdisciplinary research and profiles are a particular concern. Those of us working within DH will all have faced experiences of reviewers or interviewers judging our work or profiles according to the conventions of a specific discipline and consequently failing to understand the purpose or significance of our work. For as Klein highlights, interdisciplinarity and DH often 'fall outside conventional criteria of evaluation', with evaluators struggling to understand 'what counts as an acceptable form of knowledge production in the field' (Klein 2015).

In the UK context, the British Academy's 2016 report on interdisciplinarity highlighted that due to such obstacles many academics would advise an early career researcher against undertaking interdisciplinary research (British Academy 2016). There has nevertheless been some progress in recent years towards better recognising and valuing interdisciplinary research. The increasing focus on challenge-led research by major research funders has been accompanied by a greater emphasis on interdisciplinary approaches for tackling such challenges. The UK's research assessment exercise (REF) in 2021 also introduced an Interdisciplinary Research Advisory Panel to better support effective recognition for interdisciplinary research. As part of this new approach institutions were asked to flag interdisciplinary research in their submissions, although interestingly the panel reported significant failings with this system with institutions either using flags inappropriately or failing to flag any interdisciplinary submissions at all (REF2021 2022).

These issues point to institutions apparently both failing to understand interdisciplinarity and, particularly in the cases of institutions who flagged no interdisciplinary submissions, continuing a risk-averse approach to submitting interdisciplinary research for assessment. Similar conservatism has also been highlighted by the Hidden REF initiative – highlighting the ongoing institutional failure to submit less conventional forms of research output, which are often associated with interdisciplinary digital research (Hidden REF n.d.). These examples highlight the key challenge that while we have seen more positive discourses from funders and national bodies around interdisciplinarity in recent years, conservatism within the assessment system remains.

As Edmond has written, DH has 'found itself at the heart of a conflict between shifting practices and static structures' (Edmond 2019). The consolidation of DH departments and centres in the UK has undoubtedly helped to create a more welcoming 'home' for the kind of interdisciplinary digital research practices that the British Academy's report identified as often lacking for interdisciplinary researchers. However, DH still suffers from a level of invisibility in the UK's research assessment and funding structures, not having for example its own REF subpanel or being listed as a discipline classification on the UK Arts and Humanities Research Council's funding system. This invisibility increases the risks of DH research being sent to reviewers or assessors with a limited understanding of the specific types of research conducted in the field.

While there have been efforts to involve scholars from different disciplines in the assessment of interdisciplinary digital research, the Modern Language Association's *Guidelines for Assessing Digital Scholarship* (2024) highlight the risks of an 'epistemic mismatch', particularly if reviewers are not familiar with the intellectual traditions of the humanities. As a result it is vital that we continue to advocate for greater visibility for DH within the UK's assessment and evaluation systems, and follow the example of many US subject associations by being more proactive in developing our own evaluation guidelines and criteria for digital scholarship. This work is particularly crucial for those doing DH research outside of DH departments and centres who face even greater challenges in ensuring that departmental reward structures recognise the different nature and outputs of their research.

When considering failings in our assessment and evaluation systems, we must also recognise that failures at more advanced career stages do not necessarily have the same effects on careers as those that occur much earlier in the process, such as the failure to secure PhD funding or that crucial first academic post or fellowship. While those from more financially secure backgrounds might be able to make repeated attempts until successful, for those without such a safety net it will more quickly become necessary to stop trying and turn to other career paths. Acknowledging such inequities should not be confused with reinforcing traditional academic discourses that have suggested that the choice to move outside of academia is itself a failure. Rather, we should acknowledge the differing circumstances in which such choices are made.

Equally, feelings of 'failure' associated with such moves may be connected to the more limited number of viable research-led careers that exist for humanities researchers outside of academia. A 2022 report on doctoral graduate employment, for example, found that those with an arts and humanities PhD were less likely than those in other fields to report that they used their doctoral skills or that their job fitted their career plan (Vitae 2022). While many may go on to have fulfilling careers in other sectors, these findings point to potential feelings of frustration, disappointment or even failure in not being able to apply their research skills.

The picture appears more positive for DH, with the range of knowledge and skills gained through a DH PhD appearing to be more appealing and applicable to a diverse range of research-related roles (Cannelli et al. 2021). Within DH there is also greater openness to the experiences and approaches that researchers with different professional backgrounds and profiles bring to the field. This greater openness may provide a space for those who have faced structural barriers to undertaking the conventional academic career path and help to overcome the sense of 'make or break' that operates within traditional research careers in the humanities. In this respect, DH has a valuable role to play in sharing approaches to and experiences of cross-sector mobility with the wider humanities community and particularly doctoral students who may understandably fear the seeming cliff edge that faces them at the end of their studies. DH must also continue its work to challenge and transform the reward structures in academia to better recognise different roles and how they contribute in different but crucial ways to the success of research.

Nevertheless, despite some areas of optimism for DH, we must also acknowledge the prejudices and implicit biases in our systems and, as researchers such as Risam (2015) have highlighted, the field of DH is not exempt from these issues. A notable acknowledgement of such biases in the wider research funding landscape is the recent experiment by the British Academy to introduce partial randomisation in the selection process for their small grants scheme. Perhaps unsurprisingly, this approach has led to a more ethnically and institutionally diverse field of applicants succeeding in the scheme (British Academy 2023).

While it is promising to see funders seek to address this issue, this example highlights the significant work still needed to address the biases operating across our assessment and evaluation systems. Here, as well as working to recognise and combat our own biases, DH researchers might reflect on how the field can contribute to better understanding how these biases operate across our research systems. The Creative Informatics project has, for example, illustrated how data-driven research methods in DH can be applied to better understand the effectiveness of Equality, Diversity and Inclusion initiatives in the creative industries (Black 2023). Siddiqui in this volume also uses DH methods to highlight the geographic inequalities in Digital Humanities conferences that can hinder the career advancement of scholars, particularly in the Global South. Such examples illustrate the value of turning DH methods inwards to analyse our own institutional, national and international research structures to better understand how and why failure falls inequitably on specific individuals and groups.

In sum, while not ignoring how failure can be an individual learning experience, we must acknowledge that some of the determining factors that contribute to failure operate outside of circumstances that are within an individual's control or capabilities to overcome. This is not to promote a fatalistic approach to failure but rather to highlight that only by understanding and acknowledging these failings in our systems can the DH community identify and advocate for the changes that are needed. While failure will inevitably remain a feature of all research careers, we must ask ourselves how we can work together to tackle the wider systemic issues that make it much harder for some forms of research and some researchers to succeed than others.

References

Black, Suzanne, Anna Orme, Nicola Osborne and Melissa Terras. 'Evaluating Equality, Diversity, and Inclusion Activities within Creative Industries Clusters: A Report from Creative Informatics'. Zenodo, 2023. https://doi.org/10.5281/ZENODO.8114197.

British Academy. 'Crossing Paths: Interdisciplinary Institutions, Careers, Education and Applications'. 2016. Accessed 30 June 2024. https://www.thebritishacademy.ac.uk/documents/213/crossing-paths.pdf.

British Academy. '"Promising" Results from First Year of Innovative Grant Awarding Trial Show Greater Diversity of Awardees and Institutions given Funding'. 2023. Accessed 30 June 2024. https://www.thebritishacademy.ac.uk/news/promising-results-from-first-year-of-innovative-grant-awarding-trial/.

Cannelli, Beatrice, Jane Winters, Arianna Ciula, Paul Gooding, Justin Tonra, Charlotte Tupman, Michelle Doran, et al. 'Next Generation Careers in and from Digital Humanities', OSF Preprints, 2021. https://doi.org/10.31219/osf.io/e8tus.

Edmond, Jennifer. 'Are Para-Academic Career Paths about People or Places? Reflections on Infrastructure as the European Alt-Ac'. In *Debates in the Digital Humanities*, edited by Matthew K. Gold and Lauren F. Klein, 389–98. University of Minnesota Press, 2019. https://doi.org/10.5749/9781452963785.

Hidden REF. 'The Hidden REF', n.d. Accessed 30 June 2024. https://hidden-ref.org/.

Klein, Julie Thompson. *Interdisciplining Digital Humanities: Boundary Work in an Emerging Field*. University of Michigan Press, 2015.

MLA Committee on Information Technology. 'Guidelines for Evaluating Digital Scholarship'. Modern Language Association of America, 2024. Accessed 30 June 2024. https://www.mla.org/content/download/191995/file/Guidelines-Evaluating-Digital-Scholarship.pdf.

REF2021. 'Interdisciplinary Research Advisory Panel: Final Report', 2022. Accessed 30 June 2024. https://2021.ref.ac.uk/media/1901/idap-final-report-designed-final.pdf.

Risam, Roopika. 'Beyond the Margins: Intersectionality and the Digital Humanities', *Digital Humanities Quarterly* 9, no. 2 (2015). Accessed

30 June 2024. https://www.digitalhumanities.org/dhq/vol/9/2/000208/000208.html.

Vitae. 'What Do Researchers Do? Doctoral Graduate Employment, Activities and Earnings'. 2022. Accessed 24 November 2024. https://vitae.ac.uk/wp-content/uploads/2024/12/What-do-researchers-do-doctoral-graduate-employment-activities-earnings-2022-1.pdf.

Chapter 18

Experimental publishing: acknowledging, addressing and embracing failure

Janneke Adema

Experimenting with the ways in which academic research is published, with the processes and practices of knowledge production, has been crucial to explore more inclusive forms of humanities knowledge that are open to ambivalence and failure and to welcome the possibility of new thinking (Adema 2021). Experimental publishing comprises experiments with new publication forms and formats, from enhanced publications that include multimedia and more closely integrate the data underpinning a publication, to iterative and versioned publications that explore processual forms of publishing. It also includes experiments with collaborative, interactive and open forms of research (for example, incorporating collaborative writing practices, annotations, open peer review) and with reuse and remix. But experimental publishing also involves experimentation with the relationalities of publishing, rethinking the various roles and functions involved in the publishing process, and the configuration of the political economy that surrounds knowledge production (Adema and Kiesewetter 2022b).

Rethinking and, more crucially, reperforming the ways in which research is published, therefore involves a critical assessment of existing legacy – predominantly print and codex-based – publishing workflows. These workflows are supported and upheld by extensive scholarly communication infrastructures – which are often proprietary and controlled by one of the five major publishing conglomerates (Posada and Chen 2018) – and further buttressed by institutional assessment and valuation systems that revolve around publications as measurable outputs connected to clearly identifiable individual authors. In this context, experimenting with new forms and relationalities for publishing while speculating on different, more ethical and diverse futures for scholarly communication, comes with various risks and challenges and inevitably runs into moments of failure when testing new roles, formats and technologies.

Acknowledging failure

Yet it is important to see these failures in the context of what we want to achieve with these publishing experiments. Often what are perceived as 'failures' (for example, lack of uptake, engagement or further implementation) have to do with the lack of familiarity of authors and publishers with new publishing workflows, software, processes and roles. At the same time, incentives to experiment are further hindered by funder, institutional, publisher, infrastructural and economic requirements that tend to prioritise certain legacy types of publication and that valorise individual success (Feldman and Sandoval 2018).

Experimenting takes time (and can be costly), yet failure should be perceived as an intrinsic part of experimental publishing projects, part of an iterative process of reflection, review and – where needed and appropriate – further development. Reflecting on failure also makes the processes of knowledge production and the labour involved in its various stages more visible while highlighting the difficulty scholars and publishers are facing to facilitate engagement around research (integrally connected to the current crises in academia and reflected in ever increasing workloads and precarious labour). This unfamiliarity also extends to the relationalities of publishing, where the roles, functions and agencies involved in more traditional print-based publishing workflows will need to be reconfigured in more digital and experimental publishing workflows. This might involve incorporating and acknowledging different roles (for example, software developers and designers, the crucial role played by digital technology) or bringing in existing roles and functions at different stages in the research and publishing process. Here publishing becomes less of an afterthought at the end of a research project, and more something that becomes crucial to research design.

To conduct and support experimental (book) publishing projects, my colleagues and I have worked on creating extensive documentation to accompany a selection of pilot projects.[1] This documentation serves to demystify some of the processes involved in experimental forms of publishing, to familiarise scholars and publishers with software and tools, workflows and roles, and to be transparent about where things (can) go wrong, where barriers and inhibitions continue to exist and where improvements are still needed (Adema and Kiesewetter 2022a). The focus of this documentation is therefore less on showcasing failure as a misstep and more on seeing it as an opening to improving publishing workflows going forward, to accommodate more diverse forms of research and to entice authors and publishers to try out experimental forms of publishing for themselves.

Addressing systemic failure

Over the last few decades, the kind of research that has been conducted within the data-driven humanities, the digital humanities and the digital posthumanities (Hall 2016) in particular, has triggered a rethink of the way that humanities research has traditionally been and continues to be published (still predominantly following a humanist, print and output-based system and original proprietary authorship models (Adema 2021)). Yet experiments with new forms of publishing continue to come up against how engrained this existing publishing system remains, sustained by various vested and commercial interests, making it a fundamentally conservative system.

In addition to being more open towards failure in experimental publishing (and publishing in general) as an inherent part of its speculative and interventionist appeal, it is important to highlight that experimental publishing is in essence a response against a failing legacy system, one that has been developed based on a print hegemony which is no longer functional in an increasingly (post-)digital context where there is a clear need to share research in different ways and to explore how the digital medium can assist academics and publishers in doing so. This legacy system has a hard time accommodating different forms of distributed authorship or multimodal, processual and interactive publications, as its profit and reputation-driven economy has been built upon a commodity and object-based publishing model, based on the extraction and exploitation of intellectual property rights – often preventing further reuse and adaptation of research. A system that is buttressed by liberal humanist conceptions of individual original authorship and dominated by Global North epistemologies that are continuously reproduced and normalised in exclusionary ways, structurally excluding different voices and ways of knowing. It is this legacy system that is increasingly failing academia and the kind of knowledge sharing it requires, which makes it crucial that we experiment with alternative, more ethical and equitable ways of sharing knowledge and working together within academia and with communities outside of the academy, to better reflect the more communal and processual ways we actually conduct research, produce knowledge and share it. This would involve foregrounding a different way of engaging with research and publishing and re-evaluating what counts as scholarship.

As I outlined in the previous section, often what are perceived as failures in experimental publishing can be explained in relation to issues of (lacking) academic labour, to not enough time and funding being available to experiment with new forms of publishing. Yet again, instead of seeing this as a failure on the part of experimental forms of publishing, we could also perceive this as a systemic failure where there has been a lack of investment by academic institutions and by large publishing companies in new modes of publication. Many of the more exciting experiments in academic publishing have hence been conducted by scholarly communities and by small, not-for-profit, scholar-led publishers, often based on volunteer labour and/or with the support of forward-looking funders (Adema and Moore 2021). What is important to emphasise here is that failure is *generative*, and that the failure of the legacy system has also brought people together to imagine otherwise and to work on setting up new publishing models based on collective action, mutual reliance and cooperation.[2]

Embracing failure

While there is a need to be more transparent about failure in experimental publishing and to pinpoint where existing publishing systems are actually *failing us* as academics, there is similarly a need to think through how we can create publishing systems that are more accommodating to failure: to explore how we can introduce more focus on experimentation, process and failure into our academic communication and publishing structures and institutions, to support and encourage difference and change. To further explore this, it might be fruitful to make connections to and draw upon queer theory, as queer theorists have critiqued accepted and normative definitions of success and failure, interrogating these dichotomies and instead arguing for queer forms of failure. Jack Halberstam, in *The Queer Art of Failure* (2011), argues that failure provides openings that might allow for new challenges to normative ways of knowing (and living) to emerge. Applying this to publishing means that failure can potentially challenge and question what are commonly upheld as successful forms of research and publishing – and for what reasons. What normative ideas about success get repeated in these constructions?

As Halberstam argues, failure can function here as a counterhegemonic imaginary for knowing. What role can experimental publishing play in embracing failure, how can it offer us guides, examples and imaginaries for more non-conformist and communal forms of publishing, how can it help us try to rethink the hegemonic and humanist notions upon which our publishing systems are built?[3] Experimental publishing can play an important role here as an alternative discourse to narratives of innovation that are increasingly structuring and underlying our knowledge domains, where the focus is on creating outcomes or results that are measurable and demonstrable or that serve dynamic economic growth (see also Adema 2021, 178–85).

Similarly, it would be useful if the focus in academia was less on the individual success story (for example, as part of performance assessment systems) of the finalised and published output, product or object (a book or article) and more on the collaborative processes of failure and success that were encountered along the way. This would help emphasise that research is never an individual endeavour or achievement but is and has always been a collaborative process of knowledge production. It would help de-stigmatise personal failure and the fetishisation of individual excellence in academic audit cultures. Making the processual aspect of scholarship more visible – which includes the way we collaborate, informally communicate, review and publish our research – and highlighting not only the successes but also the failures that come with this (reclaiming the right to fail), could potentially aid in demystifying the way scholarship is produced, shared and valued.

Notes

1 We have done so amongst others as part of the Research England Development Fund and Arcadia funded research projects COPIM (Community-led Open Publication Infrastructures for Monographs) and OBF (Open Book Futures). See for more information: https://copim.pubpub.org/experimental-publishing-group (accessed 24 November 2024).

2 See the Radical Open Access Collective (https://radicaloa.postdigitalcultures.org/) and the Open Book Collective (https://openbookcollective.org/) as good examples of this (both accessed 24 November 2024).

3 Also see Kathi Weeks's work on utopian demands in this context, which function as provocations to imagine alternative futures and to incite collective action (Weeks 2011, 225).

References

Adema, Janneke. *Living Books: Experiments in the Posthumanities*. Leonardo. The MIT Press, 2021.

Adema, Janneke and Rebekka Kiesewetter. 'Combinatorial Books Pilot Case: Introduction to Project Documentation'. *COPIM*, 2022a. https://doi.org/10.21428/785a6451.ffc4307b.

Adema, Janneke and Rebekka Kiesewetter. 'Experimental Book Publishing: Reinventing Editorial Workflows and Engaging Communities'. *Commonplace*, 2022b. https://doi.org/10.21428/6ffd8432.8998ab82.

Adema, Janneke and Samuel A. Moore. 'Scaling Small; Or How to Envision New Relationalities for Knowledge Production', *Westminster Papers in Communication and Culture* 16, no. 1 (2021): 27–45. https://doi.org/10.16997/wpcc.918.

Feldman, Zeena and Marisol Sandoval. 'Metric Power and the Academic Self: Neoliberalism, Knowledge and Resistance in the British University', *tripleC: Communication, Capitalism & Critique. Open Access Journal for a Global Sustainable Information Society* 16, no. 1 (2018): 214–33. https://doi.org/10.31269/triplec.v16i1.899.

Halberstam, Jack. *The Queer Art of Failure*. Duke University Press, 2011.

Hall, Gary. *Pirate Philosophy: For a Digital Posthumanities*. MIT Press, 2016.

Posada, Alejandro and George Chen. 'Inequality in Knowledge Production: The Integration of Academic Infrastructure by Big Publishers.' In *ELPUB 2018*, edited by Leslie Chan and Pierre Mounier. University of Toronto, 22–24 June 2018. https://doi.org/10.4000/proceedings.elpub.2018.30.

Weeks, Kathi. *The Problem with Work: Feminism, Marxism, Antiwork Politics, and Postwork Imaginaries*. A John Hope Franklin Center Book. Duke University Press, 2011.

Chapter 19

Writing about research methods: sharing failure to support success

Anisa Hawes and Riva Quiroga

Traditional research outputs, such as academic articles, offer authors minimal scope to describe or reflect on their methods, prioritising instead the presentation of novel and successful results. This limitation reduces methodology to a sequence of linear steps, suggesting a straightforward path to achieving the desired outcome (Rickly and Cook 2017, 120–21). Such representations can give the impression that decision-making is simple and swift, downplaying the complexity of iterative processual adjustments, and obscuring the fact that, often, failure plays a key role. Unsuccessful attempts, or challenges encountered along the way are rarely discussed, keeping valuable insights about *what didn't work well* hidden from our academic discourse. How might a form like the *Programming Historian* lesson provide space for researchers to reflect upon their methodological failures, and support others towards success?

In 2012, *Programming Historian*, a project that had emerged four years earlier as a series of blog posts for historians wanting to learn the programming language Python, was relaunched as an open-access, peer-reviewed scholarly methods journal. Its core goal was to create a venue for sharing the computational methods becoming increasingly relevant to humanities researchers, at a time when there were few opportunities to learn or practise programming, and the digital was under-explored in university curricula (Crymble 2018). By publishing lessons that sit at the intersection of research and pedagogy, *Programming Historian* allows authors to turn their work with specific methods into case studies for lessons that demonstrate how others could use those methods themselves (Walsh 2021).

Inadvertently, discussion of the methodological work rendered invisible by other academic journals became *Programming Historian*'s point of focus. By making explicit the iterative, sometimes non-linear path towards results, these methodological lessons represent an economy of community effort because methods are open and shared for reuse, and equally present an opportunity to transform experiences of failure into productive catalysts that help others succeed.

Our open publishing workflow has also developed iteratively. We use a public GitHub repository to host the code, files and data that configure our website and serve lessons to our readers. GitHub also provides an environment where we collaborate to develop lessons and manage our open peer-review processes.[1] Working openly from the beginning, we understood how critical it is to ensure a safe space for contributors. Very early in the project's history, we implemented an anti-harassment policy which now forms part of a broader code of conduct providing community participants the assurance that acknowledging difficulties faced when learning about digital methods is welcomed, and gives people the freedom to thoroughly scrutinise ideas, ask questions, make suggestions or request clarification when reviewing a lesson.[2] We recognised this to be especially valuable considering that, at the time, many online forums such as Stack Overflow were notorious for their hostility toward inexperienced coders and people from marginalised groups (Hanlon 2018). The code of conduct has helped us enhance the positive aspects of working openly. By choosing an open peer-review process, we've reframed the role of reviewers as collaborators – who are credited in every lesson – and active contributors to shaping the content of each lesson. This has allowed us to welcome challenging questions during the review process as honest attempts to help a lesson achieve its full potential.

Embracing and encouraging writing that is honest about what is challenging, and highlights – rather than hides – parts of the research process that are difficult became one of the characteristics which made *Programming Historian* distinct. As the project's commitment to, and definition of, openness broadened to comprise global access and multilingualism, our understanding of how *failure* can support success broadened too. Creating effective learning resources for (and with) a global audience who have varying computational resources and internet connection speeds, as well as multilingual communities using different character sets and data examples, required us to increase our awareness of – and sensitivity to – circumstances where the failure of a lesson is dependent upon the technical and social context within which a method is applied. For example, during our open review process, we have realised that particular tools require a minimum amount of RAM because reviewers have failed when trying to use them on their computers.[3]

We understood a need to be more explicit about what you actually need to work through a lesson successfully. And we recognised how the process of translating lessons was helping us to understand limitations of tools and barriers to methods. As we developed our community of translation practice, we were also discovering 'localised' failures – exposing ways that certain methodologies simply fail when we apply them in languages other than English.[4] Over the years, we've encouraged editors to take a critical stance, supporting authors and translators to be upfront where there are limitations or barriers so that readers can learn to be aware of implicit bias and navigate ethical challenges.

During 2024, we published our 250th lesson. With the growth of our directory, the expansion of our contributor community and an increase in the number of lesson proposals we receive, has also come an opportunity to revisit the guidelines we provide to support good practice across the project.

An aptitude for explanation, and an interest in the reflective practice of *writing about method* aren't stated pre-requisites in our author guidelines, yet these are the qualities we've valued from the start. The ability to use a tool or a method does not automatically correlate with the ability to write to explain and demonstrate that use – these are two distinct skill sets. One of our objectives as a publisher is to provide guidance that can develop and empower those skills within our community. It was time to revisit and rethink. We needed to approach our author guidelines afresh, to *write about writing about method*. Our aim has been to find a way to clearly express what we think an effective *Programming Historian* lesson is.

At a moment when many learners are exploring the potential (and potential limitations) of programming with the help of AI, we find ourselves thinking about where the greatest strength of a methods journal, written *for*, *by* and *with* peers persists.

So, this is our opportunity to play to our strengths: explicitly encourage authors to write as though they are explaining their method to a colleague or peer, to draw in the kind of reflective, analytical discussion of decisions and workflows which we think characterises our most successful lessons. The process of rewriting our author guidelines has involved revisiting lessons to consider how that success has been attained, which characteristics those lessons share and how we might provide a scaffolding upon which future authors can build effective learning resources within this distinct form.

As our directory of published resources has grown, so too has the challenge of maintaining lessons. The work of troubleshooting errors in code, and adjusting instructions to accommodate new versions of software libraries, changing dependencies and updates in operating systems has become an increasing burden. This has prompted us to reflect on how the problem came to be. We've found ourselves thinking at length about the introductory sections of lessons which, when carefully developed, can open valuable space for authors to set out the context, requirements and conditions within which a method has been developed, and within which it can be applied. Until now, we think we've failed to emphasise the importance of this groundwork, and that is the reason it has sometimes been overlooked. One part of the future solution is prevention. How might we better support authors to write sustainably? How could a methodological lesson remain valuable after the tool at its centre becomes obsolete?

Going forwards, we want authors to provide our readers with at-a-glance statements about which operating system, programming languages and software versions each lesson has been developed for and tested within. We're providing a sequence of questions that will guide authors to set out the technical understandings and computational environment needed to complete a lesson. As much a question of clarity, the inclusion of these principle statements as a basic requirement is a question of sustainability. The answers will help us establish what the computing context is/was at the time of writing, preempting that things may change (and potentially fail) with future updates.

Our revised framework also includes an expanded overview which comprises a series of prompt questions that invite authors to discuss the contextual 'caveats' of the method or tool they're teaching, from both a technical and social perspective. For example, we want to encourage authors to explain what kinds of data or formats a particular method or tool can handle well, and to articulate how this understanding can support readers' decision making when it comes to whether the method will be suitable in their research use-case. Our prompts seek insights into common stumbling-blocks that make a software package or its libraries challenging to install, and 'known issues' that make initial set-up tricky. The idea is that these questions cue writing with the generosity of voice we use naturally when we are sharing workflow with a colleague – when we're trying to raise their awareness to what could go wrong, or admitting where we perhaps failed in our initial attempts.

At the centre of the framework we're constructing is a learning example. In our experience, a real dataset that readers can handle, accompanied by sample code they can experiment with, are key to a successful *Programming Historian* lesson. In this section, we are guiding authors to narrate their workflow in practical units so that readers will be able to follow and understand the process. In the writing, we encourage descriptions of the process in general terms, rather than details of every action, click or gesture. Here, we emphasise the value of reflective notes that draw readers' attention to specific steps which – in the author's experience – were not intuitive, proved challenging or initially failed, and we ask authors to share suggestions that will support their reader to navigate them with the benefit of this insight.

In our view, this kind of processual commentary is a great strength of peer-to-peer writing – key to equipping another researcher to learn a method that they'll be able to apply in their own work. For example, in Blankenship, Connell and Dombrowski's recent lesson 'Understanding and Creating Word Embeddings', they gently reassure their reader, as a friend or colleague might reassure us when we are doubting ourselves over a puzzling output:

> One important thing to remember is that the results you get from each of these function calls do not reflect words that have similar definitions . . . While some of the words you'll get in your results are likely to have similar meanings, your model may output a few strange or confusing words. This does not necessarily indicate that something is wrong with your model or corpus . . . It always helps to go back to your corpus and get a better sense of how the language is actually used in your texts. (Blankenship et al. 2024)

The accelerating, ever-new possibilities for AI-pair programming has contributed to our understanding that we haven't done enough to emphasise these uniquely human qualities of peer-to-peer writing which reflects, reconsiders, interprets and explains. As demonstrated by the excerpt above, in some lessons we succeed, but in others we have clearly failed to sufficiently support authors towards this kind of methodological writing, rarely sought by other academic publishers who tend to prioritise the summarisation and presentation of results.

As our lesson directories have grown, so too has the risk that rapid technological change will threaten the long-term utility of our past publications. It is likely that we will continue to face an increasing number of complex lesson maintenance challenges, unless we revise the guidance we provide to contributors. The new guidance must actively guide the production of writing which pivots away from the specific steps towards methodological overviews, discussion and reflection.

Thinking back to the project's origins, we've recognised that among our core offers is a venue for researchers to openly share the computational methods they've applied, adapted or advanced in their work – surfacing the critical processes of decision-making, failure and iterative modification so that other researchers will be supported to succeed.

Since the beginning, we have worked consciously to create an open scholarly environment where people can become part of our knowledge-exchange community. But as we've grown, we think we have failed to explicitly articulate the particular strengths and capabilities of the *Programming Historian* lesson as a unique form. If that distinctive quality becomes lost in the project's long memory, then the longevity of our journals is at risk.

The sustainability of our project depends upon re-articulating what defines the *Programming Historian* lesson, and providing a clear scaffold upon which authors, editors and reviewers can collaboratively build.

Our lesson framework and revised suite of guidelines remain in progress, and imperfect. This is not the first time the project has taken the initiative to reflect on where we have failed, and how we can make improvements. In the past, issues such as the lack of gender diversity in our contributor community have prompted us to openly recognise failure, and take action (Crymble 2017; Sichani et al. 2019).[5] This is how the project has always operated and, perhaps, what has enabled our longevity. Change is an ongoing process, necessarily involving honest conversations which reflect on shortcomings, accept failures and plan for change.

Notes

1 All the editorial work related to a lesson takes place as an issue in this GitHub repository: https://github.com/programminghistorian/ph-submissions/issues (accessed 24 November 2024). Although the entire process takes place in the open, the published lessons don't have a direct link to the peer-review process, as other venues like the *Journal of Open Source Software* do. That could be an area for improvement.

2 The first iteration of this policy on GitHub can be read in this issue: https://github.com/programminghistorian/ph-submissions/issues/3#issuecomment-196629337. Our current code of conduct is available in four languages, and can be accessed via our main repository: https://github.com/programminghistorian/jekyll/blob/gh-pages/CODE_OF_CONDUCT.md (both accessed 24 November 2024).

3 For example, this happened during the review of an original lesson in Spanish about ImagePlot: https://github.com/programminghistorian/ph-submissions/issues/254#issuecomment-594219900. This issue was then raised for discussion with the whole editorial board: https://github.com/programminghistorian/jekyll/issues/1712 (both accessed 24 November 2024).

4 You can find an example of this in the following Issue: https://github.com/programminghistorian/jekyll/issues/647#issue-271191579. This led to the discussion about which lessons are translatable from English to other languages in: https://github.com/programminghistorian/jekyll/issues/756 (both accessed 24 November 2024).

5 The open discussion about how to address the gender imbalance can be read here: https://github.com/programminghistorian/jekyll/issues/152 (accessed 24 November 2024).

References

Blankenship, Avery, Sarah Connell and Quinn Dombrowski. 'Understanding and Creating Word Embeddings', *Programming Historian* 13 (2024). https://doi.org/10.46430/phen0116.

Crymble, Adam. 'A Decade of Programming Historians'. Network in Canadian History & Environment, 23 March 2018. Accessed 24 November 2024. http://niche-canada.org/2018/03/23/a-decade-of-programming-historians/.

Crymble, Adam. 'White, Male, and North American: Challenges of Diversifying the Programming Historian'. Université de Lausanne, Switzerland (23–24 March 2017).

Hanlon, Jay. *Stack Overflow Isn't Very Welcoming: It's Time for That to Change.* 26 April 2018. Accessed 24 November 2024. https://stackoverflow.blog/2018/04/26/stack-overflow-isnt-very-welcoming-its-time-for-that-to-change/.

Rickly, Rebecca and Kelli Cargile Cook. 'Failing Forward: Training Graduate Students for Research – An Introduction to the Special Issue', *Journal of Technical Writing and Communication* 47, no. 2 (2017): 119–29. https://doi.org/10.1177/0047281617692074.

Sichani, Anna-Maria, James Baker, Maria José Afanador Llach and Brandon Walsh. 'Diversity and Inclusion in Digital Scholarship and Pedagogy: The Case of *The Programming Historian*', *Insights* 32 (2019): 16. https://doi.org/10.1629/uksg.465.

Walsh, Brandon. 'The Programming Historian and Editorial Process in Digital Publishing'. Modern Languages Association Conference 2021, 7–10 January 2021. Accessed 24 November 2024. http://walshbr.com/blog/the-programming-historian-and-editorial-process-in-digital-publishing/.

Chapter 20

Bridging the distance: confronting geographical failures in digital humanities conferences

Nabeel Siddiqui

The digital humanities has positioned itself as a field committed to openness, collaboration and the democratisation of knowledge. This vision suggests a borderless academic community where scholars freely exchange ideas across institutional, national and cultural boundaries. Academic conferences, as the field's primary sites of knowledge exchange and community building, are meant to embody these values. For instance, in 2011, the annual Digital Humanities Conference chose 'Big Tent Digital Humanities' as its theme. This metaphor was meant to suggest an aspiration of inclusivity where diverse perspectives would be welcomed and actively cultivated, traditional academic hierarchies would be flattened, and global participation would be the norm rather than the exception.

However, despite these aspirations for inclusivity, practitioners increasingly challenge this characterisation, arguing that DH has reproduced and sometimes amplified existing inequities in academic and social hierarchies (Svensson 2012). For example, studies have shown that DH contains a concentration of male scholars and a 'monoculture' of English (Fiormonte 2014; Galina Russell 2014). Likewise, postcolonial scholars note that attempts to map or highlight DH activities often privilege those with institutional support, such as centres and research labs, while leaving out much of the 'informal' DH of the Global South. I argue that these broader inequities manifest prominently in how digital humanities conferences operate and exemplify what I term a 'geographical failure' – the systematic way in which physical distance, location and territorial boundaries have created barriers to sites of knowledge production. These failures are not merely logistical challenges to be solved through better planning or increased funding. Instead, they represent fundamental structural inequities determining whose definition of 'digital humanities' gains traction.

Conferences can serve as microcosms of broader academic culture, reflecting prevailing norms and expectations that shape researchers' experiences and aspirations. Emily Henderson argues that conferences are phenomena that are simultaneously under-researched and over-experienced (Henderson 2015). While formal studies on the emotional and physical experiences of conference attendance are scarce, most academics are familiar with the demands and challenges of participation. Emma Bell and Daniel King (2010) liken presenting at a conference to an endurance test where attendees battle headaches, lack of sleep and dehydration to finally add that coveted next line to their CV. Limited access to these production sites can significantly hinder an individual's academic career advancement. In an increasingly neoliberal academic landscape, they play a vital role in establishing professional connections, disseminating research findings and increasing visibility (Nicolson 2017; Rowe 2018; Wang et al. 2017).

In digital humanities, this gatekeeping function is mainly concentrated through the Alliance of Digital Humanities Organizations (ADHO). As Roopika Risam (2017) notes,

> While digital humanities (DH) scholarship exists outside the purview of ADHO, the annual conference, the regional reach of the constituent organisations, and the number of important DH publications affiliated with it . . . gives ADHO and its constituent organisations significant influence over DH at the global scale.

Consequently, studying ADHO conferences can serve as a proxy for understanding DH's broader landscape.

Most ADHO conferences are in North America or Europe, which can be challenging for academics from other regions due to the long distance required to travel. Furthermore, scholars from the Global South may face hurdles in obtaining visas to enter countries where conferences are held, a complex and sometimes even unsuccessful process. Conference participation costs, like airfare, lodging and registration fees, can be prohibitively high, especially for scholars without institutional backing or dedicated funding for professional development. This barrier is particularly acute for early-career researchers, independent scholars and those from under-resourced institutions, who may lack access to the same level of support as their more privileged colleagues. Finally, because conferences require that attendees break from daily duties, women, who continue to bear the brunt of domestic responsibilities, are disproportionately prohibited from attending (Henderson and Moreau 2020).

To expose the hidden geography of power in digital humanities, I created an interactive visualisation mapping sixty years of travel patterns to ADHO conferences. This project reveals who attends these gatherings and who faces systematic exclusion due to distance barriers. My analysis builds on the comprehensive *Index of DH Conferences* developed by Lincoln, Weingart, and Eichmann-Kalwara (2021) – a database tracking over 500 events, 8,800 presentations, and 10,400 authors across multiple countries. While their initial analysis confirmed DH's lack of regional and gender diversity, my visualisation adds a crucial spatial dimension: by mapping the actual distances scholars must traverse, it makes visible the physical barriers that shape intellectual exchange in the field (Weingart and Eichmann-Kalwara 2017).

To create the timelapse map, I reverse-geocoded the institutional affiliations of authors in the dataset and the conference hosting institutions using the ArcGIS API. When university affiliation was missing, I used the city or country of the presenter. This method has limitations, since some individuals might submit papers from non-university affiliations, change affiliations or not live near their listed affiliation, particularly affecting marginalised scholars or those without institutional support. However, this provided a valuable method to chart travel patterns in most instances. With this data, I built a layered GIS map of the global mobility of DH conference attendees in FourSquare Studio, using data from the Index of DH Conferences until July 2024.[1]

The travel pattern data exposes geographic imbalance and a self-reinforcing cycle where conference locations systematically amplify existing power structures. Most conference-goers are from North America, Europe and Australia; only a few scholars are from other regions. This imbalance is stark compared to the global distribution of digital humanities activities, which are more evenly spread worldwide (Gil 2014). Perhaps most importantly, the map reveals the impact of hosting location on conference attendance, with major cities and research hubs

Figure 20.1: Map of DH Conferences in 2018. © Nabeel Siddiqui.

attracting disproportionate participants. For instance, Digital Humanities 2018 in Mexico City (represented in Figure 20.1) attracted a much more diverse group of participants than in other years, with a significant number from Latin America and other regions outside North America and Europe. However, this remains an exception, with most continuing to be held in the Global North.

A histogram of the haversine distance travelled by conference participants further illustrates the stark disparities in access and the importance of conference location in shaping attendance (see Figure 20.2). Most attendees travel less than 1,000 kilometres, suggesting proximity to the conference is critical in determining who can participate. Only a minority of scholars traverse distances exceeding 10,000 kilometres, many of which are from the Global North.

To address these geographical failures – including the concentration of conferences in the Global North, prohibitive travel costs, visa restrictions and care responsibilities that limit mobility – the DH community must take concrete steps to decentralise conference locations and explore alternative modes of participation. Drawing from successful examples like DH2018 in Mexico City, which demonstrated how strategic location choice can dramatically diversify participation, a key priority should be geographic redistribution through a rotating conference system that ensures regular

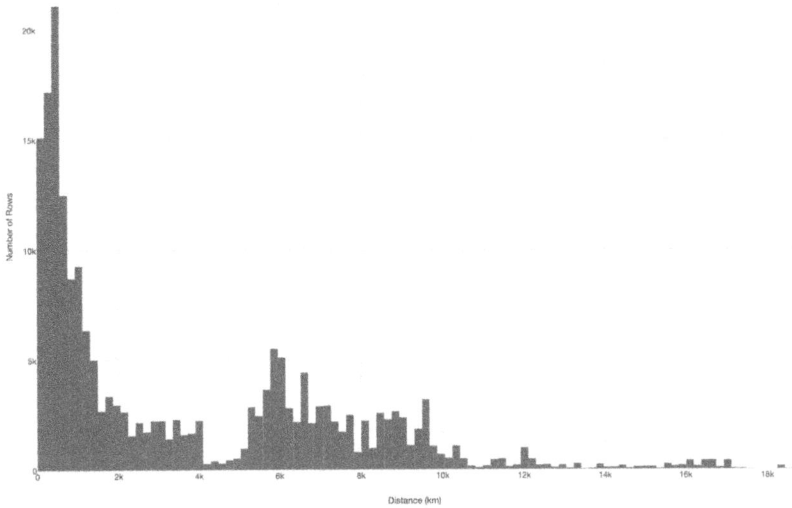

Figure 20.2: Histogram of DH Conference distance travelled. © Nabeel Siddiqui.

events in the Global South. This should be coupled with establishing regional hubs for smaller, more frequent gatherings, supported by partnerships with local institutions to build hosting capacity. Alongside this physical restructuring, the field must develop robust financial support mechanisms, including dedicated funding streams for scholars from under-resourced institutions and sliding scale registration fees based on country of origin.

Finally, the DH community should embrace virtual conferences and regional events complementary to traditional in-person gatherings. The COVID-19 pandemic has highlighted the potential of online platforms to facilitate global participation and reduce the barriers associated with physical travel. However, more research is needed to fully understand the impact and effectiveness of virtual conferences in fostering inclusivity and diversity within the field. As the DH community explores these alternative modes of engagement, critically examining their potential benefits and limitations is crucial. This examination should focus on ensuring that virtual conferences and regional events genuinely contribute to creating a more accessible and equitable 'Big Tent' that reflects the diversity of digital humanities scholarship and practice worldwide. By doing so, the field can move towards a more inclusive and representative future, where knowledge production and exchange are not as limited by territorial demarcations or institutional affiliations.

Note

1 The full interactive map is available for viewing: https://nabeelsiddiqui.net/an-undue-burden/ (accessed 24 November 2024).

References

Bell, Emma and Daniel King. 'The Elephant in the Room: Critical Management Studies Conferences as a Site of Body Pedagogics', *Management Learning* 41, no. 4 (2010): 429–42.

Fiormonte, Domenico. 'Digital Humanities from a Global Perspective', *Laboratorio Dell'ISPF* 11 (10.12862) (2014): 121–36.

Galina Russell, Isabel. 'Geographical and Linguistic Diversity in the Digital Humanities', *Literary and Linguistic Computing* 29, no. 3 (2014): 307–16.

Gil, Alex. 'Journey: Around DH in 80 Days'. 2014. Accessed 24 November 2024. https://arounddh.elotroalex.com/journey/.

Henderson, Emily F. 'Academic Conferences: Representative and Resistant Sites for Higher Education Research', *Higher Education Research & Development* 34, no. 5 (2015): 914–25.

Henderson, Emily F. and Marie-Pierre Moreau. 'Carefree Conferences? Academics with Caring Responsibilities Performing Mobile Academic Subjectivities', *Gender and Education* 32. no. 1 (2020): 70–85.

Lincoln, Matthew D., Scott B. Weingart and Nickoal Eichmann-Kalwara. 'The Index of Digital Humanities Conferences', *Journal of Open Humanities Data* 7 (2021): 12. https://doi.org/10.5334/johd.26.

Nicolson, Donald J. *Academic Conferences as Neoliberal Commodities*. Springer International Publishing, 2017. https://doi.org/10.1007/978-3-319-49190-5.

Risam, Roopika. 'Other Worlds, Other DHs: Notes towards a DH Accent', *Digital Scholarship in the Humanities* 32, no. 2 (2017): 377–84.

Rowe, Nicholas. '"When You Get What You Want, But Not What You Need": The Motivations, Affordances and Shortcomings of Attending Academic/Scientific Conferences', *International Journal of Research in Education and Science* 4, no. 2 (2018): 714–29.

Svensson, Patrik. 'Beyond the Big Tent'. In *Debates in the Digital Humanities*, edited by Matthew K. Gold, 36–49. University of Minnesota Press, 2012. https://doi.org/10.5749/9781452963754.

Wang, Wei, Xiaomei Bai, Feng Xia, Teshome Megersa Bekele, Xiaoyan Su and Amr Tolba. 'From Triadic Closure to Conference Closure: The Role of Academic Conferences in Promoting Scientific Collaborations', *Scientometrics* 113, no. 1 (2017): 177–93.

Weingart, Scott B. and Nickoal Eichmann-Kalwara. 'What's Under the Big Tent? A Study of ADHO Conference Abstracts', *Digital Studies/Le Champ Numérique* 7, no. 1 (2017): 6.

Conclusion: on failing

Anna-Maria Sichani and Michael Donnay

While developing this volume, several major cyberattacks targeted cultural heritage infrastructures, including the Internet Archive, British Library, Seattle Public Library and Toronto Public Library. These incidents of 'vanishing culture' (Messarra et al. 2024) should be seen as stark reminders of the inherent fragility of the digital realm, underscoring that digital scholarship is fraught with unexpected challenges and failures, often beyond the scope of even the most meticulously crafted contingency and risk management plans. Failure, brokenness, loss, struggle are the default, not the exception.

However, those of us working in digital scholarship are accustomed to navigating such moments of crisis and risk. Our work is full of these kinds of operational risk – alongside the conceptual risks we're accustomed to taking in our research – and so we can offer our failure as a resource to others who may be grappling with these concerns for the first time. We are used to dealing with emerging technologies and the rapidly evolving risks that accompany them, even if they elude our full comprehension. We find ways to deal with complex data and systems, even as we wrestle with obsolete media and fragile infrastructure. We manage complex relationships and navigate broken institutional frameworks. Whether successfully or not, the willingness to tackle these issues head on can be our contribution.

We embarked on this volume with a double hope: to return failure to our critical repertoire and to develop a constructive and compassionate way to speak and think about failure in digital scholarship. While we focused on four broad areas – innovation, technology, collaboration and institutions – we hope the reflections can serve as a scaffold for a rich exploration of failure in other parts of the research ecosystem.

We believe the essence of failure lies outside easy categorisation, in the hard-to-see corners of our everyday. Failure finds its natural place in the cracks between things – between innovation and technological obsolescence, between personal relationships and institutional systems. And it is through these cracks that we glimpse, not necessarily success, but a brave sense of hope for the future.

References

Luca Messarra, Chris Freeland and Juliya Ziskina, *Vanishing Culture: A Report on Our Fragile Cultural Record*. Internet Archive. Accessed 25 November 2024. https://blog.archive.org/wp-content/uploads/2024/10/Vanishing-Culture-2024.pdf.

Index

www.ingramcontent.com/pod-product-compliance
Lightning Source LLC
LaVergne TN
LVHW052029300826
846742LV00025B/99
* 9 7 8 1 9 0 8 5 9 0 9 1 6 *

List of figures

Notes on contributors

Janneke Adema (she/her) is a cultural and media theorist working in the fields of (book) publishing and digital culture and an associate professor in digital media at the Centre for Postdigital Cultures (Coventry University).

Brittany Amell (she/her) is an INKE Partnership postdoctoral fellow in Open Social Scholarship and MITACS Accelerate Industrial postdoctoral fellow in Open, Collaborative Scholarship (Arts & Humanities) at the Electronic Textual Cultures Lab (ETCL).

Arianna Ciula is director and research software senior analyst at King's Digital Lab, King's College London.

Frances Corry is an assistant professor in the Department of Information Culture and Data Stewardship at the University of Pittsburgh.

David De Roure is academic director of digital scholarship at the University of Oxford and professor of e-Research in the Oxford e-Research Centre.

Quinn Dombrowski is the academic technology specialist in the Division of Literatures, Cultures, and Languages, and the Library, at Stanford University.

Michael Donnay is a community manager with the Software Sustainability Institute.

Anisa Hawes is *Programming Historian*'s publishing manager. Beyond the project, she is a researcher and web archivist with a special interest in critical curatorial practice, and using open-source tools to preserve digital cultural memory.

Jennifer Isasi is an assistant research professor of digital scholarship at the Pennsylvania State University, where she directs the Digital Liberal Arts Research Initiative, and is also part of the editorial board of the open access journal *Programming Historian*.

Caio Mello is a postdoctoral researcher in the project Impresso – Media Monitoring of the Past at the Luxembourg Centre for Contemporary and Digital History (C²DH).

Jenny Mitcham is chief digital preservation officer at the Digital Preservation Coalition where she works closely with members on their digital preservation challenges.

Christopher Ohge is senior lecturer in digital approaches to literature at the School of Advanced Study, University of London.

Riva Quiroga is a linguist and educator by training. Since 2019, she has been involved in *Programming Historian* as an editor of the Spanish team and as a trustee of ProgHist Ltd, the charity that runs the project.

Arran Rees is a researcher and practitioner interested in museums, digital cultural heritage collections and collaborative action research processes and currently works as the Museum Data Manager for the Museum Data Service.

Jentery Sayers is associate professor of English and director of media studies at the University of Victoria, where he also directs the Praxis Studio for Comparative Media Studies.

Anna-Maria Sichani is a media historian and a digital humanist. She is currently a BRAID fellow and a research associate in digital humanities at the Digital Humanities Research Hub, School of Advanced Study, University of London.

Nabeel Siddiqui is an assistant professor of digital media at Susquehanna University, where he also serves as the director of the Center for Teaching and Learning.

Elena Spadini is a researcher in digital humanities, with a background in romance philology. Her research interests span from medieval manuscripts to contemporary authors and born-digital literary sources.

Jennifer Stertzer is director of the Center for Digital Editing and the Washington Papers and a research associate professor at the University of Virginia.

Lauren Tuckley is director of the Center for Research and Fellowships at Georgetown University, where she leads a team administering undergraduate research programmes and mentoring students and young alumni applying for nationally competitive fellowships.

Joris J. van Zundert is senior researcher and developer in the Department of Computational Literary Studies and the Digital Humanities Lab at the Huygens Institute of the Royal Netherlands Academy of Arts and Sciences (KNAW).

Naomi Wells is senior lecturer in Italian and Spanish with digital humanities at the School of Advanced Study, University of London.

Jane Winters is professor of digital humanities and director of the Digital Humanities Research Hub at the School of Advanced Study, University of London.

Acknowledgements

This project and book would have been impossible without our wonderful contributing authors; we would like to thank them for trusting us with their inspiring reflections and for their resiliency and professionalism.

We are equally indebted to those whose writing didn't quite make it into these pages. We'd like to extend our particular thanks to the original contributors of the 2022–23 seminar who we were not – for one reason or another – able to include in this collection, but whose discussions helped shape this book nonetheless.

Special thanks to our publisher, Emma Gallon, for her attentive care and invaluable role in the production of this volume. We'd also like to thank the two anonymous peer reviewers for their thoughtful feedback early in the process.

Anna-Maria would like to thank her co-editor, Michael, for being such a terrific collaborator and for helping see this project through to the end. She would like to thank Jane Winters for being an inspiring mentor and supporting us in this seminar series and publication. Special thanks go to the entire team at DHRH, as well as colleagues from the various projects she has worked on over the years, for reinforcing her belief that digital scholarship is far from a failed discourse, practice and career choice. And to Vassilis, Loukia and David, for being a positive force in her life.

Michael is grateful to Anna-Maria for being a generous and understanding co-editor, without whom this book would not have been completed. He would also like to thank Jane Winters, Naomi Wells, and the rest of the team at the University of London for being so supportive of the project. Thanks go to his parents, Michelle and Victor, for being his first and best editors and to Chris for teaching him to think computationally. And to Lily, for all her love and support.

We hope our efforts as editors of this volume have not failed. But even if they have, this failure remains a labour of love.

Introduction: reframing failure

Anna-Maria Sichani and Michael Donnay

Failure is ordinary. Paraphrasing Raymond Williams's famous quote on culture (McGuigan 2014), this book talks about failure as an everyday, common thing both in life and in digital scholarship. The truth is that no one gets through life without failing – in both minor and often significant ways. When we fail, it may feel as if we are alone in this. However, there is nothing more human than to fail: a relationship crisis, a failed exam, a career reversal, a book proposal rejection or a bungled project. To err is human – to fail is too.

Yet, for something so central to our experience, failure often sits at the periphery of our writing, training and professional discourse. This inability to see failure as an essential part of our work does not just have the potential to leave us feeling isolated. It also leaves a sizeable hole in how we understand the process of *doing* digital scholarship. Its absence can lead to an incomplete understanding of our own research, teaching and collaborations. This book encourages us to recentre failure as a core part of our scholarship.

This book aims to do two related and interlocking things. The first is to develop a vocabulary for failure that is critical, constructive and compassionate. Much of the language associated with failure draws on negative emotions or implies a personal, moral deficiency on the part of the individual who has failed. This negative discourse discourages a critical engagement with failure, while the focus on the individual can ignore the systemic issues at play. We aim to replace that language with a vocabulary that fosters critical and constructive engagement, while at the same time speaking with an appropriate compassion for those involved.

The second is to bring a renewed critical focus to failure as an object of inquiry and contribute to the growing and increasingly diverse body of 'critical digital humanities'. In many ways, failure has been a defining element of digital scholarship in the arts and humanities over the last several decades. These failures have sparked excellent reflections from practitioners like Shawn Graham and Quinn Dombrowski, who have called for the field to explore failure more critically and seriously (Graham 2019; Dombrowski 2014). Yet despite these writings and continued technical, social and institutional failures in the field, a sustained engagement with failure has not materialised.

As other fields in the humanities begin to reassess their relationship with failure and digital scholarship begins a renewed engagement with questions of technical and environmental sustainability – or lack thereof – now seems like a particularly generative moment to return to this conversation (Coleman 2023). This collection offers an updated and richly interdisciplinary set of perspectives, drawing on recent experience and developments, while remaining rooted in the critical and reflective tradition of earlier writing in the field (Greenspan 2019).

In bringing together the reflective, personal approach with a critical perspective, we want to move away from the approach that self-improvement and motivational literature takes to failure (for example, see Lachkovic 2024). We are not offering a guide on learning to fail forward or succeed at failure. We are not going to glorify the technocratic call to 'move fast and break things'. And we aren't going to offer any secret advice about how to avoid failure.

Instead, this book offers examples of real-world failures for evaluation, discussion and critical reflection. We want to showcase the various types of failure in digital scholarship. We want to normalise a discourse of open conversation (and practice) around failure in academic and professional life. And we want to remind one another that we are not alone in making mistakes, not alone in failing.

Failure in digital scholarship

The book is structured around four major conversations within digital scholarship: innovation, technology, collaboration and institutions. These groupings represent our best (and perhaps failed) editorial effort to provide structure to the collection, but there are certainly overlaps and discussions

that reach across sections. Each chapter is made up of short reflections offering the author's distinct perspective on failure relating to that issue. Every reflection stands on its own – and can be read as such – but is also in conversation with the other pieces alongside it. They are written in a variety of styles, reflecting both the practice in each author's home discipline and their personal approach to the topic.

Contributors come from a deliberately wide range of disciplinary backgrounds and work in different institutional and national contexts across the globe. Their perspectives are informed by and connected to their research, but they are also deeply grounded in their individual positionality. The reflective mode allows for a more candid approach than traditional academic writing and hopefully captures some of the generous spirit of dialogue we have found with our contributors.

While many of our contributors identify as digital humanists, not all do, and so we have chosen the more expansive term 'digital scholarship' to describe the areas of research with which this collection is concerned. Digital scholarship refers broadly to the use of digital methods and technologies, without setting a boundary around the specific disciplines they are applied to (Digital Scholarship @ Oxford n.d.). We have tried to be similarly expansive when setting the focus for this book and you will see both terms used throughout. We hope this will allow those working within digital scholarship, as well as those in other (even non-digital) communities of practice, to draw on these reflections.

When taken as a whole, the book offers a polyvocal snapshot of the 'state of failure' in digital scholarship and serves as an invitation to pull failure back from the periphery of our understanding of the field – and ourselves.

Failure and innovation

Lisa Spiro's 2012 observation – that the 'digital humanities community recognizes the value of failure in the pursuit of innovation' – also serves as a provocation for the community to examine its relationship to innovation (Spiro 2012). In many ways, the ethos of digital scholarship resembles that of the technology sector, characterised by a bias towards 'newness' (Sichani 2022). Indeed, digital humanities practitioners have often built a professional identity that celebrates risky playfulness (Nowviskie 2016) and 'screwing around' (Ramsay 2014). But when our methodological orientation

leans too far in that direction, we are at risk of adopting the same techno-optimist frameworks that prioritise novelty and (disruptive) innovation which several of the reflections in this chapter critique.

Despite the crucial role failure plays in innovation, there remains a strong taboo against publicly acknowledging that side of the coin. For example, the affordances of contemporary software development – such as version control and trackable revision histories – could allow for an open-ended, extensible and constantly updated research output. While these tools offer the potential to embrace a 'culture of the perpetual prototype' (Flanders 2015) or 'perpetual beta' (Nowviskie 2012), institutional pressure from funding bodies and universities to demonstrate concrete deliverables means there is little room for the failure inherent in prototyping to be manifested as such. Some of the reflections in this section address this challenge and consider how failure might point us in the direction of a more sustainable approach to innovation and the work required to move us there.

Failure and technological obsolescence

Technical obsolescence is quickly becoming one of the main focuses for digital researchers. The field has long been aware of the challenges involved in maintaining digital projects and data, but the topic has taken on an increased urgency in recent years as major changes to foundational technologies, like the sunsetting of Adobe Flash in late 2020, and the increase in cyberattacks on cultural heritage institutions and infrastructures (Warren 2024; Keating 2024), have made the maintenance challenges even more stark. In response, there has been a growing and vivid discussion around technical sustainability and maintenance (Holmes et al. 2023).

However, these technical conversations are only just beginning to connect to the theoretical, social and institutional contexts where failure also plays a major (unacknowledged) role (Holmes et al. 2023). Specific solutions, like static websites, still tend to put the focus on technological solutions rather than addressing the people and skills required to maintain digital objects (Dombrowski 2022). Ironically, even when systemic solutions to technical obsolescence are proposed, they rarely come with the necessary funding. So even though the funding bodies in the United Kingdom now require a data management plan, they rarely if ever allow grant funding to be used to cover project maintenance beyond the end date of the project (UKRI 2018).

The reflections in this section draw on diverse experiences of technological obsolescence to consider how we can better manage the inevitable failure of our digital objects and how we might study those objects when they have failed. They pay particular attention to the role our human infrastructure plays in sustaining tools and technical systems.

Failure and collaboration

Digital research is almost always a collaborative endeavour, and so enabling and managing collaborations is a core concern for digital scholars and practitioners. Unlike many other humanities disciplines, digital projects regularly require large teams that bring together a wide range of skills, professional expertise and communities of practice. These teams often include people working in software development, cultural heritage institutions and universities – all of whom can bring different assumptions and professional languages to a project (Neubert 2020). The discipline has long been aware of the challenges in working this way, with some of the most insightful writing on the topic coming from collaborators normally relegated to the periphery of the academy (Bell and Kennan 2021).

However, for a field that prides itself on interdisciplinarity, we still spend little time discussing how to do it well (Ahnert et al. 2023). This is, in part, because humanities scholars rarely have a professional venue to discuss their research process as opposed to outputs. It's also because we are less willing to acknowledge when these collaborations go wrong (as they often can). This can often be out of an understandable desire to protect relationships. Yet this unwillingness to discuss when and how collaborations go wrong can leave future projects ill-prepared to address similar challenges. Moreover, the informal way these challenges are discussed privileges those who have access to those professional networks and excludes those who do not. Each reflection in this section takes those 'coffee break' conversations and brings a critical and constructive lens to them.

Failure and institutions

Although not unique to digital scholarship, systemic challenges within institutions are perhaps more keenly felt because of the collaborative and interdisciplinary nature of the field (Greenspan 2019). These challenges cut across the three other areas of the book, with many of the failures of

innovation, technical infrastructure and collaboration directly tied to wider systemic issues. In many ways, the failure of institutional frameworks, from funding systems to postgraduate training, circumscribe all the work we do – a theme taken up by several reflections in this section.

As a field we continue to fall short of our aspirations for better utilising digital technology to create a more equitable research culture, despite any number of guidelines about citing digital outputs, assessing digital scholarship and acknowledging contributors' roles in research outputs (Editorial Process n.d.; Modern Language Association 2012; Allen et al. 2019). Reflections in this chapter take up some of these challenges and propose alternatives that leverage the affordances of digital publishing in particular to shift institutional cultures.

This section also acknowledges that failure brings different risks for different people. The privilege to fail publicly is still more likely to be afforded to white, male and permanently employed academics (Gupta in Graham 2019), while those with more precarious positions face additional barriers to publicly discussing their failures. These practitioners are also the ones most likely to be failed by existing institutional structures, compounding the issue. A number of contributors address these challenges explicitly and it's a thread we hope is evident throughout the book.

Reframing failure

In bringing together this community of authors, our hope is to make clear the important place of failure in scholarly life. We want to reflect on failure in the round, bringing critical attention to the (often unacknowledged) role it plays in shaping our response to some of the core questions in the field.

By proposing failure as a commonplace of our theoretical, critical and technological endeavours, this book aims to offer an unusual – hopefully not too failed – account of our everyday professional practice. By naturalising and normalising failure in its various iterations, we seek to promote a mode of digital scholarship that accepts, celebrates and cares for human creativity beyond success and innovation.

References

Ahnert, Ruth, Emma Griffin, Giorgia Tolfo and Mia Ridge. *Collaborative Historical Research in the Age of Big Data: Lessons from an Interdisciplinary Project*. Elements in Historical Theory and Practice. Cambridge University Press, 2023. https://doi.org/10.1017/9781009175548.

Allen, Liz, Alison O'Connell and Veronique Kiermer. 'How Can We Ensure Visibility and Diversity in Research Contributions? How the Contributor Role Taxonomy (CRediT) Is Helping the Shift from Authorship to Contributorship', *Learned Publishing* 32, no. 1 (2019): 71–4. https://doi.org/10.1002/leap.1210.

Bell, Emilia C. and Mary Anne Kennan. 'Partnering in Knowledge Production: Roles for Librarians in the Digital Humanities', *Journal of the Australian Library and Information Association* 70, no. 2 (2021): 157–76. https://www.tandfonline.com/doi/full/10.1080/24750158.2021.1907886.

Coleman, Simon. 'Preface', *Journal of the Royal Anthropological Institute* 29, S1 (2023): 6–7. https://doi.org/10.1111/1467-9655.13910.

Digital Scholarship @ Oxford. 'What Is Digital Scholarship?' (n.d.) Accessed 26 November 2024. https://digitalscholarship.web.ox.ac.uk/what-digital-scholarship.

Dombrowski, Quinn. 'Whatever Happened to Project Bamboo?' *Literary and Linguistic Computing* 29, no. 3 (2014): 326–39. https://doi.org/10.1093/llc/fqu026.

Dombrowski, Quinn. 'Minimizing Computing Maximizes Labor'. *Digital Humanities Quarterly* 16, no. 2 (2022). Accessed 24 November 2024. http://www.digitalhumanities.org/dhq/vol/16/2/000594/000594.html.

'Editorial Process: Reviews in Digital Humanities', *Reviews in Digital Humanities*. (n.d.) Accessed 26 November 2024. https://reviewsindh.pubpub.org/review-process.

Flanders, Julia. 'The Long Now of Digital Humanities'. Baker-Nord Center for the Humanities, Case Western Reserve University, 2015. Accessed 25 November 2024. https://case.edu/artsci/bakernord/events/past-events/2014-2015/long-now-digital-humanities.

Graham, Shawn. *Failing Gloriously and Other Essays*. With a Foreword by Eric Kansa and Afterword by Neha Gupta. Digital Press at the

University of North Dakota, 2019. Accessed 25 November 2024. https://thedigitalpress.org/failing-gloriously/.

Greenspan, Brian. 'The Scandal of Digital Humanities'. In *Debates in Digital Humanities 2019*, edited by Matthew K. Gold and Lauren F. Klein, 92–5. Debates in Digital Humanities. University of Minnesota Press, 2019. https://doi.org/10.5749/9781452963785.

Gupta, Neha. 'Afterword'. In *Failing Gloriously and Other Essays*, by Shawn Graham, 130–34. Digital Press at the University of North Dakota, 2019. Accessed 25 November 2024. https://thedigitalpress.org/failing-gloriously/.

Holmes, Martin, Janelle Jenstad and Matthew J. Huculak. 'Introduction to Special Issue: Project Resiliency in the Digital Humanities', *Digital Humanities Quarterly* 17, no. 1 (2023). Accessed 24 November 2024. http://www.digitalhumanities.org/dhq/vol/17/1/000671/000671.html.

Keating, Roly. 'Learning Lessons from the Cyber-Attack'. 8 March 2024. Accessed 24 November 2024. https://blogs.bl.uk/living-knowledge/2024/03/learning-lessons-from-the-cyber-attack.html.

Lachkovic, Josh. 'What I Learnt from My Failed Startup'. *Sifted*. 5 April 2024. Accessed 25 November 2024. https://sifted.eu/articles/learnings-from-my-failed-startup/.

McGuigan, Jim. *Raymond Williams on Culture & Society: Essential Writings*. SAGE Publications, 2014. https://doi.org/10.4135/9781473914766.

Modern Language Association. 'Guidelines for Evaluating Work in Digital Humanities and Digital Media Journal of Digital Humanities', *Journal of Digital Humanities* 1, no. 4 (2012). Accessed 24 November 2024. https://journalofdigitalhumanities.org/1-4/guidelines-for-evaluating-work-in-digital-humanities-and-digital-media-from-the-mla/.

Neubert, Anna Maria. 'Navigating Disciplinary Differences in (Digital) Research Projects'. In *Digital Methods in the Humanities: Challenges, Ideas, Perspectives*, edited by Silke Schwandt, 59–85. Digital Humanities Research. Bielefeld University Press, 2020. https://doi.org/10.14361/9783839454190.

Nowviskie, Bethany. 'Evaluating Collaborative Digital Scholarship (or, Where Credit Is Due)', *Journal of Digital Humanities* 1, no. 4 (2012). Accessed 24 November 2024. http://journalofdigitalhumanities.org

/1-4/evaluating-collaborative-digital-scholarship-by-bethany-nowviskie/.

Nowviskie, Bethany. 'On the Origin of "Hack" and "Yack"'. In *Debates in Digital Humanities 2016*, edited by Matthew K. Gold and Lauren F. Klein, 66–70. University of Minnesota Press, 2016. https://doi.org/10.5749/9781452963761.

Ramsay, Stephen. 'The Hermeneutics of Screwing Around; or What You Do with a Million Books'. In *Pastplay: Teaching and Learning History with Technology*, edited by Kevin Kee, 111–20. University of Michigan Press, 2014.

Sichani, Anna-Maria. 'Embracing Decline in Digital Scholarship beyond Sustainability'. In *The Bloomsbury Handbook to the Digital Humanities*, edited by James O'Sullivan, 317–24. Bloomsbury Publishing, 2022.

Spiro, Lisa. '"This Is Why We Fight": Defining the Values of the Digital Humanities'. In *Debates in the Digital Humanities*, edited by Matthew K. Gold, 16–35. University of Minnesota Press, 2012. https://doi.org/10.5749/9781452963754.

UKRI. 'Guidance on Best Practice in the Management of Research Data'. 2018. Accessed 26 November 2024. https://www.ukri.org/publications/guidance-on-best-practice-in-the-management-of-research-data/.

Warren, Tom. 'The Internet Archive Is Back as a Read-Only Service after Cyberattacks', *The Verge*. 14 October 2024. Accessed 26 November 2024. https://www.theverge.com/2024/10/14/24269741/internet-archive-online-read-only-data-breach-outage.

Part I
INNOVATION

Failure and innovation

Digital technologies have historically been embedded in narratives of experimentation, novelty and innovation that often pair with discourse around risk and failure. While discussions surrounding innovation and newness – whether in technology, culture or everyday life – often embrace failure as part of the journey towards a successful outcome, they simultaneously embed a narrative of rupture that discards previous modes and paradigms (Christensen 1997). Facebook's early motto – 'move fast and break things' – evocatively captures this duality (Blodget 2009).

These discourses have become more prominent among research funders, and programmes that prioritise experimentation, risk and novelty are increasingly common, at least in the United Kingdom and European contexts (UKRI 2019; Leptin 2024). This move might suggest that humanities disciplines have adopted a culture that is willing to easily accept the failures that will inevitably accompany that approach to research. Yet, as Quinn Dombrowski deftly argues, professional culture in the humanities – even to some extent within the digital humanities – remains highly risk averse. Jane Winters examines some of the reasons this conservative culture persists, including (somewhat ironically) the funding organisation's own approach to grant evaluation.

Definitions of innovation can shape the work we do in other ways. Christopher Ohge's reflection asks whether we are well served by an 'innovation-as-novelty' paradigm. He argues instead for an approach to innovation that recognises the importance of newness, but orients us towards a research ethic that values doing things well over doing things differently for the sake of it. This theme is picked up in David De Roure's contribution, which examines the 'software waste cycle' that

many innovative digital projects fall into. The reformulation of failure as play that De Roure proposes could encourage risk-taking and innovation, while incentivising the reuse of existing tools and methods.

These reflections all acknowledge the importance of innovation in research generally, and digital scholarship particularly, while drawing attention to places where our current model of innovation fails us.

References

Blodget, Henry. 'Mark Zuckerberg On Innovation'. *Business Insider* (1 October 2009) Archived from the original on 9 February 2021. Accessed 24 November 2024. https://www.businessinsider.com/mark-zuckerberg-innovation-2009-10?r=US&IR=T.

Christensen, Clayton M. *The Innovator's Dilemma: When New Technologies Cause Great Firms to Fail.* The Management of Innovation and Change Series. Harvard Business School Press, 1997.

Leptin, Maria. 'Evaluation of Research Proposals: The Why and What of the ERC's Recent Changes'. European Research Council. 2024. Accessed 24 November 2024. https://erc.europa.eu/sites/default/files/2024-02/Evaluation_of_research_proposals.pdf.

UKRI. *UK Research and Innovation Annual Report and Accounts 2018–2019*. Dandy Booksellers Ltd, 2019.

Chapter 1

Stop lying to yourself: collective delusion and digital humanities grant funding

Quinn Dombrowski

From grant applications to curricular development, digital humanities projects and programmes are shaped by the field's perceived connection with funding.[1] Projects are often awarded small grants of money or labour with the condition – implied or explicit – that the project leader will seek external funding to continue or expand this work. And yet, the process of applying for a grant can fundamentally shift both the project and the perspective of the principal investigator (PI) applicant, exposing both to varieties of failure not previously possible.

This piece discusses the impact of applying for a grant on the development of a digital humanities project, the different scales of failure that can come into play with a 'successful' grant application, and the consequences of that success on the trajectory of an individual scholar's career. Contrasting the kind of failure that comes from self-funded projects with the multiple layers of failure often at stake in grant-funded work, it proposes steps for mitigating the damage of the current model of grant funding that could be taken at the level of the individual, the funding agency and professional organisations, all of which are implicated in different ways.

Failure in self-funded projects

A grant application is almost never the beginning of a project, except in classroom contexts where writing a grant is a pedagogical activity. A digital humanities project almost always grows out of a person's own interests, passions, frustrations or problems. It is because of this personal connection to the project content that many digital humanities projects come into existence in the absence of funding, running entirely on a person's own labour in the margins of their lives and whatever financial resources they can dedicate to the work. These projects are arguably the most fortunate, despite the constraints they face: allowed to develop in their own time and manner, without a predetermined path that has been committed to the page and shared with a broader audience. Outside of the context of research-intensive institutions, self-funded projects may be the only feasible mode of project development, with initiatives taking a distinctly different shape in the absence of institutionalised structures for project development and support (Risam 2021).

This is not to say that there is no accountability in self-supported projects: collaboration of any sort generates a network of entanglements and obligations. As soon as you involve other people – be it through working with their materials, or accepting their labour (all the more so when it is volunteer labour, as is often the case in unfunded projects) – you take on the weight of responsibility to see that something comes of those materials or work (Mann 2019; Keralis 2018). Accepting volunteer labour, or being entrusted with materials important to a person or community, or building something that other people begin to rely on (or rely on the promise of) for their own future work: these are all pathways to a form of genuine failure. The failure that is worth seriously wrestling with, and letting it shape your approach to future collaborations, is the kind that involves letting down people who were counting on you. This is not to say that one should contort one's life into knots to avoid these letdowns at all costs: some projects are simply not feasible in the end, let alone sustainable. It often feels terrible to end a project (see 'How I Lost the Crowd' in Graham 2019, 71–80) but for most projects, endings are a matter of when and how, rather than if. This is partly a consequence of the fact that long-term sustainability for digital humanities projects remains an area of concern. Not only is it not widely provided as a service even at the best-resourced institutions, it is unclear what such a thing would even look like. The diversity of tools,

materials and technology underpinning digital humanities work makes it inherently resistant to any sort of automatable workflow, though a considerable amount of thought has gone into what pieces of such a thing might look like, including the work of The Endings Project.[2]

Sometimes there is truth in the meme-cliché: even if a project did not produce anything one could point to, the true digital humanities might be the friends met along the way. However, grappling with the gap between promises and results – especially when it implicates others' resources, and considering what that gap means for your collaborators – is an important kind of self-reflection for digital humanists to engage in. Particularly for projects led by faculty or senior staff, it is important to embrace honest feedback from collaborators in positions of lesser institutional power as part of this process, rather than simply speculating on the impact of the project and its demise. Done well, drawing a self-funded project to an ending can uncover lessons of value even in a project that fundamentally didn't work. When funding becomes part of the picture, however, the entire project framework shifts.

What happens when you get funding?

From the perspective of federal government grant agencies in particular, accountability is paramount when it comes to distributing funding. This is even more so in a political climate where even the existence of government-funded grants for the humanities comes under political attack with increasing frequency. It is important to be able to justify the value of the projects that are funded, and to know with reasonable certainty that the projects will, in fact, be completed.[3] Even for private funders like the Mellon Foundation where the programme officers provide more support and dialogue through the application process and after the project is funded, part of the process involves crafting a detailed set of deliverables, project plan, staffing plan and budget.

There is nothing wrong with this approach to careful and deliberate project planning, and depending on the desired scale of the project, it may be the only way forward. Problems arise when scholars feel pressured to shift their project in directions that they don't truly want in order to secure funding. This leads to grant proposals crafted out of well-meaning self-delusion: being funded, they reason, will come with a set of things they wouldn't have otherwise done, but it at least would provide institutional

legitimacy and surely there will be enough funding around the margins to do the work the scholar is actually excited about.

Compromises between a scholar's ideal project and something that aligns with funder priorities are an unavoidable and even productive tension that comes out of the grant application process. It is easy to profess support for open data and sharing code; the reality is much messier when one is faced with the prospect of diverting resources (in the form of labour) from research, satisfying technical development work, or scholarly production to the distinctly tedious and stressful task of cleaning and documenting data and metadata, and wrangling them into an institutional, disciplinary or other type of repository. Funder requirements are an effective way to enforce norms like code and data sharing that have a broader value, even when it is at odds with the immediate preferences of project teams.

However, compromises like open data requirements are not the only ones in play when scholars apply for grants. In reality, the projects that make the most sense from the perspective of a scholar's own research or teaching are rarely well-aligned with major grant programmes. Even digital humanities work itself often falls between the cracks, for example, the major Canadian agency funding the humanities does not have a dedicated category for digital humanities (DH). The reward structure of academic disciplines from the perspective of career advancement is at odds with the priorities of funders, who typically look for a broader impact. At research-intensive institutions, a well-reviewed monograph that wins an award from the disciplinary society has a much greater value for a scholar's career than building a technical tool or platform that could be used by scholars in multiple fields. The latter also requires considerably more ongoing labour and infrastructure, and the scholar then faces a dilemma. Do they devote their own time to this maintenance work, at the cost of producing additional forms of legible scholarly production that will better support their career? Here, again, scholars outside research-intensive institutions may be in an advantageous position: the self-funded DH projects developed at public access and regional comprehensive institutions tend to be better received as part of the scholar's evaluation, without forcing them to contort the project to fit a set of specific expectations and outcomes.

In this way, step by step, a scholar with a grant-funded digital humanities project is sucked deeper into the cycle of having to write grants to maintain technical work that they didn't need for their original vision, but the technical work was necessary to get the grant to fund that initial vision.

This process calls to mind the children's rhyme 'There Was an Old Lady Who Swallowed a Fly', where the old lady swallows progressively larger creatures, each to catch the prior creature she'd swallowed, until she ultimately perishes. The wiser choice, at any point in this process, would be to come to peace with the set of well-intentioned but misguided choices that led to a situation of metaphorically swallowing several animals whole (that is, writing grants) and *stop swallowing ever-larger animals*, even if it means grappling with the consequences of having a 'failed' project.

The anxiety about 'failure' runs deep, with digital humanities generally following the acculturation of the humanities rather than the technical communities with which it intersects. In the humanities, failure is deeply personal, bringing with it shame and stigma, if not ostracisation. 'Failure' to secure an academic job after a PhD can still lead to scholars being written off by their former advisors and community. An article with an analysis that people feel 'failed' can be held against the writer for years. These represent fundamental, collective cultural failures within the humanities, casually discarding the years of training and mentorship and acculturation that go into graduate work in these fields. Meanwhile, failure is culturally unremarkable on the IT side because it is inevitable: IT teams do not spend years of meticulous study and work on a focused line of argumentation that draws deeply from their own insights and personal experiences. They build things – often, new things. Some of the things they build will inevitably fall apart, or fail to even come together long enough to meaningfully be described as 'falling apart'; this is the nature of the work. There is some wisdom in the humanities' efforts to interrogate the concept of 'failure', reframing efforts that one might immediately label that way in order to centre other aspects. But a tendency towards critical analysis and reframing can easily slip into pathological avoidance of the discomfort of 'failure', downplaying it and talking around it. It is worth confronting and acknowledging.

Reframing funding

Any project that involves human labour is expensive. It is expensive if you hire specialists with expertise. It is also expensive if you hire people who are learning the skills necessary to become future specialists. Learning involves failure and waste; learning is slow, and often jeopardises project timelines. In my first encounter with preparing a grant budget as part of sustaining the Digital Research Tools (DiRT) directory (Dombrowski 2021),

I was appalled when my boss took my numbers – carefully and precisely calculated to include what I felt was a realistic buffer for delays – and told me to double them. He was right.

Digital humanists tend to suffer from a surfeit of naiveté-powered optimism, and we pay dearly by closing the gaps between that optimism and reality with time and energy that would serve us better if we were to step away from this work and take a break. It precipitates burnout, and normalises this behaviour for more junior members of the team, whether or not the project leader attempts to draw clear boundaries and expectations exempting them from heroic measures to get the project done. The fact is that the scale of funds that projects are typically awarded – where $200,000 counts as a sizeable grant – is simply not commensurate with the work we commit to taking on. This is the case even if that work matches our actual needs and desires for the project, which it often does not. The discrepancy between the scale of funding available to humanists and to the sciences is not explainable in terms of the differences in material costs between the fields: labour is a primary cost driver in both cases. We do ourselves, and our collaborators, a deep disservice by pretending otherwise.

Digital humanities is long overdue for a reality check with regard to grant funding. While funding agencies have opened the door to public feedback before, the power dynamics at play inherently put constraints on honest dialogue. Scholars who are themselves potential future applicants are reluctant to raise concerns, lest it be taken as ingratitude – or worse, a reflection of their personal incompetence and inability to execute a project that others could do with ease. I write this from a position of a twisted kind of privilege: in my current role, I am not permitted to apply for grants. With grant funding off the table, I can speak more freely about what I have seen, both as a reviewer and while supporting applicants and recipients at various stages of their journeys.[4]

Funders need to be more conscientious about the assumptions that underpin their calls for proposals (CFPs). What are the benefits to the scholars who undertake this kind of work? What kinds of scholars are even in a position to undertake the work without great cost to their own careers, or spending nights and weekends on the grant in order to do the double load of traditionally legible scholarly output and a digital project? In what discipline(s) are the priorities in the CFP actually valued, beyond the mere CV bonus of receiving grant funding? For what discipline(s) do the priorities feel 'close enough' that scholars will be tempted to contort the work

they want to do into the shape of the grant? How much time, realistically, is required to do a project that compellingly fulfils the CFP, and is the available funding adequate to do that work?[5]

Funding agencies have set out grant programmes as a form of indirect influence on the priorities of fields. However, the result has been an unresolved game of chicken between funders and fields, the latter of which have not broadly implemented changes to their tenure and promotion guidelines that reflect funder priorities. Professional organisations continue to fight to address this gap, issuing revision after revision to recommendations for greater recognition for digital scholarship. While this is better than simply leaving scholars to fend for themselves, both grant agencies and professional organisations need to take a more active stance in advocating for greater alignment between funding priorities, professional organisation recommendations and the actual requirements that scholars face in their own evaluation process. Otherwise, however well-meaning their actions may be, funders and professional organisations are setting up scholars for failure by incentivising them to pursue grants and start projects that will take time and energy away from work that will actually be rewarded in research-intensive institutions.

There is also a role here for scholars to do a better job of looking out for their own interests. If they see digital scholarship as an important part of their work, that should be included in the negotiations upfront around tenure and promotion requirements. Grant funding is alluring, particularly at institutions where the scholar has access to fewer resources to implement the kinds of projects they dream of, but it is crucial to be brutally honest with yourself about how far the grant expectations stray from what you actually want to do. What additional work are you taking on that you wouldn't otherwise? What will you be required to find in order to sustain the thing you create – assuming you are able to finish it? How much would you lose face if you're unable to complete the project, or unable to sustain it for long? What is the value of the project for you personally and your career, when weighed against these risks and challenges? What would you be losing out on – including factoring things like your own mental health – if (and, realistically, when) this project spills over into your nights and weekends, so you can meet the other professional expectations necessary to continue or progress in your job?

In 2023, the Association for Computers and the Humanities (ACH) sought to reimagine its seed grant programme in a direction that centred radical

honesty. The outcome of the reinvisioned grant programme wouldn't be any particular *thing*, but a write-up of what the project team had learned in the process – which is to say, it would reflect what is truly the most durable outcome of most grants, and be resistant to the traps of self-delusion that so commonly accompany grants. While the implementation of this programme is still under discussion as of summer 2024, the act of discussing such a different approach to grantmaking was itself generative. On the one hand, ACH is free of the kinds of public accountability constraints that national funding agencies are. On the other hand, perhaps a radical reimagining of federal government grant programmes could also stop selling a conception of digital humanities that primarily produces platforms and tools, and shift the discourse towards digital humanities as a vehicle for developing important expertise, not unlike programmes funded under US Title VI, first introduced in 1958 under the National Defense Education Act (NDEA), which has subsequently provided support for language and area studies training (US Department of Education 2011). What if we thought of technical and analytical skills at the intersection of data and human cultures as akin to language or area studies knowledge: perhaps not relevant to all citizens at all times, but important for the country to know it has well-trained people to call upon in a crisis that would need to draw upon those skills. Alpert-Abrams (2020) movingly paints a picture of 'what the humanities do in a crisis'; as a later example, Saving Ukrainian Cultural Heritage Online (SUCHO) brought together digital humanists, librarians and everyday people to preserve Ukrainian digital cultural heritage under siege in Russia's full-scale invasion (LeBlanc et al. 2022). Ironically, the perceived risks that drove SUCHO were not realised in Ukraine, but rather, in the United States, as the Trump administration quickly undertook a ham-fisted keyword-search based effort to purge government webpages and data referencing women, ethnic minority groups, and the LGBTQ+ community. In a moment where methods commonly used – with care and thought and nuance – in digital humanities circles were being adopted to wipe out an inclusive historical narrative, digital humanities scholars in the US and beyond have found themselves in a position to apply their skills towards a social good.

This is a compelling case for the digital humanities, and there are existing grant programmes focused on training opportunities. But given the often poor alignment between grants that fund projects and what is actually to the benefit of both scholars and broader communities, it may be

time to rethink the 'DH project grant' as a vehicle to prepare experts who can respond in a crisis, while simultaneously working with disciplinary organisations to develop meaningful, small-scale funding opportunities that can offset the costs of doing the kind of disciplinary digital work that can more directly lead to legible scholarly outcomes for the person doing it. If we cannot responsibly ask scholars to broaden their scope because we do not have the resources to either support or reward that kind of work, a better path forward would be to provide funding at the level where the scholar's own scope is meaningful and impactful. Even if the amount of funding were smaller, less money better targeted to the scholar's actual goals is still a better outcome than a larger grant that comes with unwanted obligations.

Conclusion

Money cuts across all disciplinary and technical boundaries, offering a form of validation legible to department chairs and deans, regardless of whether they share one's own methodological or theoretical framework. As a result, grant funding feels like the ultimate prize for many scholars, whether or not it actually makes the most sense as a way to implement the project they have in mind. The institutional value of grants – quite separate from the metrics on which scholars themselves are evaluated – further exacerbates this drive, leading scholars to partake in a collective delusion where grants are inherently good, however detrimental they may be in practice for the individual scholar.

Given the digital humanities culture of transparency and honestly reckoning with issues ranging from labour to data ethics, the role of grant funding is overdue some serious interrogation from all sides. Are funders genuinely satisfied with their existing programmes, and the incentives they lay out for scholars, even with the reasonably high probability of detrimental consequences for scholars' careers? Are scholars going into grant applications with a clear vision of metaphorically swallowing that first fly, and all the animals that are likely to follow? What are the roles of disciplinary organisations? Do they genuinely value the kinds of discipline-focused projects that scholars themselves come up with? If so, how can they support the realisation of these projects? If not, perhaps this should be made clear to scholars who can then make choices accordingly, as this has implications for their career development.

It is well past the time for looking the metaphorical gift horse of digital humanities grant funding in the mouth. Otherwise, one would be wise to recall the old lady who swallowed a horse. As the conclusion of the rhyme tells us: she died, of course.

Note from the author

This chapter was written in summer 2024. There is a painful irony in finalising a piece advocating for less reliance on grants, as a US citizen, in a moment when the Office of Digital Humanities has been eliminated from the National Endowment for the Humanities, which has experienced devastating funding cuts, along with the Institute for Museum and Library Services, another major DH funder within the US government. Regardless, I stand by these provocations, as an offering of food for thought for colleagues who find themselves in more supportive funding contexts, present and future.

Notes

1 See Allington et al. (2016) for an example of building an argument against digital humanities on the basis of that perceived connection.

2 See https://endings.uvic.ca (accessed 25 November 2024).

3 The mass cancellation of US National Endowment for the Humanities grants in spring 2025 under the Trump administration, in order to reallocate funds to a 'Garden of Heroes' featuring realistic sculptures of figures from American history from an approved list, goes to show that bad-faith political attacks are sometimes simply that. No amount of documentation and Gantt charts and carefully worked-through budgeting would have an impact on the cancellation of these grants, and the only path to reinstating these funds runs through appealing to elected representatives and lawsuits, such as ones filed by organisations including the Authors Guild, the American Council of Learned Societies, the Modern Language Association, the American Historical Association, and others.

4 Different positions come with different sets of opportunities and constraints, and in many cases, staff have a wealth of experience – across a wider range of projects than most individual faculty – and have less personally at stake in the outcome. As a result, they are more likely to be open about challenges, and can get into specifics while also maintaining an appropriate degree of anonymity.

5 The National Endowment for Humanities (NEH) has recently updated its grant application packet to require a justification of costs, which is a step in a positive direction towards surfacing how many people will be paid how much, and forcing applicants to reflect on these numbers somewhat. Programmes would benefit from even more explicit guidance about an appropriate scale for these projects.

References

Allington, Daniel, David Golumbia and Sarah Brouillette. 'Neoliberal Tools (and Archives): A Political History of Digital Humanities', *LA Review of Books* (1 May 2016). Accessed 25 November 2024. https://lareviewofbooks.org/article/neoliberal-tools-archives-political-history-digital-humanities/.

Alpert-Abrams, Hannah. 'What the Humanities Do in a Crisis'. Blog post (11 April 2020). Accessed 25 November 2024. https://halperta.medium.com/what-the-humanities-do-in-a-crisis-a7ae63263b0e.

Dombrowski, Quinn. 'The Directory Paradox'. In *People, Practice, Power: Digital Humanities Outside the Center*, edited by Anne McGrail, Angel David Nieves and Siobhan Senier, 83–98. Debates in Digital Humanities. University of Minnesota Press, 2021. https://doi.org/10.5749/9781452968346.

Graham, Shawn. 'How I Lost the Crowd'. In *Failing Gloriously and Other Essays*, 71–80. The Digital Press at the University of North Dakota, 2019. Accessed 25 November 2024. https://thedigitalpress.org/failing-gloriously/.

Keralis, Spencer. 'Disrupting Labor in Digital Humanities; or, The Classroom Is Not Your Crowd'. In *Disrupting the Digital Humanities*, edited by Dorothy Kim and Jesse Stommel, 273–94. Punctum Books, 2018.

LeBlanc, Zoe, et al. 'A Conversation with the Organizers of Saving Ukrainian Cultural Heritage Online (SUCHO)'. *Journal of Library Outreach and Engagement* 2, no. 1 (13 July 2022). https://doi.org/10.21900/j.jloe.v2i1.969.

Mann, Rachel. 'Paid to Do but Not to Think: Reevaluating the Role of Graduate Student Collaborators'. In *Debates in the Digital Humanities 2019*, edited by Matthew Gold and Lauren Klein, 268–78. Debates in Digital Humanities. University of Minnesota Press, 2019. https://doi.org/10.5749/9781452963785.

Risam, Roopika. 'Stewarding Place: Digital Humanities at the Regional Comprehensive University'. In *People, Practice, Power: Digital Humanities Outside the Center*, edited by Anne McGrail, Angel David Neives and Siobhan Senier, 304–14. Debates in Digital Humanities. University of Minnesota Press, 2021. https://doi.org/10.5749/9781452968346.

US Department of Education. 'The History of Title VI and Fulbright-Hays: An Impressive International Timeline'. 2011. Accessed 25 November 2024. https://web.archive.org/web/20240301181512/https://www2.ed.gov/about/offices/list/ope/iegps/history.html.

Chapter 2

Risk, failure and the assessment of innovative research

Jane Winters

Digital humanities research may be organised in numerous different ways within institutions – in departments, centres, hubs, institutes – but the unit of the laboratory is one that has been widely adopted. And, 'While the design lab or art studio has had a great influence on many digital humanities labs, the model of the science laboratory is most often invoked by those that imagine the digital humanities lab-space' (Earhart 2015, 392). Central to our understandings of such a laboratory is that it is a place where experiments happen, drawing on explicitly scientific methods. New knowledge is generated through experimentation, through trial and error, through what has been described as 'thinkering' – 'the action of playful experimentation with technological and digital tools for the interpretation and presentation' (C^2DH, n.d.). Such experimentation necessarily goes hand in hand not just with the potential for failure but with its inevitability. Mistakes are made. A 3D print of a complex object collapses before it is finished, the errors in a script only become apparent twenty-four hours after it was set running, a web scraper gets caught in a crawler trap, the wrong choice of stop words turns out to exclude an important set of entities during text analysis. This is the everyday experience of doing digital humanities research. It can, to say the least, be annoying, but it can also be a highly valuable learning experience or perhaps even generate new insights. The sharing of these setbacks and failures with other members of a team can prevent them from making the same mistakes, might help to explain a similar problem that has been holding them back, or might trigger a new idea or train of thought.

So far so good. This is the kind of failure that we can all get on board with. It is an acceptable, even desirable part of the research process. It is generally only talked about within a team, and often occluded by public descriptions of seamless pipelines and workflows, but there are no negative consequences were others to hear about it. But what happens when experimentation is scaled up, when it is not at the level of an individual task but at the heart of a large research project for which you are seeking funding? The stakes are suddenly much higher, both at the research proposal stage and subsequently (should you be lucky enough to get through peer review) during reporting on project delivery and outcomes. How can the possibility of failure be negotiated; how can it be acknowledged as inextricable from experimental processes, as an enabler of innovation?

To read the funding calls published by research support agencies is to be struck with enthusiasm for and interest in experimentation, innovation and interdisciplinarity. A quick glance at recent calls published by UK Research and Innovation (UKRI) open to arts and humanities researchers reveals the presence of words such as 'ambitious', 'transform', 'alternative', 'innovative', 'breakthrough', 'disruptive' and 'transcend' (UKRI, n.d.). Researchers are encouraged to think big, to push at the boundaries of current knowledge and to devise projects that will be transformative both in form and in findings. But how does this aspiration hold up in the face of traditional peer-review criteria that include value for money, feasibility and track record of success? These are, of course, important factors to consider – especially for publicly funded research – but within the strict grading systems operated by many funding bodies, they can serve almost systemically to weed out innovation and experimentation. What are the mechanisms for evaluating the feasibility of a method that cannot be fully explained at the outset of a project because it will only develop as the research unfolds? This might be the case, for example, in a project that draws on systemic action research. It is possible to outline the broad principles of the action research cycle – plan, act, observe, reflect, plan forward – but not precisely where they will lead in the context of a particular project (Heron and Reason 2006). The lack of fixity is precisely the point, but it carries with it risk, and with risk comes the potential for failure. We are encouraged to 'manage out' risk; if it is acknowledged at all it is in the reassuring form of a carefully weighted risk register. But in attempting to remove risk completely we are in danger of stifling innovative practice, discouraging interdisciplinary collaboration and holding back the development of new forms of scholarly output.

One way of addressing this challenge is to devise funding schemes that support straightforwardly exploratory and experimental research. The Curiosity Awards scheme launched by UKRI in 2023, for example, is 'intentionally flexible' and encourages proposals concerned, among other things, with 'high risk and high potential concepts' (a rare positive mention of risk!) and 'scoping and piloting . . . early-stage proof of concept for ideas or change of direction' (UKRI 2023). As might be expected, the available funding is relatively limited (up to £100,000) but that in itself removes a degree of pressure from applicants and opens the door to generative failure as a reported research finding. Such schemes will work most effectively if they are accompanied by peer-review training processes that encourage recognition of risk, uncertainty and failure as inherent in some of the most exciting and challenging research and not as an automatic indicator of unfeasibility. There has to be scope to admit that risk is present, and that a project may fail, but that it is worth supporting despite and perhaps even because of that fact.

The connection between 'high risk' and 'high potential' in some areas of research is clearly beginning to be recognised. Encouraging risk in principle, however, is not the same thing as accepting it and its companion – failure – in practice. How can institutions, funding bodies, research teams and individual researchers work together to create spaces where it becomes not just possible but essential to report on the things that have failed, and what was learnt from that failure, as well as to celebrate project successes? This is hard to do within evaluation and reporting structures that are concerned with metrics – how many journal articles were published by a project team, how many conferences did they attend, what software and datasets were created, how many people interacted with project outputs of varying kinds? There may often simply be no mechanism for telling the story of a project in official reporting, of contextualising both achievements and failure to achieve intended goals, of exploring the innovation that can arise from having to redesign an ongoing project that is not quite working.

There are, though, some positive developments in relation to the evaluation of research, including the acceptance not just that 'Research assessment shapes research culture', but that 'Funders can initiate positive culture change through careful design and implementation of research assessment' (Global Research Council 2020, 5). Initiatives such as the Declaration on Research Assessment (DORA) and the Coalition for Advancing Research Assessment (CoARA) encourage more qualitative

approaches to the assessment of research and its impact, allowing complex narratives about research trajectories to be constructed, valued and evaluated. The dial is beginning to move, but it takes a long time to change a research culture, and perhaps even longer to overcome institutional aversion to risk and the public acknowledgement of failure.

Finally, it is important to recognise that the option to talk openly about risk and failure is not available to everyone, or that the potential consequences may be different depending on career stage, gender, ethnicity or a range of other factors. Established researchers are much more able to talk about their failures, about their rejected grant proposals and publications, about the projects that had to be steered back on to the rails, without damaging their careers. This brings a responsibility to do precisely that, while acknowledging that such openness reflects privilege. We can all, however, respond to consultations from funding bodies looking to design and implement responsible research assessment processes. We can all work within our institutions to raise awareness of what it means to be a DORA signatory in both principle and practice. We can all make space within our teams for the sharing of failure without judgement or consequence. It may take time, but we can change research cultures and bring failure openly into our research and practice as a positive force.

References

C^{2}DH. 'Thinkering', n.d. Accessed 25 June 2024. https://www.c2dh.uni.lu/thinkering.

Earhart, Amy. 'The Digital Humanities as a Laboratory'. In *Between Humanities and the Digital*, edited by Patrik Svensson and David Theo Goldberg. MIT Press, 2015.

Global Research Council. *Responsible Research Assessment*. 2020. Accessed 25 June 2024. https://globalresearchcouncil.org/fileadmin//documents/GRC_Publications/GRC_RRA_Conference_Summary_Report.pdf.

Heron, John and Peter Reason. 'The Practice of Co-operative Enquiry: Research "With" Rather than "On" People'. In *Handbook of Action Research*, edited by Peter Reason and Hilary Bradbury, 179–88. Sage Publications, 2006.

UKRI. 'AHRC Responsive Mode: Curiosity Award Round One'. 2023. Accessed 25 June 2024. https://www.ukri.org/opportunity/ahrc-responsive-mode-curiosity-award/.

UKRI. 'Funding Finder: AHRC', n.d. Accessed 25 June 2024. https://www.ukri.org/opportunity/?filter_council%5B%5D=814.

Chapter 3

Innovation, tools and ecology

Christopher Ohge

Innovation may seem like a new idea, but it is a sixteenth-century term that was first recorded during an era of scientific revolutions. The *Oxford English Dictionary* defines it firstly as 'The action of innovating; the introduction of novelties; the alteration of what is established by the introduction of new elements or forms' (s.v. 'Innovation, n.'). But it also includes an obsolete sense of 'political revolution; a rebellion or insurrection' exemplified by Shakespeare's King Henry IV's warning about the 'discontents' who 'gape and rub the elbow at the newes / Of hurly burly innouation' (*Henry IV, Part 1*, v. i. 78). Nowadays many people would think of its most common usage of bringing a new product into the market, but the first sense of 'novelty' and 'new forms' speaks to the ethos of many digital researchers. That lingering sense of revolution may also suggest another reason why it is so congenial to technology, whether it was the 'revolution' of print in the fifteenth century (as Elizabeth Eisenstein put it, which has since rightly been reconsidered as overly sweeping) or the digital revolution of the past few decades (Eisenstein 2012; Johns 2000; Baron et al. 2007). When resources are scarce, though, it might also seem attractive to a humble humanist to claim that they are revolutionaries now, too. (King Henry IV might suggest danger.) This relationship between innovation and revolution brings me to the core question of this polemic: is it a failure to innovate in digital humanities (DH), or a greater failure *not* to innovate? Or, better yet, under which conditions should we innovate when the idea itself seems to partake of growth-economy logic that has perpetuated the climate crisis? Should

innovation be about newness as such, or about 'making it new' (namely, making something new out of tradition, or what has worked well before)?

The fact that 'Innovation' was a criterion for acceptance into the Association of Digital Humanities convention in 2023 shows its importance as a working principle in DH, even though there is still no consensus on what the term means. If innovation is about novelty, or about engaging in a logic that supports neoliberal hype, then it can become an albatross for a DH researcher or team. Innovations in DH have led to some important benefits (e.g. IIIF n.d) as well as failures (e.g. Project Bamboo), but the albatross is usually the resources required for maintaining the project (Dombrowski 2014). Yet some of the greatest achievements of DH tool-making are not 'innovative' in the sense of being sophisticated or flashy – like AntConc (Anthony n.d.) or Voyant Tools (Sinclair and Rockwell n.d.) – but simple and very useful and are nonetheless impactful and widely used.

As I worked as a coordinator for the Digital Humanities Climate Coalition Toolkit (Baillot et al. 2024), it became clear that an unthinking loyalty to innovation-as-novelty contributes to an increased carbon footprint. It also betrays the dual calamity of the climate crisis and precarity – *precarity*, in that many institutions simply cannot afford to be innovative, and that the people required to do this work are operating under the realities of insecure university staffing.

Given these considerations – the vexed implications of innovation, the environmental costs of innovation and precarious resources and labour conditions – innovation should be framed in pragmatic terms. By 'pragmatic terms' I mean making things that work and that help us cope better with the conditions of our research.[1] (This goes against a capitalist logic of innovation which valorises novelty and return on investment.) I can think of no better example of this in my own digital work than the development of a manuscript editor for the Herman Melville Electronic Library (hereafter, MEL).[2] When I started contributing to this project, in 2010, one of the project's main focuses was to develop an XML editor, called TextLab, initially to encode the complicated surviving manuscript of *Billy Budd*. Developed by Nick Laiacona, who had previously worked with Jerome McGann on the Juxta Commons platform,[3] TextLab was as innovative a manuscript editor as one could imagine: it matched TEI XML-encoded transcriptions of a manuscript to the coordinates of the manuscript's facsimile, allowing for a granular examination of inscriptions and revisions. It was also multilayered: it could view a diplomatic transcription (with mouseover pop-up

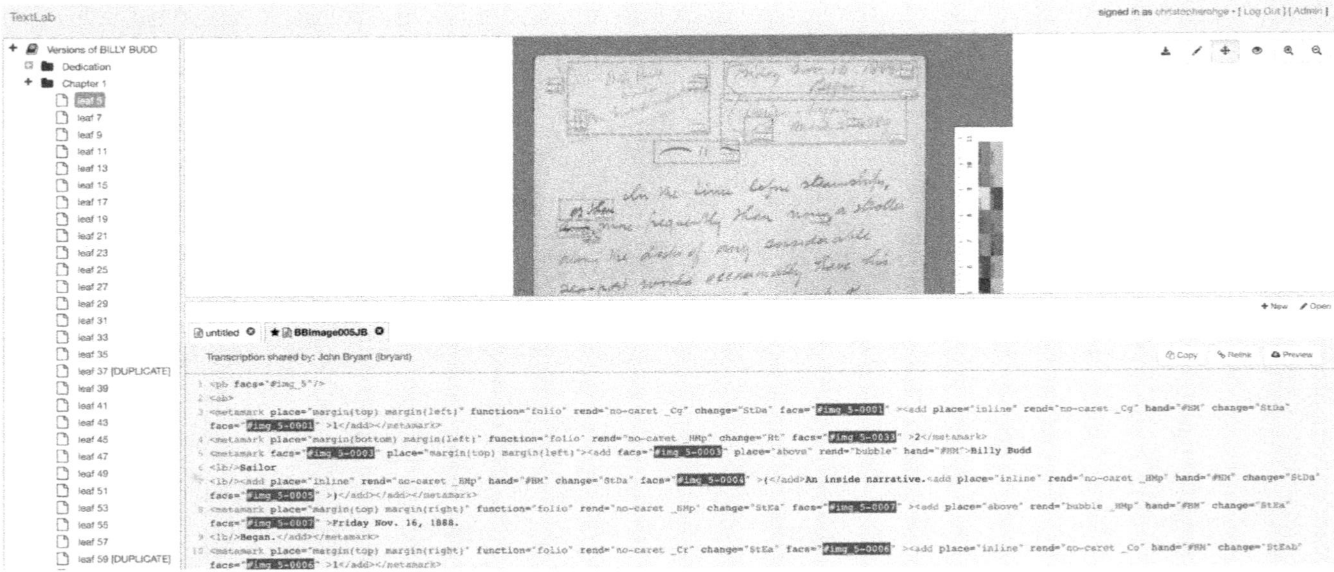

Figure 3.1: TextLab XML editing window. Public domain.

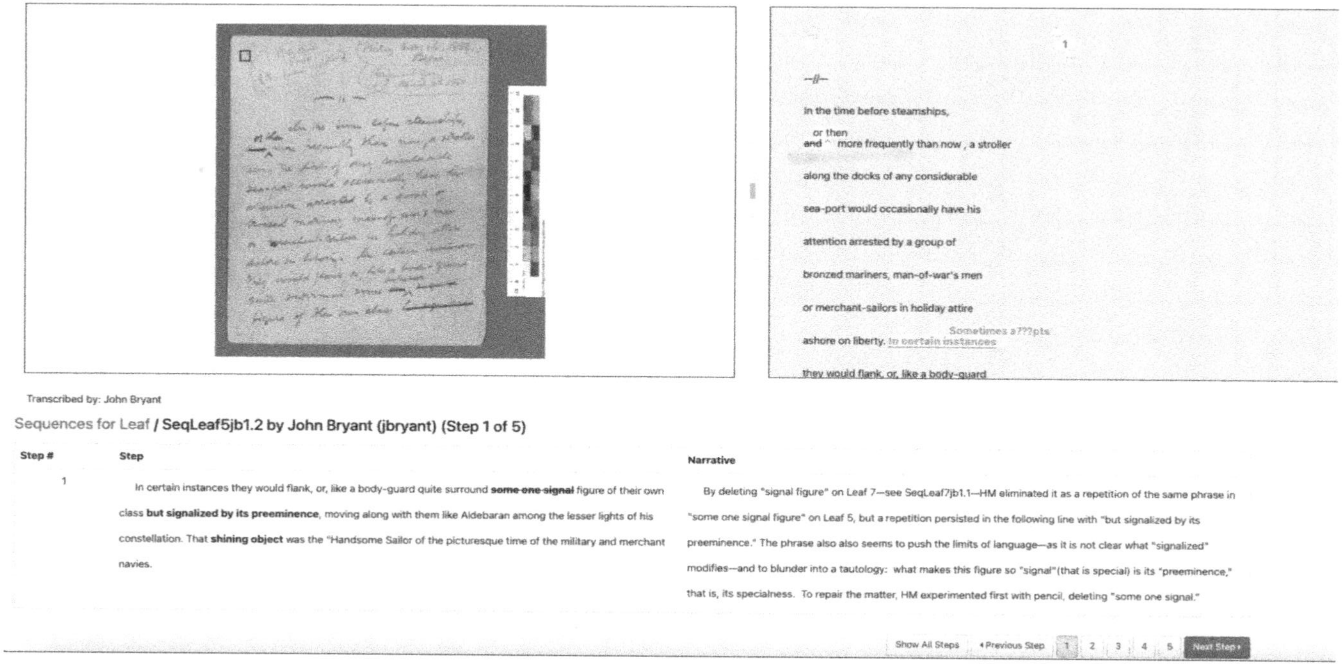

Figure 3.2: TextLab's diplomatic transcription view, with revision narrative sequences, from the Melville Electronic Library (c. 2019). Public domain.

notes that showed the TEI encoding), a base text (a cleaned-up version of the diplomatic text), as well as 'revision narrative' notes to explain how the text changed.

This all amounted to a technical implementation of John Bryant's theories in *The Fluid Text*, which argued for a new way of presenting all versions of a text in a digital interface (Bryant 2002). TextLab was brilliant: by 2019, the editors had completed a fully encoded digital edition of *Billy Budd*.

TextLab presented some serious issues, though. The first is that it was developed for one project, the Melville Electronic Library, rather than being built as a general-purpose tool. It was also a dynamic app, hosted on Heroku, that cost several hundred US dollars per month just to maintain. Then MEL lost its support from its funder. Then the director of the project, John Bryant, retired, and his former institution chose not to support the project, and its supporting research centre. MEL became the orphan that Ishmael describes at the end of *Moby-Dick*.[4] But we also faced the dilemma of innovating without being able to pay for it in the long term. By hosting a dynamic app on a third-party site, we were also not harbouring a sustainable, environmentally friendly tool. This is not the fault of anyone in particular: these were the conditions of innovation under which we were operating – conditions which were incentivised by the funding environment at the time but not supported for the long term. Like many projects that benefit from a windfall, MEL created cutting-edge tools that directly contributed to its obsolescence.

Even though we learned these lessons the hard way, we continued our conversations and collaboration with Nick Laiacona, who has since founded Performant Software to support digital humanities projects and develop tools. We agreed that what was needed was a general-purpose tool similar to TextLab but that could make use of existing innovations (such as IIIF) while also making use of minimal computing principles to ensure sustainability.[5] By combining features of MEL's TextLab with another project's lightweight manuscript interface, at the Making and Knowing Project, Laiacona released EditionCrafter in 2023.[6] Owing to the stable TEI XML source data at the Melville Electronic Library, we were able to facilitate the replacement of the TextLab software with EditionCrafter to display the *Billy Budd* manuscript.

By innovating in this pragmatic and responsible way, and with much heroic effort by Laiacona and other colleagues, we were able to build on a previous failure to ensure the stability of the project and to support a more

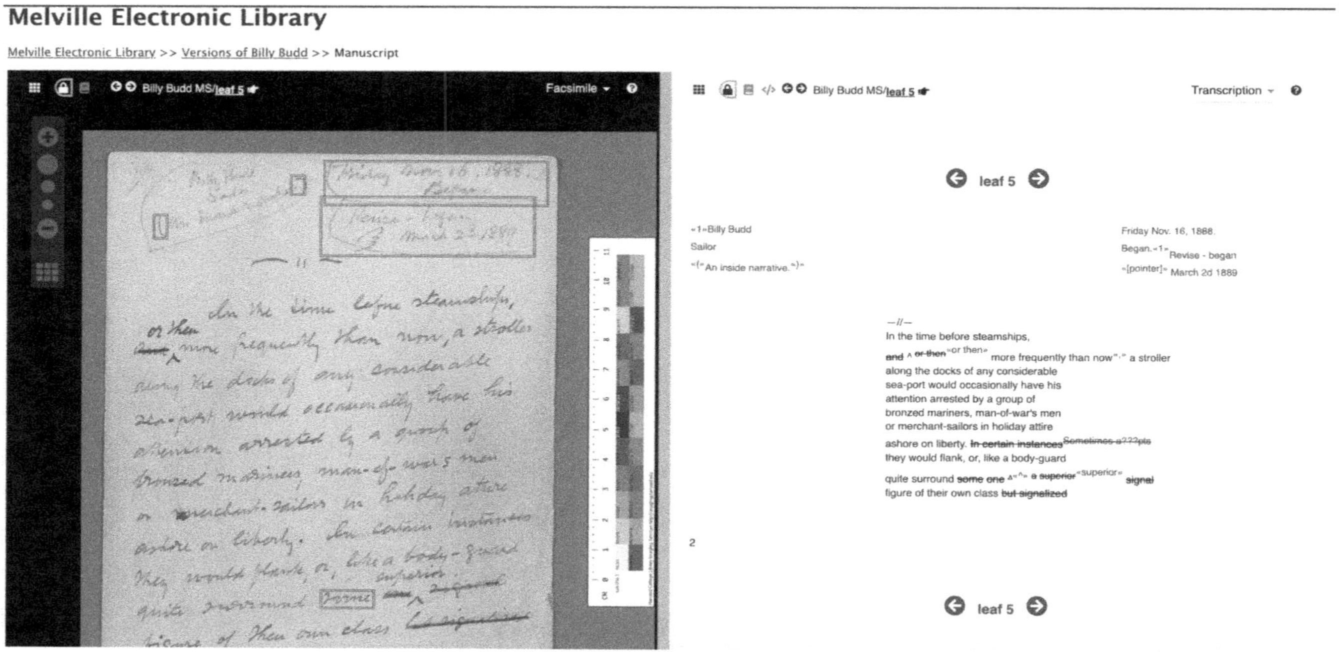

Figure 3.3: The current *Billy Budd* manuscript viewer in Edition Crafter (https://melville.electroniclibrary.org/editions/versions-of-billy-budd/billy-budd-ms.html#/ec/img_5/f/img_5/transcription). Public domain.

responsible digital tool.[7] By doing so, we were also setting an example to reduce the carbon footprint of our project.

I rather like the organic metaphor of innovation, used in botany, to describe the growth of a new shoot at the apex of a stem or branch. It reframes innovation as a process of 'making it new', or branching off from the whole – to push the metaphor further, it could entail that innovation is a new branch of the discipline which is dependent on its roots. Innovation can strengthen that which remains. What this would require, in theory, is that we innovate by branching off from what is already useful, and to think of more efficient ways of promoting healthy growth. I would hope that if we undertake the much harder work of changing our culture of innovation in digital humanities, we might see more innovative thinking instead of techno-utopian promises that contribute to the further degradation of the natural world. In practice, this would mean putting the focus on doing things well (and responsibly) rather than novelty for novelty's sake (making new things), without pressuring ourselves to introduce novelties into technology that are unnecessary to promote the core enterprise – the work, the research.

Notes

1 In Chapter 1 of my *Publishing Scholarly Editions: Archives, Computing, and Experience* (Cambridge University Press, 2021), I discuss what pragmatic approaches to editing and publishing entail.

2 See https://melville.electroniclibrary.org/ (accessed 25 November 2024).

3 See https://wiki.tei-c.org/index.php/JuxtaCommons (accessed 25 November 2024).

4 See the detailed analysis of the ongoing management, security and sustainability of roughly 100 digital humanities projects by Smithies, Westling, Sichani, Mellen and Ciula in *Digital Humanities Quarterly* (2019).

5 Minimal computing refers to computing done under some set of significant constraints of hardware, software, education, network capacity, power or other factors, as defined by the Global Outlook Digital Humanities group. See https://go-dh.github.io/mincomp/about/ (accessed 25 November 2024).

6 See https://edition640.makingandknowing.org/#/ and https://cu-mkp.github.io/editioncrafter/ (accessed 25 November 2024).

7 Before EditionCrafter was implemented, the MEL website had also been transformed into a static site, which further reduced energy usage and ensured long-term sustainability.

References

Anthony, Laurence. 'AntConc: A Freeware Corpus Analysis Toolkit for Concordancing and Text Analysis (Version 4.3.1)', n.d. Accessed 25 November 2024. https://www.laurenceanthony.net/software/antconc/.

Baillot, Anne, James Baker, Jenny Bunn, Alex Cline, Michael Faerber, Charlotte Feidicker, Josephine Lethbridge, Matthew McConkey, John Moore, Christopher Ohge, Torsten Roeder, Nicolas Seymour-Smith, Martin Steer, Jo Lindsay Walton and Elizabeth Williamson (eds). 'Digital Humanities Climate Coalition Toolkit', 2022. Accessed 25 November 2024. https://sas-dhrh.github.io/dhcc-toolkit/.

Baron, Sabrina Alcorn, Eric N. Lindquist and Eleanor F. Shevlin (eds). *Agent of Change: Print Culture Studies after Elizabeth L. Eisenstein.* University of Massachusetts Press, 2007.

Bryant, John. *The Fluid Text: A Theory of Editing for Book and Screen.* University of Michigan Press, 2002.

Eisenstein, Elizabeth L. *The Printing Revolution in Early Modern Europe.* 2nd edn of *Canto Classics*. Cambridge University Press, 2012.

Dombrowski, Quinn. 'What Ever Happened to Project Bamboo?', *Literary and Linguistic Computing* 29, no. 3 (September 2014): 326–39. https://doi.org/10.1093/llc/fqu026.

International Image Interoperability Framework (IIIF). Accessed 25 November 2024. https://iiif.io/.

Johns, Adrian. *The Nature of the Book: Print and Knowledge in the Making*. University of Chicago Press, 2000.

Ohge, Christopher. *Publishing Scholarly Editions: Archives, Computing, and Experience*. Cambridge University Press, 2021.

Oxford English Dictionary, s.v. 'innovation (n.)', June 2024. Accessed 4 November 2024. https://www.oed.com/dictionary/innovation_n?tab=meaning_and_use.

Sinclair, Stéfan and Geoffrey Rockwell. 'Voyant Tools. Web application'. Accessed 25 November 2024. http://voyant-tools.org.

Smithies, James, Carina Westling, Anna-Maria Sichani, Pam Mellen and Arianna Ciula. 'Managing 100 Digital Humanities Projects: Digital Scholarship & Archiving in King's Digital Lab', *Digital Humanities Quarterly* 13, no. 1 (2019). Accessed 25 November 2024. https://dhq.digitalhumanities.org/vol/13/1/000411/000411.html

Chapter 4

Software at play

David De Roure

Software is pervasively part of digital scholarship. Here we reflect on its role in the affordances of the digital, how it enables innovation and its vital role in what we will describe as *play* within new scholarly practice. Narratives and practices around software, experimentation and innovation have been shaped by the beneficial experience of failure, and we shall argue for permission to be creative and permission to fail.

Working with digital data and tools brings a set of affordances benefitting humanities scholarship. One of these affordances is that 'digital' doesn't respect historical disciplinary boundaries, and indeed it enables us to cross them. Practices around experimentation and innovation can flow across too, and we will look in particular at the concept of *reproducible* research, focusing on software as a medium for innovation – while also recognising a 'software waste cycle'. We will suggest that programming and computation realise digital affordances too, and that they enable a sense and practice of play.

The digital and computational

The affordances of 'the digital' are well articulated (Naughton 2014). One is the ability to bring together objects that could not come together physically, in digital juxtaposition or superimposition. Democratised access is an affordance in terms of access to content and also in terms of analysis, illustrated for example by crowdsourcing that can engage volunteers at scale. Most pervasively we have the common medium of digital data – or

the bitstream – to represent all forms of cultural artefact, and blurring a boundary between born-digital and remediated content.

An immediate critical note is needed: we are not asserting that the digital representation of an object is a replacement for its material form – for example, there is typically a loss of information associated with any selecting or encoding, of content or metadata. Furthermore, no infrastructure is agnostic, and this is as true in the digital as the analogue sphere. A common implicit presumption that 'digital' is naturally more authoritative or complete must be challenged. In other words, disaffordances of the digital can be identified too, and this balance is surely necessary in any discussion about failure. Furthermore, affordances have consequences: for example, while it is an affordance that digital content is significantly easier to copy and distribute than material goods, this also means licensing, rights and business models need to evolve.

Large-scale analysis and automation are well known digital affordances – in fact *computational* ones: the digital data opens the door to today's computational approaches and prepares us for tomorrow's. Less widespread perhaps is simulation, which enables us to explore 'what if' scenarios in our research inquiry; indeed it lets us experiment and fail safely. We might look at this affordance as close reading by digital prototyping, a kind of 'experimental' humanities (De Roure and Willcox 2017). We see adoption of simulation in augmented and virtual reality as a humanities method too, for example in historical reconstruction of buildings and 3D modelling of artefacts. Because these digital artefacts are easy to construct, we can readily try out alternatives in our process of enquiry – and in fact this process can be supported by automation.

Programming

All these affordances have digital content in common, and they are enabled by software tools. What is important about these tools is that we are able to create them, to adopt and to adapt them. This is a powerful evolution in our research infrastructure, and prompts the suggestion that *programming* is a crucial affordance of the digital too. No infrastructure is agnostic, so available software tools are a lens which might lock us into particular modes of analysis – we must not forget this, and knowing it will help us address it because software is a particularly versatile and adaptable instrument.

Software can itself be the subject of critical discourse, and its evidence in the archive – even if it no longer works – is evidence of our understanding, aims and methods. There is excellent scholarship around early software (Berry and Marino 2024) and what is now termed 'Digital Humanities' has a history as 'Humanities Computing', or even *non-numerical computing* (Michie 1963).

However, software can be hazardous too. Unsworth articulates the role of software and eloquently discusses the 'software waste cycle' (Unsworth 2020):

> Software developed by individual researchers and labs is often experimental and hard to get, hard to install, under-documented and sometimes unreliable. Above all most of this software is incompatible. As a result it is not at all uncommon for researchers to develop tailor-made systems that replicate much of the functionality of other systems, and in turn create programs that cannot be reused by others and so on in an endless software waste cycle.

This is a disaffordance but we can do something about it. The Software Sustainability Institute (SSI) was founded in the UK in 2010, dedicated to improving software in research across all disciplines – indeed to address this waste cycle, helping to ensure benefit from funder investment in software creation.[1] As well as providing training, SSI introduced the notion of the 'Research Software Engineer' (RSE): these are skilled colleagues who contribute to research by developing software and engaging with the problem. The RSE role has enjoyed significant uptake (Cohen et al. 2021) and this spread extends to arts too (Ma et al. 2024).

Software and skills

SSI undertook a large-scale survey of the UK arts and humanities research community to establish practices and skills in the use of digital tools and software (Taylor et al. 2022). The report highlights diversity of practice, evolving interdisciplinarity and collaboration, a wide spectrum of engagement and the importance of communities of practice. Recommendations also identify skills and knowledge development, data management and sustainability, and supporting careers including early career researchers and research technical professionals.

Indeed, supporting communities of practice in software creation, documentation and training may be a particularly effective intervention in the humanities context: it is a means of sharing practice from the 'early adopters' to build capacity. A strong example of this approach is the consortia of Huma-Num, the French Research Infrastructure for the Social Sciences and Humanities, where collective consultation defines communities and their technical resources.[2]

SSI itself has sustained for fourteen years to date, helped by its 'collaborate, not compete' ethos and wide disciplinary breadth. Its current work focuses on four of the software sustainability priorities we perceive today: capable research communities, widespread adoption of research software best practice, evidence-driven research software policy and guidance, and broadened access and contributions to the research software community.[3] In this way, SSI is building resilience against failure into the research community and addressing the software waste cycle.

The new primitives

While digital computational resources have grown over recent decades, so too has the engagement of citizens with the digital world – we were once a community of scholars with access to a small number of computers; now we operate in a world of crowd and cloud, and a new abundance of both data and computation.

This nexus is significant in the evolution of our knowledge infrastructure. It has, for example, catalysed the remarkable success and adoption of large language models (LLMs). Machine learning approaches are rapidly being adopted into our digital research methods, and into the infrastructure itself.

It is interesting to reflect on the various affordances we have identified in the context of scholarly primitives (Unsworth 2000). Some of them might suggest, or at least align with, candidates for new primitives; for example modelling, prototyping, crowdsourcing and training a machine learning model.

We suggest that another new affordance of the digital, and perhaps a scholarly primitive, is play (De Roure and Willcox 2020). Play involves observing, testing and trying; it involves imagination and, crucially, it is safe to fail. Newcomers to programming are often relieved to discover they don't break the computer if they get something wrong. Play encourages